Regional Studies Series

The Regional Studies Series

Africa
China
Europe
The Subcontinent of India
Japan and Korea
Latin America
The Middle East and North Africa
Russia and the Commonwealth

Africa

Regional Studies Series

Consultants

Louise Crane

Harvey Feinberg

Eleanor Berman

Susan Hall

GLOBE FEARON

Pearson Learning Group

Louise Crane

Louise Crane is former Outreach Coordinator at the Center for African Studies, University of Illinois

Harvey Feinberg

Harvey Feinberg is professor of history at Southern Connecticut State University

Eleanor Berman

Eleanor Berman is an instructor in world studies.

Susan Hall

Susan Hall was for many years with the school services division of the African-American Institute.

Area Specialists: Patricia Kuntz is with the African Studies Program of the University of Wisconsin, Madison. Habakkuk Musengezi is at the Center for African Studies of the University of Florida, Gainesville.

Reviewers: John Alex Diopoulos, Assistant Principal, P.S. 125, New York City Public Schools.

Cover Image: The picture on the cover shows a street and building in Abidjan, Côte d'Ivoire.
Maps: Mapping Specialists, Ltd.
Graphs, Diagrams, and Charts: Keithley & Associates

ISBN 0-8359-0413-X

Printed in the United States of America
9 10 11 12 13   06 05 04

Globe
Fearon

Pearson Learning Group

1-800-321-3106
www.pearsonlearning.com

CONTENTS

Maps

Graphs, Charts, and Diagrams

We delighted, my friend, in an African presence:
Furniture from Guinea and the Congo,
Heavy and polished, dark and light.
Primitive and pure masks on distant walls
    yet so near.
Taborets of honor for the hereditary hosts,
The princes from the high country.
Wild and proud perfumes from the thick
    tresses of silence,
Cushions of shadow and leisure like quiet
    wells running. . . .

—Léopold Sédar-Senghor, translated by Miriam Koshland

Africa, my Africa
Africa of proud warriors
In ancestral savannas,
Africa of whom my grandmother sings,
On the banks of the distant river. . . .

—David Diop, translated by Ulli Beier

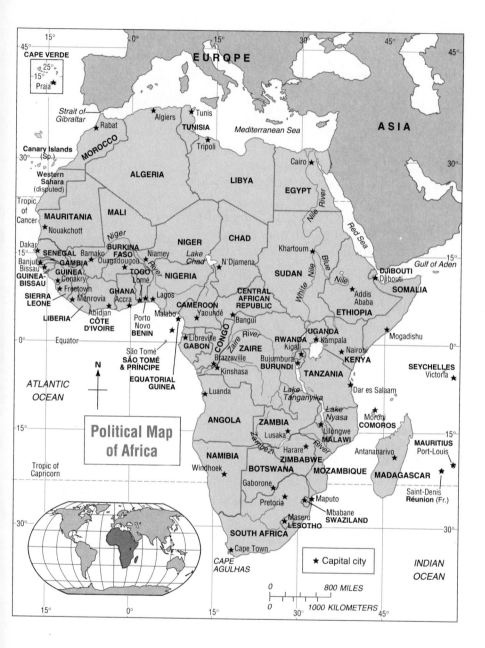

Political Map of Africa

CAPE VERDE
25°
15°
Praia

EUROPE

ASIA

Strait of Gibraltar
Canary Islands (Sp.)
Western Sahara (disputed)
Tropic of Cancer

Algiers
Tunis
TUNISIA
Tripoli
Mediterranean Sea
Cairo

Rabat
MOROCCO

ALGERIA

LIBYA

EGYPT

Nile River

Red Sea

MAURITANIA
Nouakchott
MALI
Niger

NIGER
CHAD

Khartoum

Gulf of Aden

Dakar
SENEGAL
Bamako
BURKINA FASO
Niamey
Lake Chad
N'Djamena
SUDAN
Blue Nile
White Nile
Nile
DJIBOUTI
Djibouti
SOMALIA

Banjul
GAMBIA
Ouagadougou
Niger River

GUINEA-BISSAU
Bissau
Conakry
GUINEA
TOGO
Lomé
NIGERIA
CENTRAL AFRICAN REPUBLIC
Addis Ababa
ETHIOPIA

SIERRA LEONE
Freetown
GHANA
Monrovia
Accra
Lagos
CAMEROON
Yaoundé
Bangui

LIBERIA
Abidjan
CÔTE D'IVOIRE
Malabo
Porto Novo
BENIN

Equator
São Tomé
SÃO TOMÉ & PRÍNCIPE
Libreville
GABON
CONGO
Zaire River
Brazzaville
ZAIRE
Kinshasa
RWANDA
Kigali
BURUNDI
Bujumbura
UGANDA
Kampala
Nairobi
KENYA
Mogadishu

EQUATORIAL GUINEA

ATLANTIC OCEAN

N

Luanda
TANZANIA
Dar es Salaam
SEYCHELLES
Victoria

Lake Tanganyika

ANGOLA
ZAMBIA
Lusaka
Lake Nyasa
Lilongwe
MALAWI
Moroni
COMOROS

Political Map of Africa

Tropic of Capricorn
NAMIBIA
Windhoek
BOTSWANA
Gaborone
ZIMBABWE
Harare
Zambezi River
MOZAMBIQUE
Antananarivo
MADAGASCAR
MAURITIUS
Port-Louis
Saint-Denis
Réunion (Fr.)

Pretoria
Maputo
Mbabane
SWAZILAND
Maseru
LESOTHO
SOUTH AFRICA
Cape Town

CAPE AGULHAS

★ Capital city

INDIAN OCEAN

0   800 MILES
0   1000 KILOMETERS

1 The Land

Africa's landscape is one of extraordinary contrasts. It has vast deserts—the Sahara (suh-HAR-uh) in the north, the Kalahari (kah-lu-HAR-ee or kal-uh-HAR-ee) in the south. Its landforms also include rain forests, **savannas**, or grassy plains with scattered trees and bushes, high **plateaus**, or tablelands, lofty mountains, huge lakes, and great rivers. In Africa is the longest river in the world, the Nile (nyl). Africa is also the home of an amazing variety of plants and animals and of more than 600 million people

Social scientists often divide the continent into five geographic regions—North Africa, West Africa, East Africa, Central Africa, and Southern Africa. Each region contains various nations, and off the coast of several regions are a number of island nations. The chart on page 2 shows the regions and the nations they include.

LOCATION, SHAPE, AND SIZE

Africa straddles the equator. About half its length lies north of the equator and extends beyond the Tropic of Cancer. The other half is south of the equator and extends beyond the Tropic of Capricorn. Its 23,000-mile-long coastline is relatively smooth, with few peninsulas, gulfs, or bays. The continent is shaped something like a bulging question mark, and its northwestern section is often referred to as the "heel" of Africa. The **promontory**, the pointed mass of land jutting into the ocean on its eastern side, is called the "horn of Africa."

It is about 5,000 miles from Africa's most northern point to its most southern point. Africa's greatest distance east to west is almost as far— 4,700 miles. Compare this with the distance between New York City and San Francisco—only 2,600 miles. Or compare it with the distance between the Canadian cities of Vancouver, British Columbia, and Halifax, Nova Scotia—3,000 miles. You can see how immense Africa is.

1

NORTH AFRICA

Algeria	(al·JEER·ee·ah)	Sudan	(SOO·DAN)
Egypt	(EE·jipt)	Tunisia	(too·NEE·zhuh)
Libya	(LIB·ee·uh)	Western Sahara[c]	(suh·HAR·uh)
Morocco	(muh·RAK·oh)		

WEST AFRICA

Benin	(beh·NEEN)	Liberia	(ly·BEER·ee·uh)
Burkino Faso	(bur·KEE·nuh FAH·soh)	Mali	(MAH·lee)
Cape Verde[a]	(kayp vurd)	Mauritania	(mor·ih·TAY·nee·uh)
Côte d'Ivoire	(koht dee·VWAR)	Niger	(NY·jur)
Gambia	(GAM·bee·uh)	Nigeria	(ny·JEER·ee·uh)
Ghana	(GHA·nuh)	Senegal	(SEN·ih·gawl)
Guinea	(GIN·ee)	Sierra Leone	(see·AIR·uh lee·OH·neh)
Guinea-Bissau	(GIN·ee·bi·SOU)	Togo	(TOH·goh)

CENTRAL AFRICA

Burundi	(boo·ROON·dee)	Gabon	(gah·BON)
Cameroon	(kam·uh·ROON)	Rwanda	(roo·AN·duh)
Central African Republic		São Tomé and Príncipe[a]	(SOU tuh·MAY PRIN·suh·pay)
Chad		Zaire	(zah·EER)
Congo	(KON·goh)		
Equatorial Guinea			

EAST AFRICA

Comoros[a]	(KOM·uh·rohs)	Mauritius[a]	(maw·RISH·us)
Djibouti	(jih·BOO·tee)	Somalia	(soh·MAH·lee·uh)
Ethiopia	(ee·thee·OH·pee·uh)	Seychelles[a]	(say·SHEL)
Kenya	(KEN·yuh)	Tanzania	(tan·suh·NEE·uh)
Madagascar[a]	(mad·uh·GAS·kur)	Uganda	(yoo·GAN·duh)
Reunion[a b]	(ree·YOON·yun)		

SOUTHERN AFRICA

Angola	(ang·GOH·luh)	Namibia	(nuh·MIB·ee·uh)
Botswana	(bot·SWAH·nuh)	South Africa	
Lesotho	(luh·SOO·too)	Swaziland	(SWAH·zee·land)
Malawi	(muh·LAH·wee)	Zambia	(ZAM·bee·uh)
Mozambique	(moh·zam·BEEK)	Zimbabwe	(zim·BAB·way)

[a] Island nations
[b] Réunion is an overseas territory of France.
[c] Status in dispute

TOPOGRAPHY

The largest portion of Africa south of the Sahara is a high plateau. It rises along the Atlantic coastline, crosses the continent, and slopes down to the Indian Ocean in a series of steps. This plateau is cut north to south by deep valleys, called **rifts**. There are few lowlands beyond the narrow coastal plains. These coastal plains are often less than 20 miles wide. Only in a few places are they more than 100 miles wide.

The western and northern sides of the African plateau range from 1,000 feet in elevation near the Atlantic coast to 3,000 feet inland. The eastern and southern parts of the plateau lift upward. They reach an average of 8,000 feet above sea level in some places.

Much of the African plateau is uneven. In some regions volcanic mountain peaks and highlands rise up from the land. In other regions the plateau is broken by **basins,** or depressions in the surface of the land, and by the rifts. Many lakes and rivers also cut into the plateau. The profile drawing below will give you an idea of what the landscape would be like if you were to travel the continent along the equator.

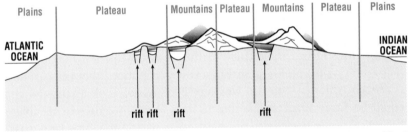

Fig 3

Great Rift Valley. Africa's most prominent geographic feature is a giant, 4,000-mile-long gash through the eastern plateau called the Great Rift Valley. Extending into Africa from the Arabian Peninsula, it stretches from Ethiopia southward to Mozambique. The Great Rift Valley varies in width from 30 to 50 miles and in depth from 1,000 to 3,000 feet. You could put 30 or more Grand Canyons inside the Great Rift Valley.

The Great Rift Valley was formed millions of years ago when movements in the earth's crust caused parts of the land's surface to crack, or **fault,** and other parts of the land to fall down between the faults. At the southern end of the western arm of the Great Rift Valley lie some of Africa's largest lakes, such as Lake Victoria. The walls of the valley plunge sharply downward in some places. Elsewhere they form huge, undulating, or waving, steps.

3

Mount Kilimanjaro, on the edge of the Great Rift Valley, is Africa's highest point. Some of the most intensive farming in Africa takes place on the mountain's fertile lower slopes.

Continental Drift. Some three centuries ago, while looking at a world map, the English philosopher Francis Bacon noticed that the east coast of South America and the west coast of Africa look as though they could be fitted together like pieces of a jigsaw puzzle. He speculated that at one time these two continents were part of the same land mass.

Since that time scientists have determined that Bacon's theory was correct. Geographers now believe that all of the world's continents were once part of one supercontinent, which they named Pangaea (pan-JEE-uh). The southern part, called Gondwana (gond-WAH-nuh), included what is now Africa and South America.

About 180 million years ago, scientists believe, Pangaea began to break apart. Its pieces, our present continents, slowly moved away from one another. As they moved, their surfaces were subjected to various pressures. An upward thrust created by the pressure of the earth's moving crust, for example, caused the formation of mountain chains. Africa, however, was subjected to less pressure than the other continents were. It therefore has fewer major mountain chains. This relative lack of pressure also explains why Africa has such narrow coastal plains.

Africa moved relatively little. Other continents broke off from it. Not until Gondwana broke up was Africa surrounded by oceans.

CLIMATE AND ENVIRONMENT

Africa's climate ranges from tropical near the equator to temperate north and south of the equator. At the extreme northern and southern ends of the continent and in the highlands, the climate is cool. There are also a range of tropical climates. It is warm and wet at the equator and becomes drier and hotter toward the Tropics of Cancer and Capricorn. A look at a climate map of Africa (page 6) shows that there is a pattern to Africa's climate. The climate gets drier and drier in regular belts as you move away from the equator in either direction northward or southward.

Climate is an important factor in determining how land is used. Where crops can be grown and livestock raised depends on the climate, particularly on the amount of water available. In Africa rainfall is distributed unevenly. Basically there are two seasons: wet and dry. In many parts of Africa, all the rain falls in the wet season, while almost none falls in the dry season. Because of this, farming and livestock raising are limited.

Rain Forests.   Rain forests cover less than one-fifth of the continent. They are dense and dimly lit. If you stood in one, you would see broad-leafed trees of many kinds forming a solid green canopy overhead. This canopy prevents sunlight from reaching the forest floor, so there are few low-growing plants.

A rain forest is one of the most complex biological communities on earth. It contains thousands upon thousands of different species of plants and animals. Among the trees are African mahogany, kola, and ebony. Among the plants are orchids, begonias, and ferns. Feeding and living in the tree tops are numerous monkeys, chimpanzees, squirrels of many varieties, forest leopards, hornbills, parrots, and numerous other birds. Living on the forest floor, which is moist and spongy and littered with fallen leaves and twigs, are giant forest hogs, okapis, bongos, and many kinds of rodents, snakes, frogs, and lizards.

There are two main sections of rain forest in Africa. Both straddle the equator in the western and west central part of the continent. As you can imagine, the climate is warm, wet, and humid. Rainfall is heavy every month of the year.

Much of the rain that falls in the rain forest soaks into the ground. The rest drains off the land and collects in the many streams that run through the region. These streams eventually feed into larger rivers, which in turn empty into inland lakes or the sea. Though the soil of

5

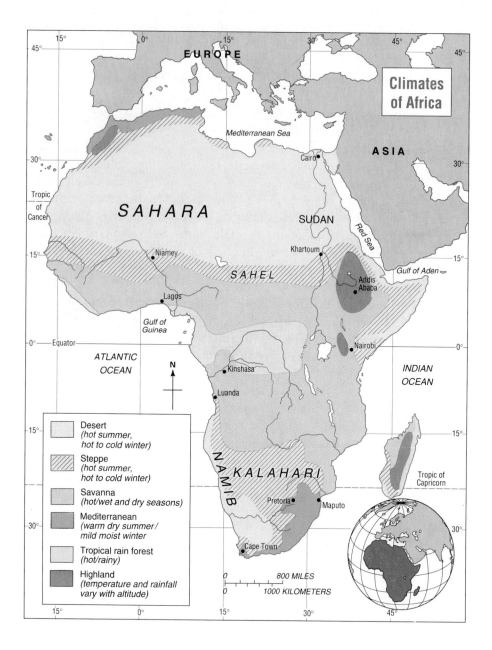

Climates of Africa

EUROPE

ASIA

Mediterranean Sea

Cairo

Tropic of Cancer

SAHARA

SUDAN

Red Sea

Niamey

Khartoum

Gulf of Aden

SAHEL

Addis Ababa

Lagos

Gulf of Guinea

Equator

Nairobi

ATLANTIC OCEAN

N

Kinshasa

INDIAN OCEAN

Luanda

NAMIB

KALAHARI

Tropic of Capricorn

Pretoria

Maputo

Cape Town

Desert
*(hot summer,
hot to cold winter)*

Steppe
*(hot summer,
hot to cold winter)*

Savanna
(hot/wet and dry seasons)

Mediterranean
*(warm dry summer/
mild moist winter*

Tropical rain forest
(hot/rainy)

Highland
*(temperature and rainfall
vary with altitude)*

0   800 MILES

0   1000 KILOMETERS

Many Africans live in rain forest regions. They clear patches of trees and plant their crops in the forest because rain and natural fertilizers are abundant there.

the rain forest is deep and full of decaying plant and animal material, it is not very fertile. The constant rainfall **leaches** (washes away) many of the soil's nutrients, or valuable ingredients.

Savannas.   As you move north or south away from the equator, the climate becomes progressively drier. Eventually it becomes too dry to support many trees. Grasses become the dominant land cover. This is the savanna. Savanna woodlands and grasslands cover more than two-fifths of Africa and occur in two belts north and south of the rain forest. Parts of the African savanna are almost treeless and resemble the American prairie. Other parts, where low trees are abundant, look almost like parks. Trees common to the savanna include acacias, baobabs, and palms.

The savannas have two seasons: the rainy season, when the climate is hot and wet, and the dry season, when little or no rain falls. During the dry season the savanna grasses turn brown, and before long most

7

On the Tanzanian savanna, women use short-handled hoes to weed their crops. Farming is the main economic activity of the African grasslands.

trees lose their leaves. Then, when the rains return, almost overnight the grasses turn green, and the trees begin to bud. The savannas are where most Africans farm and raise livestock, such as cattle, sheep, and goats. Farmers on the savannas can grow crops only during the rainy season, which lasts about five or six months of the year.

The savanna is the home of most of Africa's large animals. The lion, elephant, rhinoceros, giraffe, gnu, zebra, cheetah, hyena, jackal, and many forms of antelope make their home there. In waterholes throughout the region, hippopotamuses and wading birds congregate.

In the past, large populations of animals inhabited the savanna. Today, because of an expanding human population, with its need for more farming and grazing land, the number of animals is declining. Large herds of African wildlife, however, can be found in national parks and game preserves in East and Southern Africa. Four such protected areas are Kruger (kroo-GUR), Tsavo (tsav-OH), Lake Nakuru (NAH-koo-roo), and Serengeti (ser-un-GET-ee).

Deserts and Semideserts.   Moving north and south from Africa's two savanna belts, the climate continues to become drier. Eventually it becomes too dry even to support grasses, and belts of desert and semidesert occur.

The largest desert in the world, the Sahara, lies north of the northern savanna zone and makes up most of North Africa. It stretches from the Atlantic coast to the Red Sea, and it covers an area almost as large as the United States. A zone of semidesert, called the Sahel (suh-HEL), separates the Sahara from the savanna area to its south. The Sahel is covered by short, sparse grass.

8

Lying south of the equator beyond the savanna are the Kalahari **steppe** and semidesert lands. The steppe is an area that is even more arid than the savanna but still supports vegetation. In the southwest is the coastal Namib (nuh-MIB) and an area of short grasses, or veld (velt), known as the South African High Veld. Rainfall in the true desert is less than 10 inches a year. In the steppes and semideserts there is 10 to 15 inches a year.

The Sahara, one of the most desolate areas in the world, is a region of shifting sands and rocky formations. Except where it is crossed by the Nile River, it is practically barren. It is only habitable where groundwater close to the land's surface has created oases. The Namib Desert, along the coast of Namibia, is also largely barren. The Kalahari Desert, in the central part of Southern Africa, is a desert plateau. With an average altitude of about 3,300 feet, the Kalahari supports scrubby vegetation.

Temperatures in the African deserts, especially in the Sahara, can get high, especially during the middle of the day. Nighttime temperatures, however, are quite low, as heat radiates away from the land's surface under clear skies. Daytime temperatures commonly reach 120°F, and nighttime temperatures often fall as low as 50°F.

What scientists call desertification is a serious problem in the semiarid regions of Africa, especially in the north. *Desertification* means that semidesert land on which the livestock of nomadic herders could once graze is turning into a true desert. Prolonged drought in regions such as the Sahel is one cause of desertification. Another cause is soil erosion (the wearing away of the topsoil) that results when too many animals are allowed to graze or too many crops are harvested. When rainfall was plentiful, the people increased the size of their herds of cattle and sheep. They built more water holes, and the improved

Because farming in the Sahel has been disrupted so often by lack of rain, most people living there cannot afford modern equipment or fertilizers.

water supply encouraged even larger herds. People also began to farm more land, thus using up the nutrients in the soil. When drought struck, the crops withered, the grazing land did not produce enough grass to feed the herds, and the water holes dried up. The soil, already poor, turned to dust.

Mountains and Highlands.   The highlands of eastern Africa, part of the Great Rift Valley, stretch from the Red Sea in the north to the Cape of Good Hope at the southern tip of the continent. Here the climate is cool, with adequate rainfall. The highland areas are farming regions, where grain crops and coffee are grown extensively.

Africa's two highest mountains, Mount Kilimanjaro (kil-uh-mun-JAR-oh), 19,340 feet high, and Mount Kenya, 17,058 feet high, lie in the Great Rift Valley region and are of volcanic origin. Not far away are the Ruwenzoris (ro-wun-ZOR-ees), or Mountains of the Moon. Two of their peaks, Margherita (mar-guh-REE-tuh) and Alexandra (al-ig-ZAN-druh), are well over 16,000 feet high. Other mountains in Africa are the Mediterranean Atlas on the northwest coast, the Ahaggar (uh-HAG-ur) and the Tibesti (tuh-BES-tee) ranges in the central Sahara, and the Drakensberg (DRAK-unz-burg) Mountains in southeastern Africa. The highest mountain in West Africa is the volcanic Mount Cameroon, which is 13, 354 feet high.

Basins.   Several great basins occur throughout the African plateau. Many of these depressions were once inland seas that have long since dried up. Africa's greatest basin is the Zaire in Central Africa. North of the equator, in the western Sahara, is the Al-Juf (al-JOOF) Basin, which is mostly sandy desert.

In the northeast lies the large Sudan Basin. It is desert in the north, and in the south is a vast swamp, called the Sudd (sud). Between these basins lies the Chad Basin, containing tiny, shallow Lake Chad and the deep Bodele (boh-DAY-lee) Depression. The southernmost great basin, the Kalahari, is mostly a sandy, steppe grassland, which is seasonally wet. Small divides, plateaus, and hills separate the basins from one another.

Cooler Environments.   Rain forests, savannas, and deserts—these are the environments most typical of Africa. They all have an equatorial climate. As you have read, some parts of Africa also have some temperate and highland climates.

Rimming parts of Africa's northern and southern coasts are areas of evergreen shrubs, grasslands, and a Mediterranean climate. This means that winters are cool and rainy, and summers are warm and dry. These regions support a luxuriant cover of low, dense shrubs, some grasses, and scattered trees.

Africa's mountains and highlands are cooler than the areas around them and often wetter. Some of the high areas support evergreen forests. Others are topped with meadows of short grasses and wild flowers. Only the South African High Veld and Africa's highest plateau, in Ethiopia, have truly temperate climates, the result mostly of high altitude and/or high latitude.

WATERWAYS

Two of Africa's river systems rank among the top in the world. Africa can also boast of having the world's second largest freshwater lake and several of its deepest lakes.

Rivers.   If you look at the physical features map on page 12, you will see that most of Africa's major rivers begin in rainy highlands and then flow to

Boats transport people and cargo up, down, and across the Zaire River. Fishermen catch meals from it and women use the water for their household needs. This bridge is one of six that span the Zaire.

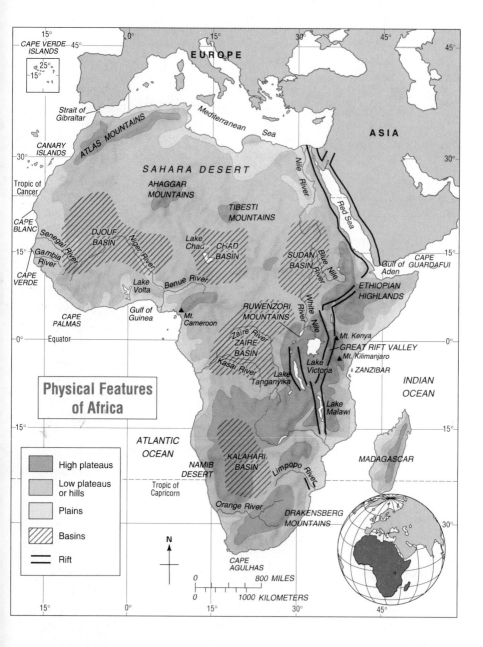

Physical Features of Africa

Legend:
- High plateaus
- Low plateaus or hills
- Plains
- Basins
- Rift

CAPE VERDE ISLANDS
EUROPE
Strait of Gibraltar
CANARY ISLANDS
Mediterranean Sea
ASIA
ATLAS MOUNTAINS
Tropic of Cancer
SAHARA DESERT
AHAGGAR MOUNTAINS
Nile River
Red Sea
CAPE BLANC
Senegal River
DJOUF BASIN
Niger River
TIBESTI MOUNTAINS
Lake Chad
CHAD BASIN
SUDAN BASIN
Blue Nile River
Gulf of Aden
CAPE GUARDAFUI
Gambia River
CAPE VERDE
Benue River
Lake Volta
White Nile River
ETHIOPIAN HIGHLANDS
Gulf of Guinea
Mt. Cameroon
RUWENZORI MOUNTAINS
CAPE PALMAS
Zaire River
ZAIRE BASIN
Mt. Kenya
Equator
Kasai River
GREAT RIFT VALLEY
Mt. Kilimanjaro
Lake Tanganyika
Lake Victoria
ZANZIBAR
INDIAN OCEAN
Lake Malawi
ATLANTIC OCEAN
NAMIB DESERT
KALAHARI BASIN
MADAGASCAR
Tropic of Capricorn
Limpopo River
Orange River
DRAKENSBERG MOUNTAINS
CAPE AGULHAS
N
0   800 MILES
0   1000 KILOMETERS

the sea. More of them flow to the Atlantic than to the Mediterranean or to the Indian Ocean. As they drop from the highlands to the plateau and then again from the plateau over **escarpments,** or steep cliffs, to the coastal belt, most of them form waterfalls and rapids. The cascading waters make navigation difficult or, in some cases, impossible.

Africa's most famous river, the Nile, is 4,187 miles long, making it the longest in the world. The Nile rises from two main sources: the Blue Nile and the White Nile. The Blue Nile begins in the highland of Ethiopia, and the White Nile rises in Uganda. The White Nile flows through Sudan, where it joins the Blue Nile in the city of Khartoum (kar-TOOM). Together the two form the Nile River, which flows northward into Egypt and empties into the Mediterranean Sea.

Shorter than the Nile, but larger in terms of the volume of water it carries from land to sea, is the Zaire River. With seven large **tributaries,** or streams that feed into rivers, plus numerous smaller ones, it forms a huge river system that drains a basin of about 1. 5 million square miles in the center of the continent's rain forest. The Zaire flows north from its source in the Ruwenzori Mountains, crosses the equator, and then swings around in a wide curve to the west. Here it turns south, crosses the equator again, and finally tumbles into the Atlantic Ocean in a series of waterfalls and rapids. Some of these powerful waterfalls have been harnessed by the Inga I Dam, a modern **hydroelectric** system. (A *hydroelectric* system uses water power to create electricity.)

Where the Zaire enters the Atlantic, it forms a large **estuary,** or inland sea. The town of Matadi (muh-TAH-dee), Zaire, at the head of the estuary, is one of the largest harbors in Central Africa.

The Niger is largely a rain-forest river. It rises in Guinea, only 200 miles from the Atlantic coast. Mountains prevent this 2,600-mile-long river from flowing directly to the ocean. Thus it is forced to flow first in a wide curve northeastward, then east and south to the Gulf of Guinea. Here it forms a broad delta of 14,000 square miles, the largest in Africa. The Niger contains more water than the Nile. Yet because its volume of water varies so much during the year, navigation is limited to short periods. The river is an important source of hydroelectric power and irrigation.

The most important river in Southern Africa is the 1,650-mile-long Zambezi (zam-BEE-zee). It is one of the few rivers in Africa that flows into the Indian Ocean. It is navigable for long stretches in its upper section. Then, about halfway to its outlet, it suddenly plunges into a deep chasm a mile wide, forming the spectacular Victoria Falls, the world's largest. The Kariba (kuh-REE-buh) Dam has been built here.

Africa has numerous rivers that are totally dry most of the year but fill up during rainy periods. These **wadis** (WAH-dees), as they are called, cross the drier areas. When they are full, they provide Africans with much needed water and are also frequented by many animals. Yet because people never know when the wadis will fill up, they remain an undependable resource.

Lakes. All of Africa's major lakes lie south of the Sahara, mostly in East Africa within the Great Rift Valley. Most of these lakes are remarkably long, narrow, and deep. Lake Tanganyika (tan-gun-YEE-kuh), 420 miles long, the world's longest freshwater lake, is only 30 to 45 miles wide. It is believed to be the world's deepest lake—in some places it reaches a depth of 4,708 feet. Other lakes within the Great Rift Valley are Lake Malawi and Lake Turkana (toor-KAH-nuh).

Lake Victoria, also called Victoria Nyanza (nee-AN-zuh), covers an area of 6,820 square miles. It is the second largest lake in the world. Only Lake Superior in North America is larger. Victoria lies in Central Africa in a shallow depression on a high plateau between branches of the Great Rift Valley. Its greatest depth is only 270 feet.

Lake Chad, a shallow body of water in the Sahel region, varies in size according to the season, from 4,000 to 10,000 square miles. Much of Lake Chad is surrounded by swamp.

NATURAL RESOURCES

Africa is rich in plant, animal, and mineral resources. It is the world's largest producer of cocoa beans, cashews, and yams and is a major source of the world's bananas, peanuts, coffee, and cotton. African herders raise nearly a third of the world's goats and about one-seventh of its cattle and sheep. Africa is also rich in the kinds of mineral resources, such as oil, needed for industrial economies. Much of **sub–Saharan Africa**—that is, Africa south of the Sahara—has great energy potential in its waterways.

Minerals. The first mineral resources mined in Africa were salt, gold, copper, tin, and iron. As long as 2,000 years ago, these minerals were used and traded. Large deposits of them still exist in Africa. Mineral products account for more than half of Africa's total exports, yet the mining industry employs less than 1. 5 million people.

The continent's minerals are unevenly distributed. Oil is a major export, with production in Egypt, Libya, Algeria, Cameroon, Gabon,

Nigeria, and Angola. Of all the world's gold outside Russia and the Commonwealth nations, 70 percent comes from South Africa. South Africa is also a leading producer of diamonds, zinc, manganese, and coal. The continent produces nearly three-fourths of the world's cobalt and about a third of its chromite. (Cobalt is an important element in the manufac-ture of industrial cutting tools and in jet engines. Chromite is the chief source for chromium, which is used with other metals, such as steel, to give a material strength, hardness, and resistance to heat.) These minerals are found in Southern Africa, along with large deposits of copper and nickel. (Copper is used extensively in wire and metalwork. Nickel is used for making stainless steel.)

Africa is also a leading producer of phosphate (used in making fertilizer) and uranium (the radioactive element that provides the fuel for nuclear energy). Oil, cobalt, chromite, copper, nickel, and other mineral resources of Africa are all used in great quantities by the industrialized nations of the world. The map on page 24 shows where the major minerals of Africa are found.

Water Power.   To the average tourist the sight of one of Africa's cascading waterfalls represents scenic beauty at its best. To an electrical engineer, however, the same falls also represent kilowatts of energy—millions of them. Waterfalls are excellent sources of hydroelectric power.

Although most of its waterfalls remain untapped, Africa has about 40 percent of the world's potential hydroelectric power. In recent years,a number of hydroelectric projects have been built on Africa's rivers.The most recent is Cabora Bassa (kuh-bor-uh BAS-uh) on the Zambezi River in Mozambique. As you have read, dams have also been built along several of Africa's other rivers. These projects provide water for irrigation and also are used to control flooding.

LAND USE

Africa's size, climate, landforms, vegetation, and soil have all had a major effect on the history, culture, and activities of the people. In general, Africa's environment has not been hospitable. Because of its boundless deserts, irregular and unevenly distributed rainfall, and limited and overused soil, much of Africa's land is marked by low productivity.

As you have read, some of Africa's land is threatened by desertification. Another serious problem is depletion of the forests. Logging companies gather vast acres of trees for export. On a smaller scale, people from the edge of the forests cut down trees for firewood. The continued loss of forest land can cause serious problems of soil erosion, especially as the deserts and savannas expand into the forest regions.

Agriculture. About 75 percent of Africans are farmers, and agriculture is the leading economic activity on the continent. In the past, most farmers were **subsistence** farmers, growing only enough for their own use. This has changed, however, and today farmers grow such crops as bananas, plantains, rice, yams, and cassava for their own use and for markets in Africa and the rest of the world.

African nations need foreign money for development. Therefore they encourage the cultivation of agricultural products for export. More and more African farmers are raising **cash crops,** or crops produced primarily for sale on the market. Yet because prices on the world market change often, farmers who raise cash crops cannot always rely on a steady income. This fact also applies to larger farming complexes, a number of which have appeared in the highland areas in South Africa. These huge farms produce such cash crops as sugar, tea, and coffee.

By studying the climate map on page 6, you can get an idea of the ways Africans use the land. Agriculture takes place in all regions except the desert. In the drier areas grain crops such as sorghum, millet, wheat, and corn are grown. African rice is produced along rivers. In the

Picking tea in Tanzania. Tea is usually grown on large plantations. At harvest time, extra workers add to their incomes from their own farms by picking the ripe tea leaves.

humid areas root crops, such as yams, sweet potatoes, cassava, and cocoyams, plus tree crops, such as plantains and bananas, are the most popular. Tea, coffee, and cocoa beans are raised for export in western, eastern, and northeastern Africa.

Other Activities.   Much of the savanna and Africa's semidesert grassland is suitable for grazing. Cattle, sheep, goats, and camels are among the animals raised by African herders in these areas.

Forestry is practiced within parts of the African rain forest and its woodland areas. Products of the African forest include timber, rubber, palm oil, and palm-oil products.

ENVIRONMENTAL PROBLEMS

The uneven distribution of water in Africa continues to be a major agricultural problem. For example, although Kenya, in East Africa, has a favorable climate and fertile soil in the highlands, only 20 percent of its land is suitable for farming because of the lack of water. To open additional land for farming, major irrigation projects are needed.

Africa's lack of navigable rivers has retarded development and industrial growth since products and goods cannot be transported easily. The physical features of the continent have helped make transportation between regions poor. Highways and railroads have been built in some areas. Most of these serve only to move goods from inland areas to the coast, however, where they can be shipped overseas.

Health Problems.   Another environmental factor that has influenced the development of Africa is widespread disease. It is estimated that millions of Africans are unwell throughout their entire lives. Malaria, carried by mosquitoes, and sleeping sickness, carried by the tsetse (TSET-see or TSEE-tsee) fly to humans and livestock, sap people's energy and affect their ability to work. Many insects, such as locusts, also cause great damage annually to crops, reducing the food supply. Thus one of Africa's most pressing problems is the eradication of disease related to the environment. The cost of such efforts can be enormous, however.

One particularly devastating environment-related disease is river blindness. Spread by a small black fly, it affects at least a million people in the Volta (VOHL-tuh) River Basin of West Africa alone. The disease is found especially among those people who live along river banks where the black flies breed. Victims of the disease suffer physical deformities,

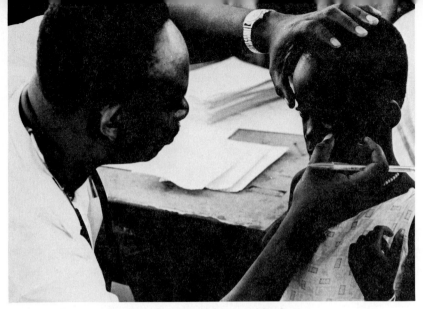

Recently a cure has been discovered for river blindness.
Other eye diseases, however, still present problems. Here
a doctor checks a young patient at a clinic in Tanzania.

weight loss, and, eventually, partial or total blindness. The following report from the United Nations describes some effects of the disease:

> Over the worst black fly regions, you see green, well-watered land that looks ideal for agriculture and animal raising. But you see little sign of [people]. When you do, it will be a deserted village, grass roofing collapsed and mud walls crumbling . . . . Having begn forced to surrender their fertile land to the black fly, people crowd on to the plateau, where uncertain rains and thin soils produce violent fluctuations in crop yields . . . . Soil exhaustion, and then erosion, often follow. These less favored areas often lack roads, clinics, or even markets.

Drought, or lack of rain, and its consequence **famine**, a serious shortage of food, have plagued Africa over the years. In the 1980s and 1990s there were terrible famines in Ethiopia, Sudan, and Somalia in which hundreds of thousands died. Efforts at relief were complicated by local wars, which hampered food distribution.

In recent years the spread of AIDS has brought a new and serious health problem to many parts of Africa (see page 272).

Population Growth.   Africa south of the Sahara is one of the least densely populated regions on earth. At the same time, its population is growing rapidly, at the world's highest rates. During the latter part of

18

the 1980s, Africa's population increased more than 3 percent each year. A British magazine article predicted:

> If things continue as they are Nigeria will, by the year 2000, have as many people as the whole of Africa today. Kenyans are proliferating faster still—at 4. 2 percent a year—and will, if they keep this up, double in number to 40 million in 17 years. This rate is challenged only by Zimbabwe and Mozambique.

Much of this increase was due to medical advances over several decades, which have reduced deaths and increased life expectancy. In addition, a much higher proportion of babies are surviving infancy now than ever before.

Other Problems. A rapidly increasing population causes major problems for African nations. Food production has not kept up with the population increase. And the more the population increases, the more demand there is for food. As you have read, the need for foreign money for development has caused many African nations to encourage the raising of cash crops. This means that more and more Africans are growing food for export rather than for their own consumption. African governments today must import food for their rapidly growing populations.

Although Africa has considerable mineral wealth, it has relatively few manufacturing industries or centers. Historically, Africa did not benefit from the technological advances of the Industrial Revolution. In the late 1800s, when Europeans moved into Africa, they did so to sell their own products and to extract Africa's mineral wealth. Thus Africans' contact with inventions and new technologies came later. Mining and manufacturing operations were financed and run by Europeans. Today, Africa's natural resources—gold, diamonds, platinum, chrome, and oil—are in demand in the world market. They need to be exploited for African advantage.

Africa's location, climate, and landforms have profoundly affected its history, perhaps more so than such conditions have affected any other continent. Today, these environmental factors continue to be significant. Drought, leaching, soil erosion, hunger, and disease are challenges that must be solved so that the continent can realize its potential. To a large extent, the degree of control that African nations can gain over environmental factors will influence their economy and political development. In later chapters you will read about the efforts being made by African countries to control their future.

CASE STUDY:

Feelings for the Land

African literature often tells a great deal about peoples' feelings for their land and their relationship to their environment.

THE DRY SEASON

The year is withering; the wind
Blows down the leaves;
Men stand under eaves
And overhear the secrets
Of the cold dry wind,
Of the half-bare trees.

The grasses are tall and tinted,
Straw-gold hues of dryness,
And the contradicting awryness,
Of the dusty roads a-scatter
With pools of colorful leaves,
With ghosts of the dreaming year.

And soon, soon the fires,
The fires will begin to burn,
The hawk will flutter and turn
On its wings and swoop for the mouse,
The dogs will run for the hare,
The hare for its little life.

Kwesi Brew [Ghana], *The Shadows of Laughter.* (London: Longmans, 1968), p. 38.

1. What are the fires that "will begin to burn" in the poem?

2. What can you learn about one African environment from this poem?

3. How do you think the writer feels about the dry season?

REVIEWING THE CHAPTER

I. Building Your Vocabulary

In your notebook, write the correct term that matches the definition.

hydroelectric	savanna	basin
desertification	plateau	rift

1. an elevated, flat land area

2. a deep valley

3. the process of semidesert land changing into true desert

4. a system that uses water power to produce electricity

5. a depression in the surface of land

6. a grassy plain with scattered trees and bushes

II. Understanding the Facts

In your notebook, write the numbers from 1 to 5. Write the letter of the correct answer to each question next to its number.

1. What is the distance between Africa's northernmost and southernmost points?
   a. 2,600 miles b. 5,000 miles c. 4,700 miles

2. What is Africa's most prominent geographic feature?
   a. the rain forest b. the coastal plains c. the Great Rift Valley

3. Where do most Africans farm and raise livestock?
   a. in the savannas b. in the rain forests c. along the rivers

4. Which of the following is a potential source of energy for sub-Saharan Africa?
   a. its rivers b. its mineral deposits c. its lakes

5. Which of the following has held back Africa's development?
   a. lack of mineral resources b. lack of water power c. widespread disease.

III. Thinking It Through

In your notebook, write the numbers from 1 to 5. Write the letter of the correct conclusion to each sentence next to its number.

1. The African rain forests
   a. produce numerous cash crops.
   b. cover three-fifths of the continent.
   c. contain soil that is not very fertile.
   d. support most of the continent's large animals.

2. The most important river in Southern Africa is
   a. the Zambezi.   b. the Nile.
   c. the Niger   d. the Zaire

3. In the 1800s, Africa did not benefit from the European presence because the Europeans
   a. were mainly interested in preventing conflicts among Africans.
   b. came to colonize and extract Africa's mineral wealth.
   c. were mainly interested in cheap African labor.
   d. wanted only to establish military bases.

4. Africa's lack of navigable rivers has retarded development because
   a. there are no other means of transportation.
   b. their waters cannot be used for irrigation.
   c. products and goods cannot be transported easily.
   d. their stagnant waters produce various diseases.

5. Which statement below best describes the African continent?
   a. The climate of the continent limits human enterprise.
   b. Africa's climate, landforms, irregular and uneven rainfall, and overused soil have not been hospitable.
   c. The nations of the continent have not exploited their resources.
   d. The existence of so many states makes cooperation impossible.

DEVELOPING CRITICAL THINKING SKILLS

1. Explain how Africa's landforms have significantly affected its history.

2. Discuss the role that health problems have played in the development of the African continent.

3. Describe the causes of desertification in the semiarid regions of Africa.

4. Show how the climate of Africa determines how land is used.

INTERPRETING A MAP

The map on page 24 shows where Africa's natural resources are to be found. Use it to answer the questions.

1. If you were building a pipeline to move the largest amounts of crude oil from wells to a port, in what part of the continent would you build it?
   a. The northwest   b. the south
   c. the west   d. the northeast

2. Timber is harvested in only one area of the continent. What characteristics of climate can you assume exists in that area?
   a. The area is completely dry.   b. The area is cool and wet.
   c. The area is completely wet.   d. The area is hot and dry.

3. If you wanted to obtain such minerals as gold, chromium, diamonds, platinum, nickel, and uranium in one general area, which section of the continent would you concentrate on?
   a. below the Tropic of Capricorn
   b. between the equator and the Tropic of Cancer
   c. above the Tropic of Cancer
   d. along the equator

ENRICHMENT AND EXPLORATION

1. Consult an atlas. Find a physical map of the African continent. Then draw on a sheet of paper a rough outline of the Great Rift Valley. Label all important mountain ranges, peaks, lakes, and rivers. In a separate table, identify the heights of principal mountains within the Great Rift Valley and the areas and depths of the major lakes. Use your map and collected information in a class discussion of the Great Rift Valley.

2. Identify the major environmental areas of Africa and describe the location of each. Gather information on the climate, the land use, the major landforms, the natural vegetation, and the products produced

in each area. Present your collected information in the form of a chart.

3. Consult a detailed political map of Africa. Plan an imaginary trip across the continent from east to west or from north to south. Prepare a preliminary plan for the trip. Take note of the places where you will stay and of the transportation methods that you can

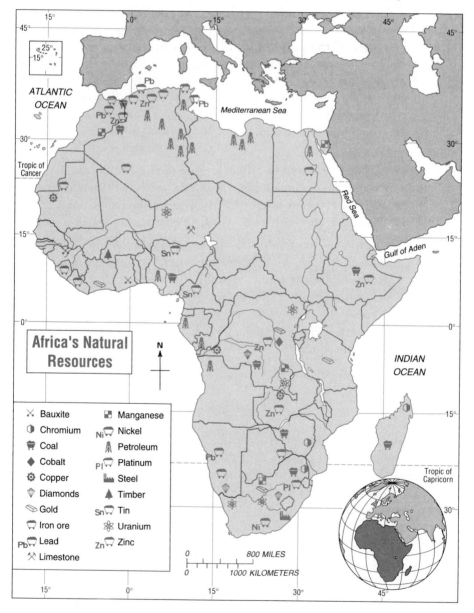

Africa's Natural Resources

✕ Bauxite
◑ Chromium
☗ Coal
◆ Cobalt
✿ Copper
♢ Diamonds
▱ Gold
▱ Iron ore
Pb▱ Lead
✗ Limestone
▰ Manganese
Ni▱ Nickel
♣ Petroleum
Pl▱ Platinum
▥ Steel
▲ Timber
Sn▱ Tin
✺ Uranium
Zn▱ Zinc

0   800 MILES
|—+—+—+—|
0   1000 KILOMETERS

use. Pay particular attention to the availability of roads and railroads. Prepare a report that describes the travel difficulties that you are likely to encounter.

4. Prepare a series of graphs that depict (a) Africa's production and (b) world production of such commodities as gold, diamonds, coffee, cocoa, cotton, copper, and uranium products. Locate the necessary statistical information that you need for your graphs by consulting a recent almanac or encyclopedia.

5. Choose one of the animals that inhabits the African savannas. Prepare a report for your class about the animal that tells where it lives, what it eats, how it rears its young, and what its enemies are. If the animal is an endangered or threatened species, explain why it is endangered or threatened and describe the steps that are being taken to preserve it. Illustrate your report with pictures or drawings.

2 *People and Culture*

It is morning on the continent of Africa, and people are beginning the day. On a high plateau in East Africa, a group of herders round up their cattle and drive them out to graze in the open grassland beyond their village. In a coastal town along the Indian Ocean, a shopkeeper prepares for the day. Facing north, he kneels on a small mat and chants his morning prayers to God.

In Johannesburg (joh-HAN-is-burg), in South Africa, a young computer expert guides his car through the busy morning traffic. He works for one of Africa's largest banks.

In the heart of the Zaire River Basin, fishermen cast delicately woven nets into the water. As they begin the day's fishing, they call on the spirits of the river to bring many fish.

In southwestern Nigeria women walk to the fields outside their town. They are going to begin the harvest of millet, their staple crop. Meanwhile, in a city not far away, the son of one woman prepares for an examination. A student at the university there, he hopes someday to be an engineer.

These are some of the people of Africa, who are of many cultures, traditions, and ways of life. In this chapter you will learn about Africa's people—where and how they live and some of their differences and similarities.

WHERE PEOPLE LIVE

projected 1.3 billion by 2025

933 million

Africa's population of more than 600 million is spread out over more than 11 million square miles of land. The population density is about 147 people per square mile. In contrast, Europe, with a population density of 324 people per square mile, is much more crowded.

26

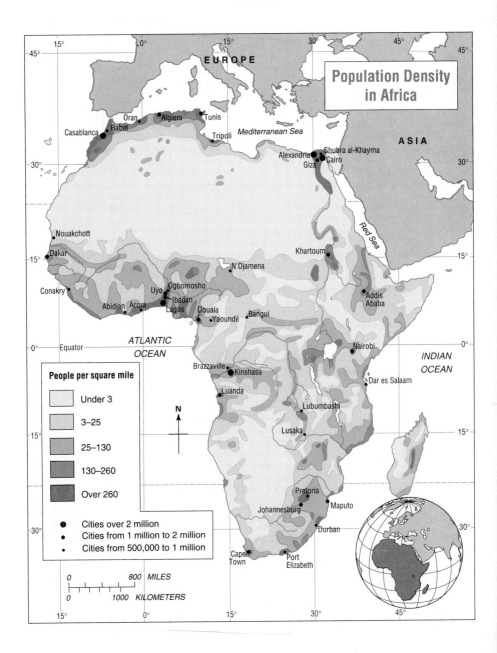

Population Density in Africa

EUROPE

ASIA

Mediterranean Sea

Oran
Casablanca Rabat Algiers Tunis
Tripoli

Alexandria Shubra al-Khayma
Giza Cairo

Red Sea

Nouakchott

Dakar
Khartoum

N'Djamena

Conakry
Uyo Ogbomosho
Ibadan
Abidjan Accra Lagos
Douala
Yaoundé Bangui

Addis
Ababa

ATLANTIC
OCEAN

Equator

Nairobi

INDIAN
OCEAN

Brazzaville Kinshasa

Luanda

Dar es Salaam

People per square mile

Lubumbashi

Lusaka

Under 3

3–25

25–130

130–260

Over 260

N

● Cities over 2 million
• Cities from 1 million to 2 million
· Cities from 500,000 to 1 million

Pretoria

Johannesburg Maputo

Durban

Cape
Town
Port
Elizabeth

0   800 MILES

0   1000 KILOMETERS

27

Because of the climate and land conditions Africans have not settled across the continent evenly. Large areas of Africa's deserts and rain forests are largely uninhabited. The majority of the people live in highlands areas, along rivers and lakes, and along the coasts. About 30 percent of the people live in large towns and cities. The map on page 27 shows the population distribution of Africa.

projected
37% urban   52% in 2025

Cities.   In Africa south of the Sahara, there are thirteen cities with populations of more than one million. In recent years, Africa's cities have grown tremendously as people have left rural areas to look for work and better opportunities. Africa's growing birth rate, now the highest in the world, has contributed to the rapid growth of the continent's cities. It is estimated that Africa's birth rate will continue to increase by almost 10 percent every three years for the rest of the twentieth century.

causes of pop. growth

Because of public health programs begun by governments throughout the continent, health conditions have improved in recent years. This means that the death rate (the number of people per 1,000 who die in one year) has decreased, and life expectancy has been extended. The migration of people from rural to urban areas has placed a strain on the cities. It is difficult for governments to provide adequate housing,

A busy street in Abidjan, Côte d'Ivoire. What does this picture tell you about life in an African city?

transportation, education, health-care facilities, and water supplies for the rapidly growing urban population.

Cities have always been a part of Africa. The city of Aksum (AK-soom) in Ethiopia is probably 2,000 years old. Timbuktu (tim-buk-Too), present-day Tombouctou, in Mali, and Kano (KAH-noh), in northern Nigeria, were thriving cultural and economic centers in the 1400s. Today many of Africa's cities are a mixture of the old and the new. Open-air markets, small shops, and houses line crowded streets in the older neighborhoods. In the newer parts of the cities, you can see tall skyscrapers, government buildings, supermarkets, movie theaters, and large shops.

The migration of people from rural areas to the cities has meant that many cities include neighborhoods of poor people, who have low-paying jobs or are unemployed. A large number of such people are migrant laborers, who work temporarily in the cities and then return to their farms and villages. Overcrowding in poor neighborhoods is common, and services such as electricity, water, and sewers are limited.

Villages and Towns. In spite of rapidly increasing urbanization, most Africans remain in rural areas. About 75 percent of all Africans south of the Sahara live in the countryside, mostly in villages and towns. In Africa a village or town may vary in size from 50 people to hundreds or thousands. Most often the people in the smaller villages form a close-knit community. The village or town may be a small settlement of houses surrounded by farms or grazing land for animals. A larger town may have a school, a health clinic, shops, and the traditional open-air markets.

Styles of housing vary greatly in rural Africa. Culture, tradition, climate, and available materials usually influence the style of homes. Many village houses are of sun-dried mud and thatched roofs of grass. In some areas, such as western Africa, homes may be of clay and covered with decorative designs. South Africa is well known for its ornately decorated houses. In some African villages and towns more prosperous people use modern materials, such as concrete blocks and metal roofs, to build their homes.

Many villages have a community square. In small villages the families gather there, around the communal water tap, to cook, share meals, and talk. In larger villages and towns the square is the center of ceremonies and celebrations that mark special occasions, such as marriages, births, deaths, and planting and harvest times.

29

THE MANY PEOPLES OF AFRICA

The majority of the people south of the Sahara are black Africans. They share a long history, dating from prehistoric times. With a few exceptions, they also share a history of colonial domination by the European powers, which controlled most of Africa from the late nineteenth century to the third quarter of the twentieth century. Yet the people of Africa are also diverse in their cultures, traditions, religions, and language. This diversity exists not only between nations, but within many African nations.

Ethnic Groups.   An ethnic group is a group of people who generally share a common tradition, language, religion, and way of life. Among black Africans, there are some 800 ethnic groups. (The map on page 31 shows some of the ethnic groups of Africa.) In the past, such groups were often referred to as tribes. This is not how Africans think of themselves, however. The term *tribe* as it has been used to describe African peoples was imposed by the European powers that colonized Africa in the 1800s (see Chapter 5). For instance, in Kenya today the Abaluyia (ah-bah-LOO-yuh) people are a mixture of several ethnic groups from different parts of East Africa. Once they had different customs and spoke different languages. British authorities, who ruled Kenya as a colony, decided to use the language of one of these groups, the Abaluyia, as a standard. Thus they referred to several different ethnic groups as the Abaluyia tribe without regard to the differences in language and culture.

Besides the African ethnic groups, the population also includes Arabs, Europeans, and Asians. The majority of people north of the Sahara are Arab, and many are followers of the Islamic religion. The majority of Europeans on the continent, somewhat more than five million, live in South Africa. Most are Afrikaners (af-rih-KAH-nurs), descendants of early Dutch, French, and German settlers. About two million white South Africans are descendants of British settlers. There are also about one million Asians in South Africa, descendants of people from the Indian subcontinent, and several hundred thousand Asians elsewhere in Africa. (You will read more about South Africa and its people in Chapter 9.)

Most African nations have a number of ethnic groups within their borders. In Zaire there are more than 40, while in Nigeria it is estimated that there are close to 300. In addition, people of one ethnic group may be found in more than one nation. For instance, the Somali

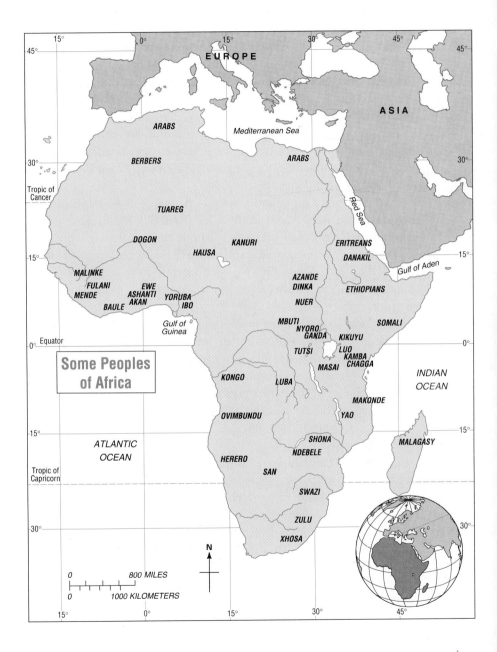

Some Peoples of Africa

EUROPE

ASIA

Mediterranean Sea

ARABS

BERBERS

ARABS

TUAREG

Red Sea

DOGON

KANURI

HAUSA

ERITREANS

DANAKIL

Gulf of Aden

MALINKE

AZANDE

FULANI

EWE

DINKA

ETHIOPIANS

MENDE

ASHANTI

AKAN

YORUBA

NUER

BAULE

IBO

Gulf of
Guinea

MBUTI

NYORO

SOMALI

GANDA

KIKUYU

Equator

TUTSI

LUO

KAMBA

MASAI

CHAGGA

KONGO

LUBA

INDIAN
OCEAN

MAKONDE

OVIMBUNDU

YAO

ATLANTIC
OCEAN

SHONA

MALAGASY

HERERO

NDEBELE

Tropic of
Capricorn

SAN

SWAZI

ZULU

XHOSA

N

0   800 MILES

0   1000 KILOMETERS

31

(soh-MAH-lee) people live not only in Somalia but also in neighboring countries. This came about because the European powers set arbitrary boundaries for their colonies, cutting across the lands traditionally held by ethnic groups. The borders of many African nations are based on these colonial patterns and continue the scattering of ethnic groups.

Languages.   The languages spoken in Africa can be grouped into four large language families: Niger-Congo (NY-jur-KONG-go), Nilo-Saharan (ny-loh-suh-HAR-un), Afro-Asiatic (af-roh-ay-zhee-AT-ik), and Khoisan (KOI-san). Languages of the Indo-European family are also spoken in Africa. The roots of the African language families developed thousands of years ago. Taken together, the language families of Africa include as many as 1,000 different languages.

The Niger-Congo language family is the largest. In addition to many languages in West Africa, it includes about 300 Bantu (BAN-too) languages. The term *Bantu* refers to a **linguistic**, or language, group. Among Bantu languages are Swahili (swah-HEE-lee), Zulu (ZOO-loo), Kikuyu (ki-KOO-yoo), Sotho (SOO-too), Kongo (KONG-goh), and Ndebele (un-duh-BEE-lee). Bantu languages are spoken by most people in southern and eastern Africa.

Nilo-Saharan languages are spoken in parts of East Africa and the Sudanic region. Dinka (DING-kuh), Masai (muh-SY), and Nuer (NOO- ur) are major languages in this group.

Afro-Asiatic languages are spoken throughout Africa north of the Sahara and in parts of East Africa. Arabic and Berber (BUR-bur) are the major languages of this family. About 100 million Africans speak Arabic. The Afro-Asiatic group also includes Amharic (am-HAR-ik), Hausa (How-sah), and Somali.

Languages of the Khoisan family are spoken in southwestern Africa. Khoisan languages are sometimes called **click languages** because their words include a series of hard, clicking sounds.

Languages of the Indo-European family are widely spoken in southern Africa. They include English and Afrikaans (af-rih-KANS), which is derived from Dutch and spoken by the Afrikaners of South Africa.

Tanzania has more than 80 languages, and there are more than 250 in Nigeria. African languages are not confined to national borders. Some are spoken by millions of people. Hausa and Swahili, for example, are widely used. Swahili is a major language in eastern and southern Africa. It is spoken by about 100 million people. About 15 million Africans speak Hausa, the language of the Hausa people of northern Nigeria. Other languages, however, might be spoken by only a few hundred people, perhaps only by the people of a single village or town.

To help communications between peoples, many nations of Africa have adopted official languages, which are used in government and business. The local languages are still spoken, however. The official language of African nations largely reflect their former domination by the British, French, or Portuguese. In Kenya, for example, the official languages are English and Swahili, while the language most frequently spoken is Swahili. In Angola, once a Portuguese colony, the official language is Portuguese, but several other languages are spoken by the various ethnic groups of that nation. In other countries once under French control, such as Chad and the Central African Republic, French is the official language. English and Afrikaans are the official languages of South Africa. Africans in South Africa speak one or both of these in addition to their mother tongue, which might be Zulu, Xhosa (KOH-suh), Ndebele, Sotho, or another.

50%

Traditional Religions. About one-half of the population of Africa south of the Sahara practices some form of traditional African religion. There is no single traditional religion with a single body of beliefs and practices, however. Rather, there are as many different forms of traditional religion as there are cultures in Africa. Nevertheless, certain characteristics are common to most. For instance, most groups believe that God as the creator gave to all living and nonliving things a life force or spirit that cannot die. In addition, everything, living and nonliving, is connected to every other living thing. Thus there is a central unity of the universe.

African traditional religions are systems of belief that give their followers not only a rich spiritual life but also a moral and ethical philosophy. They teach what is right and what is wrong and how to live a good life and avoid that which is evil or harmful. Most traditional religions include reverence for ancestors. This aspect of religion is important to most Africans, including those who are Islamic or Christian. Each group interacts with ancestral spirits in a different way. Among all of them, however, spirits of ancestors can be called on to approach God to help the living. Among most peoples, death is not seen as a departure from the world of the living but, rather, as a change of status or position, just as the change from childhood to adulthood is a change of status. The relationship between the dead and the living is believed to be like that among the members of a family.

In some African religions, the spirits associated with things and events in nature such as thunder, water, soil, fertility, and crops are believed to be always present and are part of everyday life.

Islam. Nearly 150 [25%] million Africans are Muslims, or Islamic, followers of the religion of Islam. In the nations of North Africa, Islam is the state religion. It is also a major religion in such nations as Sudan, Niger, Mali, and Chad, as well as in the coastal regions of East Africa.

Islam was founded by the prophet Muhammad in the 600s. He was recognized as the prophet of God who is known as Allah. Muhammad's followers moved out of the Arabian Peninsula to the Mediterranean world and into Africa, particularly northern Africa. Muslims founded great cities in northern Africa and spread their influence to sub-Saharan Africa through trade and commerce. Followers of traditional African religions came in touch with the beliefs of Islam and adopted them. In early African empires many non-Muslim rulers employed Muslims as advisers and officials to help them in their relations with foreigners. Muslims wrote Arabic, and African kings understood how useful a written language is for purpose of taxation, commerce, and politics.

Today, in towns and cities, particularly along the eastern coast, one hears the sounds of African Muslims being called to prayer throughout the day. *Mosques*, Islamic houses of worship, dot the horizon. Like Muslims around the world, African Muslims observe the duties known as the Five Pillars: witnessing the oneness of God and Muhammad, prayer, charity, fasting, and making a pilgrimage to Muhammad's birthplace. They revere the Quran (koor-AN), the holy book of Islam. The Quran contains Muhammad's most important moral teachings and sets down rules for behavior that his followers must follow.

Students learn the Quran in an Islamic religious school. They copy the verses on tablets, chant, and memorize them.

Christianity. 25%   The number of Christians in Africa is estimated to be nearly 160 million. In nations such as Nigeria, Uganda, Lesotho, and South Africa, Christians form the majority religious group. There are also large and sometimes powerful Christian communities in almost every other sub-Saharan nation.

Christianity in Africa dates back about 1,500 years, when a form of the religion, known as **Coptic** Christianity, took hold in Egypt and Ethiopia. It was brought to the area by followers of the Eastern Orthodox Church of the Byzantine empire.

During the European colonization of Africa in the late 1800s, Protestant and Roman Catholic missionaries spread Christianity. In Southern Africa, missionaries who followed the British and Dutch merchants and settlers brought Protestant Christianity to the region. In Central Africa, where the French and Belgians established colonies, Roman Catholicism was introduced.

As in Western Christianity, African Christian practices and rituals differ from sect to sect, and African Christianity has its own character. Many **indigenous** Christian churches and sects have developed; these are churches and sects that have originated in Africa. For example, among the Yoruba (YOR-uh-buh) people of Nigeria, the Aladura (AL-uh-dur-uh) sect is concerned with water and the healing power of prayer. When water is blessed, it is believed to have divine power. The Aladura movement is particularly strong in urban areas.

Among African Christians, music and dance have often been incorporated into religious practices. This probably stems from the role of music and dance in traditional religion, where these arts have always been used to express religious ideas. Among the Yoruba, Christians as well as Muslims take part in a traditional festival celebrating the sacred shrine of the goddess Osum, the protector of cities. In fact, a song among the Yoruba says that

> Modern religion does not forbid it,
> We shall perform our traditional rites.

THE ARTS

Art in Africa is closely tied to the traditional beliefs and values of the African peoples. Painting, sculpture, dance, music, drama, and literature are part of everyday life. Art is everywhere in Africa. It is in the decoration of everyday objects—clothing, baskets, boats, jewelry, houses—and in the performance of traditional rituals and ceremonies. Each group has its own artistic traditions.

Sculpture. Much of African sculpture is created for use in ceremonies, where it is combined with music, dance, songs, and poetry. The symbols and styles that an African artist uses are those familiar to the community. Thus in Ghana, when an Ashanti (uh-SHAN-tee) staff is topped with the figure of a bird looking backward, all who see it know that this is the *Senkofu* (sen-KOH-foo) bird. They are reminded of the proverb that tells them never to forget their past.

African artists use many different materials for their work. In the old kingdom of Benin, sculptors perfected the **lost-wax technique** and created splendid bronzes for kings and nobles. In the *lost-wax technique* a clay sculpture is coated with wax and then covered by another layer of clay. The wax is heated to melting and poured out, and a liquid metal—usually bronze—is poured into the space left by the wax. When the clay mold is broken away the hardened bronze statue remains. Earlier, artists in Ife (EE-fay), a town in West Africa, fashioned their works from **terra-cotta**, a brownish orange clay. Today, wood is usually used for

A Benin sculpture of the 1500s shows a chief with ceremonial sword flanked by two soldier-bearers and several other attendants. Today Benin bronzes are admired in museums around the world.

traditional sculpture. It is often decorated with *raffia* and other ornamental grasses, cloth, plant dyes, and pieces of mirrors or glass.

Other carved art is created for everyday use—wooden spoons for cooking, decorated covered bowls for serving food, dolls and other toys, stools, headrests, and other household objects. While these pieces often display symbols as well, their decorations are sometimes executed merely to please the eye. In Zaire, for example, a woman might present dinner to her husband in a bowl whose cover suggests a proverb, telling him that she has important news to share with him after he has eaten. And in South Africa, a child's doll is trimmed with colorful bead necklaces because the little girl who is to receive it likes the colors.

Music.   Africans use song in just about every kind of human activity. There are songs for harvesting crops, for hunting, for traveling, for paying homage to a leader. There is music for pure entertainment, for dance, and songs that recount a people's past. There is traditional music that sounds much as it has for centuries, and there is the up-to-the-minute popular music recorded in the urban areas. Music, like other arts, is often a major form of religious expression in Africa.

Africans play a variety of instruments. Rhythm is highly developed in African music, and thus the dominant instruments are usually drums and other percussion instruments. A musical group often has several types of drum, each with its own sound and pitch. Much of African music is **polyrhythmic**. This means that several overlapping and interlocking rhythms are played at once, producing a rich percussion sound not commonly heard in other parts of the world. Melodic instruments are important, too. Various types of harps and guitar-like instruments are used in traditional music. A harp-guitar called the *kora* is especially important to the oral historians of West Africa.

African music has had a great influence on the world. From the 1600s to the 1700s, millions of Africans were captured and forced to go to other lands as slaves. Wherever they went, they took their musical traditions with them. In the United States, the music of the slaves formed the foundations of gospel music, blues, and New Orleans jazz. Rhythm and blues, rock and roll, and jazz—most of the kinds of popular music we enjoy today—evolved largely from African music.

These kinds of music have in turn influenced African music. Popular African musicians now use electric guitars and saxophones alongside their traditional instruments, and strains of soul music, reggae, and Latin music from the United States and the Carribean can be heard in their work.

*African drummers usually begin learning their
instruments at a young age. They play for many years
before they are considered masters.*

Through radio and television, music from many parts of the world
is heard in Africa. Many of the most prominent foreign musicians are
well known to young Africans. African bands also play on the streets
and in the discos of the cities. In popular musical groups one finds
electronic instruments combined with more traditional instruments to
make a distinctly African sound.

Dance.   Dance is a cherished art form throughout Africa, and dancing
is an intimate part of life. Africans dance at funerals, weddings, christ-
enings; at celebrations honoring the passage to adulthood; or just for
the fun of it. A dance can tell a story with a moral or reenact an
important event in history. Or it can express emotions, such as sorrow
or joy. Dance is an important part of community life, in which everyone

participates. Africans usually dance in groups, rarely as couples. The dancing is also polyrhythmic; that is, dancers move different parts of their bodies in time with the different rhythms being played.

Traditional Literature.   Literature consists of histories, legends, folktales, stories, proverbs, poetry, and drama. An abundance of traditional material exists in Africa and has been passed orally from one generation to the next. Most African oral literature, or **oral tradition,** is both entertaining and educational. It often teaches a lesson or carries a moral. Some stories explain the mysteries of the creation of the universe or recount the origins of the people.

As it is everywhere, story telling is loved in Africa. Generally stories are told and acted out in front of an audience. Individual storytellers have a repertoire of familiar stories. Often, they change them to suit the moment and the audience. Stories are communal—that is, there is a call from the storyteller and an appropriate response from the onlookers. The result is living theater that must be seen and experienced rather than read.

In parts of Africa, generations of *griots* (GREE-ohs or GREE-ots) have kept alive cultural traditions, memories, and stories of the past through an astonishing capacity to remember and recite huge quantities of information. These recitations are often musical performances, with the *griot* singing and accompanying himself on an instrument. A *griot* is a historian, journalist, teacher, musician, and storyteller all rolled into

Women in Mali dance to celebrate the end of a drought.

one. In some places famous or powerful families had their own griot, whose frequent recitations reminded them of their ancestors' accomplishments and urged them to uphold the family honor.

Poetry, another important literary form in Africa, has been used extensively by traditional historians. One traditional type of poem is called a praise poem. It is used to sing the praises of an important person or hero. Other African poetry is recited to entertain or to satisfy the creator of the poem. Many of the herding peoples have a tradition of composing poems to sing or chant while watching their flocks. Thus they keep themselves company and keep away animals that might prey on their herds. The subjects of these poems are often the cattle that they are guarding.

Modern Literature.   Today, African writers produce works in various African languages as well as in English, French, and Portuguese, the languages of their former European rulers. In an effort to combat what they see as the demeaning of African culture by the colonial powers, writers often turn to the roots of their own heritage as the basis for their work. They write about the unity of all of African life and about its customs and traditions. They praise the Africans' love for the land and their respect for their ancestors and their history.

A number of African authors focus on their concern for the problems of modern Africa. One theme is the family and the particular stresses encountered growing up in contemporary Africa. Another theme is the difficulties young people experience finding work and beginning careers. Often, writers are critical of the contemporary governments and their approaches to solving Africa's problems.

Drama.   Traditional theater in Africa combines elements of stage plays and opera. Often the dialogue is directed toward the audience. Spectators will call out to the actors, answering questions the actors have asked.

At important festivals special dramas are enacted that remind people of their history. Actors practice for months, often secretly, the intricate dance patterns and songs that are part of the play. On the day of the festival, they dress in elaborate costumes, which might include a carved mask, symbolizing an ancestor or an important historical figure. As the masked figures dance out their story, musicians accompany them. The audience does not just sit by and watch quietly, however. Frequently men, women, and children join the "masks," turning the drama into a community celebration. Wole Soyinka, (WOH-lay-soy-lN-kuh), the Nigerian dramatist who won the 1987 Nobel Prize for literature, has used many of these traditional dramatic devices in his plays.

In urban centers entertainment is frequently in the form of comic theater, which is especially popular. Here the actors not only rely on humor but also present a moral. Often, they improvise as they perform, not sticking to a rigid format. They, too, encourage audience participation. Dancers, drummers, mimes, and actors are all part of comic theater. Sometimes, as in the case of the Mufwankolo (moo-fwan-KOH-loh) Theater Group in Lubumbashi (loo-BOOM-bah-shee), Zaire, they perform in Swahili so that they can reach a larger audience.

ECONOMIC ACTIVITIES

Economic activity is the way a people or a nation satisfies its basic needs, or the way it makes its living. More than 75 percent of the African people south of the Sahara are involved in farming and herding. The rest are engaged in such activities as mining, manufacturing, commerce, and government work.

Farming.   Farming has been the main economic activity of most Africans for thousands of years. As you have read, much of Africa's soil is not rich in the minerals essential for productive farming. In many areas Africans have developed procedures for **shifting cultivation**. By these methods farmers have planted grains, beans, and other vegetables in rotation. Each crop that is cultivated is selected because it replaces nutrients that the other crops have taken from the soil. At the end of a cycle, the land is cleared, sometimes by burning, and allowed to lie unused for a period of time, during which its organic matter and nutrients return.

The introduction of cash crops has in many places upset this balance. The best farmland is usually devoted to the growing of crops to be exported—coffee, tea, tobacco, peanuts, and cotton, to name just a few. The growing of food crops is also taking place on less productive land. This endangers food production for the local people. When the rains fail, the food crops are first to suffer.

African women are very much affected by this situation. They have always been responsible for feeding their families and, therefore, have also played a major role in farming. While men usually clear land for cultivation, it is the women who plant, weed, and harvest. They are also responsible for food preparation. And in some areas, especially in

West Africa, women sell their surplus crops to buy food they do not grow and other household necessities.

While in some regions land is owned communally by the people who farm it, individual ownership is increasing in Africa. In many countries land ownership and land use are growing concerns for governments. They understand the danger of being dependent on other countries to feed their populations. Almost all African countries, therefore, set land distribution and agricultural research as priorities.

Herding.   In all grassy areas of Africa where the tsetse fly is not a problem, herding is the main economic activity. Most African herders raise a tough breed of cattle. On the fringe of the Sahara, camels are raised. Elsewhere herders tend large flocks of sheep and goats. Most herders raise their animals for milk and other dairy products, not for meat. Rarely—except for ceremonial purposes—do they kill their animals, because the herds are their investment and their wealth. Besides dairy products, most herding peoples include a starchy staple, such as grain or potatoes, in their diet. This they raise themselves or buy.

Most herding people live in scattered villages surrounded by open grazing lands. The women tend gardens and manage the households, and the men do the herding. Some herders are **nomadic,** moving from place to place in search of grazing land and water. Nomadic herders such as the Masai, the Fulani (FOO-lah-nee) and the Dinka, tend to have definite routes they follow over a period of years. People such as the Nuer of the southern Sudan follow a seasonal cycle of movement. They live in one location during the rainy season and move to another for the dry season.

In some areas of Africa, grazing lands are in short supply, and overgrazing has resulted. Some African governments are trying to persuade herders to settle in one place and raise smaller herds of higher-quality cattle that can be sold for cash. Many traditional herders reject such proposals, arguing that to do so would destroy their way of life.

Mixed Agriculture.   Among a growing number of peoples, a combination of farming and herding is practiced. Herding is usually the main economic activity, but when rainfall is ample, crops are also planted. One group of people in southern Kenya, the Kamba (KAM-buh) combine hunting, farming, and cattle herding.

Fishing.   Fishing is an ancient and important economic activity along Africa's coasts and on the shores of many of its rivers and lakes.

In Mali, along the West African coast, fishing is a communal activity. Many men, using large nets and boats, fish together, dividing the catch among themselves.

Commercial fishing is a growing economic activity in Africa. For centuries only people near bodies of water ate fish. The warm tropical climates caused fish to spoil rapidly and discouraged its transport. Today, with improving transportation and refrigeration, governments are encouraging people to eat fish. The high-quality protein in fish will improve diets. Governments in Zaire, Zimbabwe, and Nigeria have been especially active in helping to develop commercial fish farms.

Other Occupations.   Mining is an ancient and still-important industry in parts of Africa. Forestry is an increasing activity, and, in urban areas, manufacturing is growing. Each year larger numbers of Africans leave the rural areas to take jobs in industry. They are being employed as bus and truck drivers, sanitation workers, office clerks, secretaries, bank tellers, construction workers, hotel clerks, and salespersons. Others are going to work for their government. Growing numbers have become lawyers, doctors, engineers, and teachers, while others have started businesses of their own.

SOCIAL ORGANIZATION

Every society is organized in different ways to raise children, produce food, provide for the common good, and govern itself. Among most peoples the basic unit of society is the family. It is at the family level

CASE STUDY:

African Hospitality

Africans across the continent take pride in being hospitable to visitors. This reading describes how a visitor is treated among the Ibo of southeastern Nigeria. The Ibo believe that God will only help people who are themselves kind and welcoming.

Neighbors come together in the evening to chat. . . . Women are even more hospitable than the men. Each housewife who prepares new soup sends a spoonful or two to the housewives living nearby. She asks them to tell her whether or not there is enough salt in the soup, or if there is too much pepper.

On important occasions every family sends food to the neighboring families. If a family has a visitor the neighbors will all entertain the visitor in turn. The wife goes to the house where the visitor is lodging and asks the host or hostess to bring the visitor to her house. Secretly she will find out what the newcomer likes and then prepares that food. When the guests arrive, kola* is served and food is brought. . . It is a sign of disrespect for the visitor to refuse the food. On the other hand, visitors are not supposed to finish all the food. They are expected to leave morsels of it. Otherwise the impression is created that the guest has not had enough food to eat for a long time. As a rule enough food is provided. Children who wash plates and dishes are unhappy if they do not find remnants of food on the plate or dish.

---

*The kola nut is used as a food. It is often ceremonially split and shared, particularly in West Africa, as a sign of friendship.
Rems Nna Umeasiegbu, *The Way We Lived* (London: Heinemann, 1969), p. 39.

1. How do the writer's people show that sharing is an important tradition?

2. Compare and contrast American habits when guests are present with those of the Ibo.

that children are born, brought up, educated, and taught the rules of the group. In Africa the family is often also the primary economic unit of society. The family is the basic unit of production, distribution, and consumption.

The Family.   The family is especially important in African society because it has the basic responsibility for the training and development of the young. If you ask an American young person how many people are in his or her family, most likely the answer will be somewhere between two and six. The average American family includes one or two parents plus one to four children.

If you ask the same question of an African teenager, the answer might well be a larger number. For an African defines his or her family to include not just parents, brothers, and sisters, but grandparents, uncles, aunts, and cousins. Indeed, Africans frequently live close to their relatives or have relatives living with their immediate family. For example, a teenager who qualifies for high school in a distant town will often live in the family of an uncle or aunt in that town in order to attend the school.

When a family includes three or more generations of relatives living together or near one another, it is called an **extended family**. Members of an extended family live and work together. **Kinship,** or the way in which one is related to other family members, is an important concept among African families. It is the way in which families trace their ancestry. Africans may trace their family history through both their mother and father or only through their mother. Most groups, however, are linked by their descent through male members of the family. These kinship ties are particularly strong—the relatives provide support for individuals and for families, and Africans have a kinship word to describe almost every family relationship.

Marriage and Parenthood.   Because the family is so important, marriage and parenthood are vital to an African's life. Marriage is not just the union of individuals, but of families. The children of a marriage guarantee that the kinship group will survive another generation. Typically, a young woman's family must approve her choice of suitor. In general, the family is concerned that the young man be of a good family and able to provide well for her and her children. Once the suitor is approved, a payment of **bride-wealth** to the young woman's family is expected before the marriage takes place. This is a token payment of money, goods, or livestock to guarantee the stability of the marriage. If the marriage breaks up, the bride-wealth must be returned. Thus both families have a stake in helping the marriage succeed. Payment of bride-wealth is a traditional practice that is today controversial. Several African governments oppose it.

Polygyny, having more than one wife, is an ancient practice in Africa. Typically, though, only a small number of Africans practice polygyny. In general, before a man marries a second wife, he must prove that he can afford to. Among some African people today, particularly in Islamic areas, men of status and wealth may have two or more wives. To those African women who accept this arragement, it is seen as means of sharing household and child-rearing chores.

Among most African peoples, the husband is the head of the family. After marriage, newlyweds live with or near the husband's family. Living arrangements among married people vary greatly from group to group, however. Among the Ibo (EE-boh) farmers in Nigeria, a polygynous husband provides a separate dwelling for each of his wives. He has a small house of his own in which he sleeps alone most of the time. The children of each wife sleep with their own mother. Among the Luo (loo-OH or LOO-oh) herders of Kenya and Tanzania, each wife has her own dwelling, but the husband has none for himself.

Women are not without power. As you already have seen, they do most of the planting, cultivating, and harvesting, and they sometimes control the extra money earned from trading. Where kinship is traced through the mother, property is inherited through the mother's brother, linking family members through the female line. In certain regions, particularly in West Africa, conflicts over land and inheritances began to arise when the colonial powers imposed their own property laws on African traditions. Today the courts in Nigeria, Ghana, and other countries are crowded with cases of disputes related to the clash between traditional African inheritance practices and the newer legal systems.

EDUCATION

In African society education is the primary responsibility of the family, but all adults in the community take an interest in the children. Within the family children learn their culture, history, and responsibilities. Girls learn from their mothers how to cook, plant, and care for children. Young boys learn about herding by tending the goats and other animals. In the time they spend doing these chores, the boys and girls also learn about their environment. By the time they are teenagers, most African youngsters are considered capable of taking their places as adults in the community.

In the nineteenth century formal schools were established by missionaries to teach reading and writing. The colonial powers considered these skills essential for African workers who would work for the government or for foreign-owned businesses and industries. Only a small number of students were educated in these schools. Significant advances in education did not occur until more recent times.

CHANGING PATTERNS

The people of Africa, as they change and develop, are adapting their traditional patterns to more modern ways. Town and city dwellers retain their kinship ties. When a person goes to the city, he or she still seeks out relatives. City dwellers who return to their villages take with them many aspects of urban life, such as modern music, transistor radios, and new fashions. And those who have lived in large towns and cities for many years still return to their relatives at home for important occasions, such as marriages and funerals.

For thousands of years, Africans have adapted to their environment and adopted the changes brought about by their history. As they face the future, it seems likely that they will continue to fuse together the old and the new.

At a women's educational center in Nigeria, an instructor teaches a new knitting stitch. Her students will return to their homes and share their knitting skills with their neighbors.

REVIEWING THE CHAPTER

I. Building Your Vocabulary

In your notebook, write the correct term that matches the definition.

kinship   polygyny   ethnic group
nomadic   extended family   indigenous

1. the practice of having more than one wife

2. moving from place to place in search of water and grazing land

3. originating in a particular area

4. the way in which one is related to other family members

5. a group of people who share a common languauge, tradition, religion, and way of life

6. a family that includes three of more generations of relatives living near one another or together

II. Understanding the Facts

In your notebook, write the numbers 1 to 5. Write the letter of the correct answer to each question next to its number.

1. How many ethnic groups exist among black Africans?
   a. 300   **b.** 800   **c.** 950

2. What is the largest language family in Africa?
   a. Nilo-Saharan   **b.** Niger-Congo   **c.** Afro-Asiatic

3. What instruments are the most dominant in African music?
   a. drums   **b.** harps   **c.** guitars

4. What is the main economic activity of most Africans?
   a. mining   **b.** farming   **c.** herding

5. Through what do African families trace their ancestry?
   a. bride-wealth   **b.** generations   **c.** kinship

III. Thinking It Through

In your notebook, write the numbers 1 to 4. Write the letter of the correct answer to each question next to its number.

1. More than 75 percent of the people south of the Sahara are involved in
   a. government work.   b. manufacturing.
   c. farming and herding.   d. mining.

2. Africa's need for cash crops has resulted in
   a. the total neglect of herding.
   b. the overuse of the soil.
   c. the use of the best farmland for crops to be exported.
   d. the use of large pieces of land for industrial development.

3. To counter the influence of the colonial powers, many modern African writers
   a. attack European governments in their works.
   b. turn to the roots of their own heritage.
   c. ignore the past completely.
   d. develop themes that have nothing to do with Africa.

4. Which of the following statements would most Africans *not* agree with?
   a. The family is especially important.
   b. Song should be a part of every human activity.
   c. The past has little to teach modern people.
   d. Everything living and nonliving is connected to every other living thing.

DEVELOPING CRITICAL THINKING SKILLS

1. Describe the role of the extended family in African life.

2. Explain how song in Africa is a part of virtually every kind of human activity.

3. Discuss the characteristics that are common to most traditional religions in Africa.

4. Show how the people of Africa are adapting their traditional patterns to more modern ways.

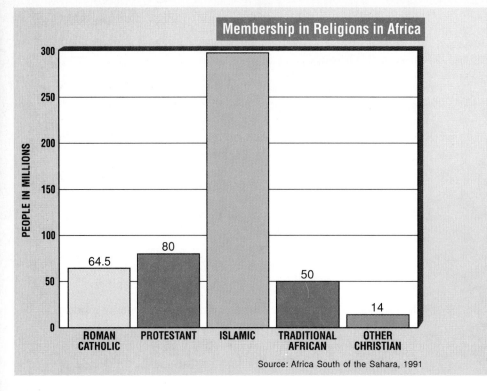

Source: Africa South of the Sahara, 1991

INTERPRETING A BAR GRAPH

Study the graph below. Answer the questions that follow the graph in your notebook.

1. What is the total number of Christians in Africa?

2. How many Africans follow the traditional African religions?

3. How many Africans are Muslims, and how many are not?

ENRICHMENT AND EXPLORATIONS

1. Locate recordings of African music and play them in class. Conduct a class discussion of the features of the music.

2. As a class project, collect illustrations of African sculpture. Make copies of interesting examples. Present and explain each in class. Identify the section of Africa that each item comes from.

3. Conduct a research project into the types of instruments that were used by African musicians. Obtain pictures of the instruments or make drawings of them. Present your findings in class, and develop a bulletin board display of the illustrations and explanatory material.

3 *Early History*

Africa has been described in many ways—a miracle of diversity, a cultural bazaar, the cradle of humanity. These phrases all have their roots in Africa's early history. Many of the patterns of living that exist in Africa today developed on that continent long ago.

THE PEOPLING OF AFRICA

Africa's human past is a lengthy one—perhaps the longest in the world. Fossil findings, by famous anthropologists, such as Louis and Mary Leakey, their son Richard, and Donald Johnson, have uncovered remarkable evidence of human origins. Scientific analysis of these findings indicate that **hominids**, or humanlike species, first walked upright in Africa. Today, most scholars agree that humankind was born in Africa more than two million years ago—some say as long ago as four million years. What this means is that the ancestors of modern humans developed there, in the Great Rift Valley region of eastern Africa. In this sense, Africa is the cradle in which humankind developed.

Earliest Ancestors.　Several humanlike types emerged in Africa. The most important in human evolution is *Homo habilis* ("skillful man"), who appeared about two million years ago. *Habilis* looked apelike but was more like modern humans than any ape. These hominids walked upright and had hands with **opposable** thumbs and forefingers, which made it easier to grasp and manipulate objects. Evidence indicates that they may have made and used simple pebble tools, such as choppers fashioned from sharp-edged pieces of stone. They lived in small, nomadic bands, apparently surviving mostly on plants that they gathered. They may also have occasionally eaten animals that they stalked and killed.

AFRICA AND THE WORLD
1000 B.C.–A.D. 350

5000–4000 B.C.	Settlements develop along Nile River.
c. 4000 B.C.	Knowledge of agriculture reaches Egypt.
c. 3500 B.C.	Nile settlements achieve civilization.
c. 3100 B.C.	King Menes unifies Egypt, becomes pharaoh. Hieroglyphics developed.
2850–2360 B.C.	*Earliest Mesopotamian Civilization*
2615–2175 B.C.	Old Kingdom
c. 2000 B.C.	Egyptians conquer Kush. Agriculture develops in sub-Saharan Africa.
c. 2000 B.C.	*Civilization flourishes in Indus Valley.*
1991–1786 B.C.	Middle Kingdom
1786–1570 B.C.	Second Intermediary Period
c. 1720 B.C.	Hyksos establish dynasty in delta region.
1570–332 B.C.	New Kingdom
1503 B.C.	Hatshepsut declares herself pharaoh.
c. 1500 B.C.	Pharaohs of 17th dynasty drive out Hyksos.
1350 B.C.	Amonhotep rebels against state religion.
1050 B.C.	Palestine and Kush independent from Egypt.
c. 1000 B.C.	Farming and herding spread throughout Africa.
c. 750–671 B.C.	Kush rules Egypt.
671 B.C.	Assyrians drive Kushites from Egypt.
480 B.C.	*Golden Age begins in Greece.*
332 B.C.	Alexander the Great conquers Egypt.
323–31 B.C.	Rule by Ptolemy and his descendants
200 B.C.	Meroë prospers.
31 B.C.–A.D. 192	Roman Empire at Its Peak
c. A.D. 1	Bantu speaking people expand territory.
c. A.D. 350	Ezana defeats Kush.

Over thousands of generations, *habilis* slowly began to change. Around 1. 5 million years ago a more advanced human type emerged. This was *Homo erectus* ("erect man"), who may have been the direct ancestor of modern humans, though scientists are not certain of this. Much more study is needed before scientists understand and agree on the evolution of human beings.

Erectus had a larger and more complex brain than *habilis* and a more humanlike appearance. *Erectus* made more advanced tools, such as hand axes, and could control fire. With these skills, this species was able to gain greater control over its environment, and thus its numbers increased. As the population grew, *erectus* moved beyond Africa, reaching China, India, and Southwest Asia.

Modern Humans Emerge.   No one knows exactly when or where modern humans, *Homo sapiens* ("thinking man"), first developed. Remains have been found in Africa, Europe, and Asia. Experts believe that the first species of modern humans appeared about 300,000 years ago. From these hominids, modern humans began to develop around 35,000 years ago.

Early *Homo sapiens* were nomadic hunters and gatherers, establishing temporary campsites in caves and rocky shelters. More intelligent than *Homo erectus*, they rapidly acquired new skills for survival. They developed smaller, more efficient tools for carving, piercing, and chopping. They used weapons such as bows and arrows, and they used

Louis and Mary Leakey were the first to discover and document human origins in Africa. Their pioneering efforts are still pursued in East Africa.

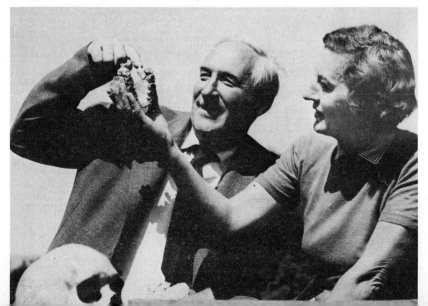

animal and plant products to make clothing, rope, and shelters. They divided their labor: men hunted and fished; women gathered and cooked and cared for the children. They developed articulate spoken languages and began to decorate or dress themselves. The prehistoric period in which humans developed from *Homo habilis* to *Homo sapiens* is called the Old Stone Age. It was a period of enormous length—it lasted at least two million years— and dramatic change.

ORIGINS OF FARMING IN THE NILE VALLEY

Only after more than two million years of human evolution did agriculture begin to develop. This was about 10,000 years ago. It was the most revolutionary and far-reaching achievement of these early times. How humans learned to grow crops and domesticate animals—that is, tame them for human use—is unknown. But that this knowledge changed the way humans live is undeniable.

With agriculture, early people had a more reliable food supply. Now they could give up nomadic life and establish permanent settlements. This change in turn led to population increases and new ways of living together. People established larger communities and organized themselves so that different people did different jobs. They began to look beyond the present to the future. For example, they stored food for future consumption. They also began to spend more time in pursuits unrelated to survival. They practiced religion and created works of art. We call this period, in which humans learned to grow crops and domesticate animals, the New Stone Age.

The New Stone Age began in different parts of the world at different times. Evidence indicates that people first developed agriculture in the Middle East some 10,000 years ago. There is also evidence that by this time, agriculture had reached Egypt.

"The Gift of the Nile."   The Nile valley was an ideal environment for the cultivation of such grains as barley, sorghum, and millet. Its great fertility was due to the river that created it.

The Nile River in northeastern Africa is part of a much larger river system. Its main source, called the White Nile, begins far to the south in Rwanda. The White Nile provides the Nile valley with a steady flow of water throughout the year. The tributary called the Blue Nile rises in the Ethiopian Highlands. It affects the Nile valley in a different way. In summer, heavy rains in the Ethiopian Highlands turn the Blue Nile into a torrent of moving water. This torrent gains even greater force as the

Egyptian farmers today work their irrigated fields in the same way as did their ancestors in ancient Egypt. The barren hills of the Sahara rise in the background.

Blue Nile and the White Nile join to form the Nile at modern-day Khartoum (kahr-TOOM). The flood is then carried along the Nile as it crosses six rocky rapids called **cataracts**. In ancient times, the land where the cataracts are located was called Kush. (Today it is called Nubia.) To the north, in the Nile valley north from Kush to the Mediterranean Sea, lay Egypt

Today the flood water is caught behind a giant dam at Aswan, near the site of the northernmost cataract. In ancient times, however, the flood reached the lower Nile valley in August, when Egypt's dry desert air is at its hottest. Every year it broke over the river banks and covered the parched earth with water. When it receded in October, it left behind a muddy deposit of rich soil. No wonder the ancient Egyptians called their country *Kemet*, or "Black Land."

In this rich soil, seeds could be planted and grain harvested before the land dried out again. These strips of land covered an area one to 12 miles wide on either side of the Nile as well as the entire **delta** region. The delta is the triangle-shaped region near the Mediterranean Sea where the Nile divides into a number of channels. It takes its name

55

from the shape of the Greek letter delta [Δ]. Each year the Nile could be counted on to flood again, once more bringing its rich gift to the farmers. The Greek historian Herodotus called Egypt "the gift of the Nile." The Egyptians themselves cosidered it a gift from a kindly god they called Hapi.

The Agricultural Revolution. The Nile valley became a rich farming region when people learned to cultivate crops and domesticate animals. To **domesticate** is to tame animals and breed them for human use. These discoveries were made at different times and at different places throughout the world. They proved so momentous that they are called the **Agricultural Revolution.** The period that followed these discoveries is called the **New Stone Age.**

Egypt's Agricultural Revolution was certainly one of the earliest. Archaeological evidence now shows that certain types of wild barley were probably cultivated by the ancient peoples of Egypt and Kush by 10,000 B.C. and possibly as early as 16,000 B.C.

This Agricultural Revolution did not take place overnight, however. It was a slow, haphazard process. At first, Old Stone Age hunters may have wandered into the Nile valley in search of animals and wild grain. After finding places where the grain grew in abundance, the next step may have been to protect it from birds, insects, and wild animals. In time, the gatherers discovered the need to leave some seed behind for next year's crop. They also learned to remove weeds with a simple stone hoe and to improve the quality of the soil by working it with a simple plow. When they finally learned to choose seeds from the strongest plants to sow, true farming had begun.

The domestication of animals must also have taken place slowly and accidentally. People who once had hunted animals for meat and hides somehow learned that by taming cattle, sheep, and goats, they could obtain continuing sources of meat, milk, and leather. As their methods of farming improved, it occurred to them that the larger animals could be trained to pull plows. Smaller animal also proved useful. Dogs could be trained to herd sheep and goats. Cats could be used to catch the mice that often ate the stored supplies of grain.

As the people of the Nile Valley made these revolutionary discoveries, they began to gather into communities. This process also was probably slow. No doubt some people preferred to continue their hunting and gathering lives. Even those who settled down often hunted, gathered, and fished for some of their food supply.

Scenes of harvesting in ancient Egypt. These paintings are from the wall of a tomb at Thebes.

Growth of Permanent Settlements. Between 5000 and 4000 B.C., a number of small, permanent settlements developed along the Nile and in the delta region. The oldest remains yet discovered of the early settlements were unearthed at Al Fayyum (al FAH-yoom; see map, page 60). There archaeologists identified grains of wheat and barley, some simple tools of stone and bone, and pottery that was used for cooking and food storage. Finally, these early farmers perfected methods of irrigation and flood control.

In many ways, this last development was the most crucial to the later development of civilization. Before irrigation and flood control, farmers had been **subsistence** farmers. In subsistence farming, each farming family can produce only enough to feed itself. Larger crops led to the production of surpluses. A **surplus** is an amount of something beyond what is needed. Food surpluses made it possible for some members of the community to abandon farming. They could then take up such pursuits as pottery making, building, trading, and administration.

Taming the river taught the villagers important lessons in cooperation and group living. One anthropologist put it this way:

> Whole villages or groups of people had to turn out to fix dikes or dig ditches. . . . There also had to be hard and fast rules. The person who lived nearest the ditch . . . must not be allowed to take all the water and leave none for his neighbors. It was not only a business of

learning to control the rivers and making their waters do the farmer's work. It also meant controlling men. . . . This learning to work together for the common good was probably the real germ of the Egyptian . . . civilization.

Surpluses also created class differences. Generally, the managers or chiefs who controlled production grew rich and powerful. Those who did the actual producing often remained poor.

Over the centuries, some of these manager-chieftains assumed control over their **clans**, or groups of families. In time, a few such leaders gained greater control over wider areas, containing a large number of clans. This process continued until by 3500 B.C. the communities along the Nile had been formed into two kingdoms, each ruled by a strong leader. One of these, Upper Egypt, extended from Aswan in the south to the beginning of the delta. The other, Lower Egypt, occupied the delta region.

EARLY EGYPTIAN CIVILIZATION

For many generations small farming villages existed along the Nile. Then suddenly something extraordinary happened. In a remarkably short time—"Almost overnight," as one historian has observed—the Egyptians made a number of important inventions and discoveries. They invented a system of writing. They worked out an accurate calendar. They began to construct large buildings and monuments of stone. And they accumulated enough wealth to permit some, at least, of the people to live more comfortably than had been known before.

Scholars agree that by 3500 B.C., societies along the Nile River had developed all the elements needed to be called a civilization. These included a city-dwelling population with specialized professions; a system of writing; a way of measuring, weighing, and calculating; monumental buildings; long-distance trade; a well-developed religion; and a highly organized form of government. No one knows exactly why or how this civilization developed so quickly.

The Religious Structure. Religion was the central force in early Egyptian civilization. Out of it evolved much of Egypt's government, art, medicine, astronomy, and literature.

The Egyptian religion is an example of **polytheism** (PAHL-ee-thee-iz-um). Polytheism is the belief in many **deities**, or gods and goddesses. The Egyptians believed that the spirits of these deities dwelled in such natural forces as the sun, the sky, the earth, and the Nile. They also believed that each clan had been founded by a special deity who would continue to protect the clan if treated with respect. They believed that the spirit of the deity sometimes inhabited the body of an animal, such as a bird, a jackal, a crocodile, or a cow.

Belief in an afterlife was important in Egyptian religion. This belief may have originated in watching nature in action. Each night the sun died in the west and was reborn in the east. Each year the cycle of flooding, planting, harvest, and dying brought thoughts of human death and renewal.

Egyptians believed that each person had a soul and that if a person was good and just in this life, his or her soul would find happiness in the next. To ensure a resting place for the soul after death, the Egyptians developed the practice of preserving the bodies of the dead. Through a complicated process, they created what are called mummies. A **mummy** is a dead body that has been preserved by embalming and wrapping. The mummies of kings and noble persons were buried with rich treasures for their personal use in the afterlife. The tombs were usually hidden to protect their treasures from grave robbers.

Strong Central Goverment.   Religion also provided the basis for the Egyptian government. Egyptians believed that their king was a god. His name was rarely spoken aloud. Instead, his subjects referred to him as **pharaoh** (FAIR-oh), a word that means "great house" or "palace." The pharaoh was identified with control of the Nile flood, an event that was crucial to the lives of all Egyptians.

A pharaoh's control over Egypt's people and territory was absolute. The pharaoh made the laws, and he appointed the officials who administered the laws. The pharaoh was judge and jury, deciding who would prosper or fail, who would live or die. The pharaoh owned the land and everything on it. The pharaoh expected absolute obedience. A person approaching the pharaoh threw himself on the ground and crawled toward him, singing his praises and exalting his beauty.

Pharaohs took their responsibilities seriously, trying to be the kind and just rulers that their subjects believed a god-king should be. Here are words of advice of one early pharaoh to his son:

> Be not evil; it is good to be kind. . . . Do right. . . . Calm the weeper, oppress no widow, expel no man from the property of his father. . . . Don't promote the son of a noble over the son of a man of lower birth, but consider a person's worth on the basis of his actions.

The First Dynasties. At first, Egyptian civilization centered on two pharaohs, not one. In Upper Egypt (the south), the pharaoh was identified with the god Set. The pharaoh's white crown bore the symbols of the vulture and the lotus plant. In Lower Egypt, the delta region, the pharaoh was identified with Horus, the falcon god. This pharaoh's red crown was adorned with a cobra.

About 3100 B.C. a king of Upper Egypt named Menes (MEE-**neez**) conquered the delta country, unified Egypt, and proclaimed himself Pharaoh of the Two Lands. He crowned himself with a double crown, which superimposed the white crown of Upper Egypt onto the red crown of Lower Egypt. He also merged the gods and customs of the two regions. He established his capital at Memphis, a convenient site on the border between Upper and Lower Egypt.

Menes founded the first Egyptian **dynasty**, or ruling family. Over the next 3,000 years, 31 dynasties would rule over the longest-lasting civilization the world has yet known. Until the very end, the pharaohs

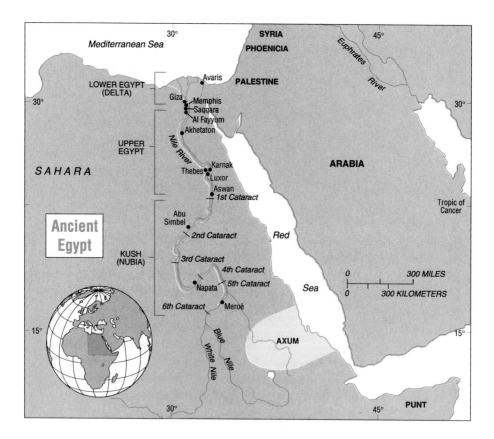

called themselves Pharaohs of the Two Lands and wore the double crown.

Trade in the Early Dynasties.　Menes and his successors exercised absolute control over the trade that was beginning to develop. In fact, some historians believe that it may have been Menes' desire to control such riches that led him to unite the two kingdoms. At first most trade was domestic, or within the country. Simple boats made of reeds carried local goods from village to village along the Nile. As the boats headed north, the rowers' task was aided by the river's current. On the trip south, the boats probably were towed by donkeys on the shore. Later, sails were invented, so that boats could take advantage of the prevailing winds from the north to propel them upstream.

Foreign trade began to develop when farmers were able to produce even larger crop surpluses and when Egyptian artisans were able to create products that people in other lands desired. Throughout the early dynasties, most foreign trade was carried by caravans of donkeys. From Kush in the south came gold, **ebony** (a hard black wood), ivory, and ostrich feathers. From Syria in the east came copper, which was important for crafting tools, pots, and even statues. Also from the east came the luxuries of spices, incense, and precious gems. In return, Egypt exported its most valuable resource: grain. Gold, imported from the south and west, often was reexported to other lands.

After the Egyptians learned to build large wooden seagoing vessels, they were able to carry their trade to more distant shores. In return for their grain, they imported much-needed timber from Phoenicia (present-day Lebanon) and olive oil from Palestine.

Trade brought new people to Egypt. It is not clear who the first Egyptians were and where they had come from. What is clear, however, is that as Egypt increased its contact with neighboring lands, people from these lands moved into Egypt. The result was a population of great diversity. In Lower Egypt, there were people from lands along the Mediterranean and from Mesopotamia in Asia. In Upper Egypt, many people from the African lands to the south became Egyptians through conquest or migration.

THE OLD KINGDOM

Historians divide the dynasties that followed the reign of Pharaoh Menes into three main periods: the Old Kingdom (about 2615-2175 B.C.), the Middle Kingdom (about 1991-1786 B.C.), and the New

The Sphinx stands guard before the Great Pyramids in the desert near Giza.

Kingdom (about 1570-332 B.C.). During these eras, a unified Egyptian government grew powerful and immensely rich. However, there were times when the pharaohs lost control and the kingdom fell into chaos, conflict, and poverty. These years of disunity are called Intermediary Periods.

The era now known as the Old Kingdom began about 2615 B.C. with the Third Dynasty. It lasted more than 400 years. The grandeur of this period's civilization is best shown by the pyramids that still loom over Egypt's desert sands. In fact, the Old Kingdom is sometimes called the Age of Pyramids.

Master Builder of the Pyramids.   A pyramid is a burial chamber for a pharaoh. Because the Egyptians believed in an afterlife, a pharaoh's tomb took on great significance. It was meant to serve as a residence for his *ka*, or life force, throughout eternity. As the kingdom became richer and more powerful, royal burial chambers began to serve an additional purpose. They became advertisements of the pharaoh's wealth and power.

The first of these monumental burial chambers was built for Zoser, a pharaoh of the Third Dynasty. Its architect was the pharaoh's chief advisor, Imhotep (im-HOH-tep), who has been called "the first real person in known history." Imhotep was a man of many talents. In

62

addition to his roles as political leader and chief architect, he achieved fame as a writer and physician.

To build Zoser's pyramid, Imhotep started with the basic rectangular shape that had long been used for royal tombs. But instead of using mud and bricks, he employed huge rectangular stones. This was the first known use of stone as a building material. Imhotep stacked these rectangles on top of one another to form a pyramid that towered some 210 feet into the sky. Later generations called the structure the *Step Pyramid* because its sides looked like six gigantic steps. Imhotep's masterpiece can still be seen at Saqqara, near the ancient capital of Memphis. It is the oldest building in the world that is still standing.

Imhotep's pyramid was the inspiration for many more. The most famous are the pyramids built for the pharaohs of the Fourth Dynasty. The greatest of all is the Great Pyramid, built for Pharaoh Khufu (KOO-foo), also known as Cheops (KEE-ops), on a plain at Giza near modern Cairo. Near Khufu's pyramid are several smaller pyramids and a colossal sphinx. A **sphinx** is a figure with the body of a lion and the head of a man, ram, or hawk. In this case, the sculptured head is that of Khufu's son. Sphinxes were a common way for the ancient Egyptians to depict the power and majesty of a pharaoh.

Building these huge monuments required a tremendous amount of labor as well as the development of amazing engineering skills. For constructing the Great Pyramid, more than 100,000 workers were needed. Without benefit of wheels or cranes, they were able to haul into place millions of stone blocks, each weighing about two and a half tons. Even today the Great Pyramid, built more than 4,500 years ago, is the largest stone building in the world.

The Social Structure. A pyramid can also be used as a way of describing the social organization of the Old Kingdom. Facts about the lives of many of the groups that made up ancient Egyptian society can be deduced from the many paintings and **reliefs** that line the walls of tombs in both Upper and Lower Egypt. A relief is a sculpture in which figures stand out from a flat background.

At the top of the social pyramid was the all-powerful pharaoh. Directly beneath the pharaoh were members of the pharaoh's extended family and the nobles who had inherited their wealth and property from their fathers. These privileged few lived a life of ease in spacious walled houses containing lush gardens. They spent much of their time hunting birds along the Nile, taking boat trips, playing games, and enjoying elaborate feasts at which they were entertained by dancers and musicians.

At the base of the pyramid were the thousands of peasants who lived in small mud houses close to the floodplain of the Nile. Throughout most of the year they farmed the land, herded cattle and goats, and fished in the Nile. The surpluses they were able to produce were given mainly as taxes to the government. During the months when the Nile was in flood, many of the peasants were recruited for othergovernment duties, such as large-scale irrigation projects, the building of pyramids and palaces, and working in state-owned gold and copper mines.

Between the nobles and the peasants were the government administrators. These civil servants carried out the many tasks of government, such as the supervision of irrigation, assessment of taxes, oversight of public works, regulation of foreign trade, administration of the temples, and attention to the pharaoh's personal needs.

During the Old Kingdom, it was sometimes possible for members of the lower classes to rise to positions of power and privilege. The key to success was the ability to write.

Egyptian Writing.   The ancient Egyptian system of writing is called **hieroglyphics** (hy-uhr-oh-GLIF-iks), a Greek word meaning "sacred carving." Hieroglyphics first came into use around 3100 B.C. and was refined and perfected throughout the Old Kingdom.

Writing in Egypt probably originated out of the need to record crop yields and tax assessments. At first, the picture symbols, called **hieroglyphs**, were used to represent specific objects. A stylized hieroglyph of a bird, for example, simply stood for the bird itself. In time, however, the Egyptians also developed hieroglyphs that stood for abstract ideas. A stylized cross, for example, came to stand for the abstract idea of *life*. A circle with a dot in the middle came to stand for *Ra*, the name of the sun god. Finally, as additional time passed, the Egyptians used hieroglyphics **phonetically** (foh-NET-ih-kuh-lee), that is, to stand for sounds, somewhat as we use our alphabet. A falcon, for example, represented the sound of our letter "m"; a swallow represented the sound of our "W." However, these phonetic hieroglyphs represented only consonants, never vowels. For this reason, scholars can make only educated guesses as to what ancient Egyptian vowel sounds may have been.

On the walls of many Old Kingdom temples, palaces, and tombs, hieroglyphic carvings recorded the names of pharaohs and the major events of their reigns. In this way the earliest written histories of Africa have come down to us.

For ordinary business, the hieroglyphics proved more complicated than was necessary. For this purpose, a new variety of writing, called **hieratic** (hy-uhr-AT-ik), was developed. It resembled our cursive, or longhand, script.

Very few people in ancient Egypt knew how to read and write. This skill, called **literacy**, was reserved for a special class of people called **scribes**. To become a scribe, it was necessary to attend a special school in which students learned their craft by painstakingly copying long passages from a textbook. At advanced levels, students copied works of literature, letters, poems, and speeches, thus learning the conventional forms and styles for these various documents. For a pen they used a sharpened **reed**, the hollow stem of a piece of grass. For inks they dissolved red or black pigments in water. They painted their symbols in lines running from right to left on sheets made from the pulp of a reed called **papyrus** (puh-PY-ruhs). Our word *paper* derives from the word for this ancient Egyptian material.

After a scribe graduated, perhaps as early as age 12, he could enter government service by purchasing a position. From then on, his future was assured. He paid no taxes, but often he collected them from others. He might practice law or diplomacy or architecture or engineering. If he showed outstanding ability, he could even become chief advisor to the pharaoh. As one ancient hieroglyphic text tells us, "The scribe orders the destinies of everyone."

Practical Siences. In addition to the skills needed for writing and monumental building, Egyptians of the Old Kingdom developed a number of other talents, all calculated to meet their everyday needs in practical ways .

They developed mathematics and geography, for example, to meet such agricultural needs as surveying the land and recording the size of the harvest. A system of weights and balances was developed, as well as a system for mathematical calculations. Ancient handbooks have been found that show the use of a decimal system in which separate symbols represent 10, 100, and 1,000. Many examples of a special measuring device called a **nilometer** have been unearthed. Nilometers were used to record the level of the annual flood, which was a fairly accurate indicator of the size of harvest that could be expected in any given year.

In surveying, the Egyptians learned to make precise 90-degree angles by what they called a "magic 3-4-5" triangle. A rope would be divided by knots into 12 equal sections. By forming the rope into a triangle with three segments on one side, four segments on a second side, and five segments on the third, a triangle was formed that always had a right (90-degree) angle between the three- and four-segment sides. This is the earliest known application of the Pythagorean theorem.

In order to know when the Nile would flood, the Egyptians invented a calendar. First, they observed that the flood occurred each year after the star Sirius appeared in the sky. Then, by keeping track of the waxing and waning of the moon, they divided the year into 12 months, each having 30 days. When they checked these calculations against Sirius and discovered that the calendar was off by five days, they corrected the error by adding five days to the month that we call September.

To measure time, the Egyptians invented the water clock. A small hole was drilled in the bottom of a stone bowl. The bowl was then filled with water, which passed slowly through the hole at the same rate all day. Daylight was divided into 12 equal segments, so that by drawing 12 equally spaced lines on the side of the bowl, the hours of the day could be identified.

The Egyptians also studied diseases. Although their religion taught that disease was a punishment sent by the gods and goddesses, some individuals began to look at illness in a more scientific way. One papyrus document indicates that Egyptian doctors knew much about body functions and could perform simple operations. Other texts show that there were specialists for diseases of the eyes, teeth, and internal organs. Throughout antiquity, Egyptian doctors were invited to serve at the courts of foreign kings. At the height of the Roman Empire (31 B.C.–A.D. 192), for example, Egyptian doctors were considered the empire's finest.

THE MIDDLE KINGDOM

The Old Kingdom lasted some 500 years. By 2200 B.C., however, Egypt had sunk into a long period of chaos and decline, called by historians the Fkrst Intermediary Period.

What happened to cause the collapse of the central government? One possibility is that the Old Kingdom's building programs drained the national treasury. Another possibility was that, as government jobs became hereditary, fees were no longer paid by people to buy their jobs. Yet another possibility is that a long dry period throughout Africa diminished Egypt's harvest. It may also have caused people living on the border of the Sahara to push into Upper Egypt.

Whatever the reasons, the power of the pharaohs was broken. Nobles established independent, self-sufficient estates and refused to pay taxes. With no income, the central government could no longer maintain its irrigation projects. Without irrigation, less food was produced and an economic depression resulted. Gangs of looters roamed the land, robbing estates and royal tombs. A papyrus text of the period describes the country's mood of despair:

> The wrongdoer is everywhere. . . .
> Plunderers are everywhere. . . .
> The Nile is in flood, yet no one plows. . . .
> Laughter has perished, and grief walks the
>   land. . . .
> The storehouse is bare.

Recovery.   After more than 200 year of troubles, a powerful prince of Upper Egypt seized control of the government. He declared himself the new pharaoh, established a new capital city at Thebes, and made the worship of a local southern god named Amon into a new state religion. These moves ushered in a long period of peace and prosperity known as the Middle Kingdom.

The pharaohs of Middle Kingdom dynasties worked hard to reassert central authority, establish a sound financial base for government operations, and keep the ambitious nobles at bay. They introduced the world's first **census**, or counting of the population, for taxation purposes. They developed a huge new irrigation project at Al Fayyum that reclaimed many acres of desert land and resulted in greater farm surpluses. They set up the world's first known spy network, called the Eyes and Ears of the Pharaoh, to detect threatening activities on the part of the nobility and to report on general conditions throughout the kingdom.

In the continuing power struggle between the pharaohs and the nobility, the common people often emerged the winners. To gain popular support against local princes, pharaohs sometimes gave the peasants their own land. In this way, people whose ancestors had been tied to the land during the Old Kingdom were now free farmers, artisans, and scribes.

Trade and Colonization.   As the Middle Kingdom economy recovered, trade resumed and expanded, most notably with Kush. Kush, now called Nubia, is the part of Africa south of the First Cataract. Its people,

Fighting men from Kush pay tribute to the pharaoh. This wall painting, completed about 1355 B.C., is from the tomb of an official in the New Kingdom.

then as now, were black Africans related to other African peoples farther to the south.

From earliest times Egyptian traders had ventured into Kush in search of ebony, ivory, gold, silver, incense, wood, and precious gems. Texts dating from the Old Kingdom's Fourth Dynasty also record an Egyptian invasion of Kush in which 7,000 Kushites were taken prisoner. Later, in the Sixth Dynasty, another pharaoh sent four peaceful expeditions into Kush, this time with the purpose of exploring beyond Kush to a country called Yam. Records left by the expedition leader tell how he returned to Egypt with 300 donkeys loaded with incense, ebony, ivory, panther skins, and such curiosities as "throw sticks," or boomerangs.

After the decline of the Old Kingdom, Egyptian trade with Kush had been disrupted. However, with the political and economic revival of the Middle Kingdom, a new campaign in the south was launched. This time a canal was cut around the rapids of the First Cataract. With improved navigation, a large Egyptian military force entered Kush. After subduing the local population, the Egyptians established a series of forts and walled towns along the Nile as far as the Third Cataract, 400 miles upstream from the southern border of Egypt. These forts were not only military garrisons but also trading posts where goods were stored before being transported back to Egypt. The large number of these forts suggests that, although Kush had been conquered, its people were still independent enough to give the invaders trouble.

The Second Intermediary Period. After 1786 B.C the authority of the pharaohs was once again weakened, the nobles took power into their own hands, and Egypt sank once more into chaos. In this era, called the

68

Second Intermediary Period, Egypt was invaded by a group of Asiatic people called the Hyksos (HIK-sos). The Egyptians had already been weakened by civil strife. Now they were no match for the Hyksos, who fought with horse-drawn chariots, chain armor, and bronze weapons— all new military technology to the Egyptian. By 1720 B.C. the Hyksos had established their own dynasty in the delta region.

Sometime during this period, a prince of Kush overthrew his Egyptian rulers and joined an alliance with the Hyksos against the Egyptians. The lament of one Egyptian prince has been found in an ancient text:

> I would like to know what good my power is when a (Hyksos) chief is
> in Avaris (the Hyksos capital) and another is in Kush, and I sit with an
> Asiatic and a Kushite, each with his slice of Egypt, and I cannot
> travel as far as Memphis.

THE NEW KINGDOM

Sometime before 1500 B.C., the pharaohs of the Seventeenth Dynasty rose up against the Hyksos. Employing the same weapons that the Hyksos had once used to defeat the Egyptians, they drove out the conquerors and reunited the two lands under the double crown. Now, however, the pharaohs were more warlike. Making Egypt's borders secure was not enough for them. Instead, they pushed beyond their own borders into foreign lands. Within 200 years, the Egyptians subdued state after state as far east as the valley of the Euphrates River, in modern Iraq, and as far south as the Fourth Cataract in Kush. The New Kingdom was an age of empire.

Monuments to Glory.   With each new conquest, Egypt grew more powerful and wealthy. In Kush alone, the gold mines yielded about 48 tons of ore a year, a level of world production not reached again for another 3,000 years. Yet this was only a fraction of the wealth brought from abroad. Every country that fell under Egyptian domination was required to pay an annual **tribute**, or tax to the conqueror, in the form of a valuable natural resource.

The pharaohs spent much of this wealth on monuments that proclaimed their personal power and glory, as well as the power and glory of the god Amon. Huge new temples and palaces arose at Luxor and Karnak in Upper Egypt. Sculptors carved colossal statues of pharaohs and gods to line the walls of these buildings. Artisans erected towering

69

*Two of the immense statues of Ramses II that gaurd
the temple at Abu Simbel in Kush. The Pharaoh is
shown both with and without a beard. In the
foreground is Nefertari, Ramses' Kushite queen.*

four-sided pillars called **obelisks** (AHB-uh-lisks), carved with hieroglyphics that told of the victories and exploits of the pharaohs.

Today many of these splendid New Kingdom monuments have
been reconstructed and can be seen by tourists visiting Egypt. One temple at Abu Simbel (AH-boo SIM-buhl) was actually moved, 30-ton block
by 30-ton block, to a position 200 feet above its original location so that
water from a new dam would not flood it. This temple honors Pharaoh
Ramses (RAM-seez) II, believed to be the pharaoh in the Bible's book of
Exodus. Other monuments of the period show Ramses with his queen,
a princess from Kush named Nefertari (neh-fuhr-TAH-ree).

By the time of the New Kingdom, pyramids had fallen out of fashion. Now pharaohs and their queens constructed more secure burial
chambers hidden in rocky cliffs on the west bank of the Nile. The most
famous group of these tombs was located in the Valley of the Kings,
across the Nile from the capital city of Thebes. In modern times,
archaeologists have unearthed many of the royal burial chambers. Most,
however, were found to be empty, looted long ago by robbers. Only
one, the tomb of a young and relatively unimportant pharaoh,
Tutankhamon (toot-ahnk-AH-muhn), was found almost intact in 1922
by the archaeologist Howard Carter. It yielded objects of such artistry
and splendor that it staggers the imagination to think of the other treasures that once lay hidden in the tombs of the Valley of the Kings.

The Woman Pharaoh.   The New Kingdom was a time of mighty warrior pharaohs. Many scholars, however, are more fascinated with the lives of two pharaohs of the period who fought no battles. One, a woman, became the ruler of a country in which women had few rights and very little power. The other, a philosopher and poet, rebelled against the religion of his day.

The pharaoh Hatshepsut (haht-SHEP-soot) was the daughter of a pharaoh. After her father's death, she became the queen of the new pharaoh. But when he also died and Hatshepsut's young nephew was proclaimed heir to the throne, she became his **regent,** or guardian. As regent, she held the power of the ruler. After nine years, in 1503 B.C., she declared herself ruler in name as well as in fact. She took the male title of pharaoh and was often pictured in the traditional male attire of double crown, kilt, and ceremonial artificial beard.

Pharaoh Hatshepsut set about winning fame through peaceful means. She organized a great expedition by sea to the southern kingdom of Punt, which some scholars believe to have been in modern Somalia. This African kingdom was rich in gold, ebony, furs, rare animals, and myrrh trees. All these precious goods were brought back to Egypt in Hatshepsut's ship.

At home Pharaoh Hatshepsut, like other pharaohs of the New Kingdom, launched an ambitious building program, partly to repair damage done during the Hyksos period. In this work she was aided by her advisor and chief architect, Senmut, a commoner like his long-ago predecessor, Imhotep. Together, Hatshepsut and Senmut designed and built what is considered the jewel of Egyptian architecture, an airy, many-colored temple nestled at the foot of rock cliffs not far from Thebes.

The Rebel Pharaoh.   One other New Kingdom pharaoh was not cast in the traditional mold of Egyptian pharaohs. He, like Hatshepsut, had been born into the royal family. He was given the name Amonhotep (ah-muhn-HOH-tep), meaning "Amon is satisfied." This name reflected the importance given to the god Amon as the chief deity of the state religion. It also reflected the respect even the pharaohs paid to the priests of Amon, who had grown extremely rich and powerful during the early years of the New Kingdom.

In the sixth year of his reign, about 1350 B.C., Amonhotep rebelled against the state worship and the priests who controlled it. He proclaimed Aton, an obscure sun god, as the only god. He closed the temples of Amon and ordered the god's name scratched out of all inscriptions. Then he changed his own named to Akhenaton (ah-kuh-

NAH-tuhn), which means "It is well with Aton." As a final act of defiance, he moved his entire court to a new capital, Akhetaton, known today as Amarna (uh-MAHR-nuh).

Akhenaton brought artists and scribes with him to Amarna to create a revolutionary new art and literature, freer and more lifelike than the classic Egyptian style. Statues of the rebel pharaoh depict him not as a godlike monarch but as a real person, with a long, thin face, drooping shoulders, and wide hips. Instead of being shown in heroic poses, he is usually shown playing with his children or relaxing in a cushioned chair beside his wife, the beautiful Nefertiti (neh-fuhr-TEE-tee). One sculpture shows him worshiping his god. Aton is depicted, not in human or animal form, but as the sun. The sun's rays end in tiny hands clasping looped crosses, the hieroglyphic symbols for life.

Akhenaton spent much of his time writing poetry. He composed ardent poems to Nefertiti and a hymn to Aton that is considered one of the finest pieces of Egyptian literature. In one stanza he writes:

When you set in the western horizon . . .
Every lion comes forth from its den,
The serpents they sting. Darkness reigns. . . .
Bright is the earth when you rise. . . .
The two lands are in daily festival. . . .
How manifold are all your works!
They are hidden from us.
0 sole god, whose power no other possesses,
You created the earth according to your desire while you
   were alone:
Men, all cattle, and wild beasts;
Whatever is on earth that goes by foot
And whatever is on high that flies with wings.

The Twilight of Empire. Akhenaton's new religion was not destined to last. His successor, once more under the influence of the powerful priesthood, restored the worship of Amon and other traditional Egyptian deities and resumed the military policies of his predecessors. However, much foreign territory had been lost. While Akhenaton sat on the throne in Amarna, absorbed with his family and his new religion, the eastern borders of the empire began to crumble. Archaeologists have unearthed more than 300 letters containing urgent messages begging Akhenaton to send troops to put down local rebellions. There is no record of any replies.

The pharaohs of the Nineteenth Dynasty were unable to restore order. Libya, sensing an opportunity, invaded the Nile delta. The

CASE STUDY:

Praising a River's Bounty

Every summer the ancient Egyptian celebrated the Nile River's flooding with a feast, a procession down the Nile, and a temple ceremony. This hymn of praise was written around 1500 for the annual festival.

> Praise to you, O Nile, that comes forth from the earth to nourish the dwellers of Egypt.
> Secret of movement, a darkness in daytime.
> You water the meadows which Ra [the sun god] has created to nourish all cattle.
> You give drink to the desert places which are far from water; your dew it is that falls from heaven.
> Beloved of the Earth-god, controller of the Corn-god, you make every worship of Ptah [the chief god] flourish.
> Lord of fish, you make the waterfowl go upstream, without a bird falling.
> You make barley and create wheat, you make the temples keep your festival.
> If you are sluggish, men's nostrils are stopped up, and they are brought low;
> The offerings of the gods are diminished, and millions perish from among mankind.
> When you arise, earth rejoices and all men are glad; every jaw laughs and every tooth is uncovered.
> Bringer of nourishment, plentiful of sustenance, creating all things good.
> Lord of reverence, sweet of savor, appeasing evil.
> Creating herbage for the cattle, causing sacrifice to be made to every god . . .
> Filling the barns and widening the granaries; giving to the poor.
> Causing trees to grow according to the uttermost desire,
> So that men go not in lack of them.

A *Comparative Study of the Literature of Egypt, Palestine, and Mesopotamia* (New York: Oxford University Press)

1. What are the gifts of the Nile mentioned in the hymn?

2. How were the ancient Egyptians attempting to control the river? How do you suppose modern Egyptians attempt to control the river?

3. What evidence does the hymn contain that fear played a part in the Egyptians' attitude to the river god?

Libyans were followed by a group of raiders from Europe and western Asia called the Sea People. Although the pharaoh was able to drive the Sea People out of Egypt, they remained in the Middle East and caused the empire in that part of the world to crumble. By 1050 B.C. Palestine and Kush had both broken away. For the next 700 years a succession of dynasties and invasions took place within Egypt itself, interspersed with periods of peace and recovery. The last native Egyptian dynasty came to an end in 332 B.C. In that year, Alexander the Great, a Greek, conquered Egypt and made Egypt part of his empire. After Alexander's death, the Egyptian throne passed to Ptolemy, one of his Greek generals. Ptolemy's descendants, including the famous Cleopatra, ruled as the Thirty-first Dynasty until the Romans conquered Egypt in 31 B.C.

THE KINGDOMS OF KUSH AND AXUM

During the New Kingdom, the pharaohs had brought Kush under direct control. The frontier had been extended south beyond the Fourth Cataract. New forts and towns had been established, and large garrisons of Egyptian soldiers, as well as Egyptian civilian administrators and traders, came to settle.

At first the Kushites resisted this colonization. Military action was needed to keep the restless population under control. Indeed, some Kushites living in the desert remained fiercely independent throughout the New Kingdom. In time, however, most Kushite city-dwellers adopted Egyptian ways. They worshiped Egyptian gods, built Egyptian-style pyramids and temples, and wrote in hieroglyphic script. Many served in the Egyptian army and held government positions.

The Rise of Kush. As Egypt began to weaken, Kush took the opportunity to break away and establish an independent kingdom. The capital was at Napata (NAP-uh-tuh), on the east bank of the Nile downstream from the Fourth Cataract. As Kush grew stronger, its kings began to look toward Egypt as a possible area for conquest. By the 700s B.C. a Kushite king named Kashta was leading armies northward. "I will take it [Egypt] like a flood of water," he declared. However, Kashta got only as far as Upper Egypt. The conquest was completed by his son Piankhi (PYAHN-kee) between 751 and 716 B.C. Piankhi's brother Shabako (shah-BAH-koh) became the new pharaoh, known throughout the ancient world as King of Kush and Egypt. He and his Kushite succesors were the Twenty-fifth Dynasty of Egyptian pharaohs. They ruled Egypt for almost 100 years.

The remains of an ancient building at Axum. Finds such as this reveal the high degree of these early peoples' knowledge of architecture and building skills.

The Iron Kingdom of Meroë.   In 671 B.C. the Kushites were driven from Egypt by Assyrians (uh-SEAR-ee-uhnz) from western Asia. Armed with iron weapons, the Assyrians overpowered the Kushite and Egyptian army. The Kushites retreated southward, but they had learned from the Assyrians an important lesson about the importance of iron. Soon they were making iron tools and weapons of their own.

As the Kushites grew richer and more powerful, their culture moved away from that of the Egyptians. They created an architecture and stunning painted pottery that showed both Egyptian influences and strictly local touches. The shapes of their hieroglyphics changed, and eventually they developed a new script, which no modern scholar has yet been able to decipher.

The Kushites established a new capital at Meroë (MEH-roh-way). By 200 B.C. it was the capital of a prosperous trading empire and one of the largest iron-producing centers of the ancient world. Caravans from throughout North Africa, the Sudan, and the Middle East came there for iron products and other goods, including ivory, ebony, wood, ostrich feathers, leopard pelts, and slaves.

The kingdom of Kush was well known to the ancient world. Its wealth came from trade along routes that connected it to northern Africa and the Middle East. It was cut off from the rest of sub-Saharan Africa, however. Many scholars believe that when the knowledge of iron-working spread to other parts of Africa, it came not through Meroë but by another route.

The kingdom of Kush thrived for 200 years before it began to weaken. In A.D. 350 it finally was defeated by an army from the kingdom of Axum (AK-soom), located in the highlands of what is now Ethiopia.

The Kingdom of Axum was a rich and powerful kingdom founded by traders from the Arabian peninsula who had mixed with the original inhabitants of the area. In time Axum became a center of trade along the Red Sea. It's chief item of trade was ivory, but it also dealt in gold, iron, emeralds, incense, spices, and other goods. Axum's trade placed the kingdom in contact with peoples throughout northeastern Africa, the Mediterranean world, and western Asia. In the fourth century A.D., missionaries from Egypt and Syria traveled in Axum and converted the kingdom to Christianity.

The people of Axum were accomplished farmers. They grew grains and other crops on terraced hillsides, which they irrigated. **Terraces** are flat platforms of earth on the side of a hill, rising one above the other. They were also superb stonemasons, well known for their great churches, monasteries, monuments, and obelisks. Axum had a law code, and it developed its own alphabet and written language.

The kingdom reached the height of its power and glory in the fourth and fifth centuries A.D. It was during this period that its armies, under a king named Ezana (AZ-zah-nah), defeated Kush. Yet with the rise of Islam in the seventh century A.D., Axum lost its trade routes on the Red Sea, and the kingdom declined.

REVIEWING THE CHAPTER

I. Building Vocabulary Skills

In your notebook write the correct term that matches the definition.

subsistence	clan	domesticate
polytheism	tribute	dynasty

1. a group of families

2. the belief in more than one god

3. producing only enough for one family unit

4. a ruling family

5. a tax paid to a conqueror

6. to tame animals and breed them for human use

II. Understanding the Facts

In your notebook, write the numbers from 1 to 5. Write the letter of the correct answer to each question next to its number.

1. What is the period called during which human beings learned to grow crops and tame animals?
   a. Old Kingdom b. New Stone Age c. Intermediary Period

2. What above all else did the initial success of Egypt depend upon?
   a. The climate   b. mineral resources   c. the Nile

3. What was the capital of the Middle Kingdom?
   a. Cairo b. Memphis c. Thebes

4. Who caused the last Egyptian dynasty to fall?
   a. Alexander the Great   b. Hatshepsut   c. Cleopatra

5. Who were the original inhabitants of the Kingdom of Kush?
   a. Arabian traders b. Egyptian artisans c. black Africans

III. Thinking It Through

In your notebook, write the numbers from 1 to 5. Write the letter of the correct answer to each question next to its number.

1. The scribes in ancient Egypt held great power because they
   a. were members of the nobility.
       b. owned land near the Nile.
   c. knew how to read and write.
   d. were close relatives of the pharaoh.

2. We would know less than we do about early African history if
   a. the Egyptians had not invaded Kush.
   b. the Old Kingdom had not fallen.
   c. the trade routes to the north had remained closed.
   d. the Egyptians had not invented writing.

3. "Calm the weeper, oppress no widow, expel no man from the property of his father." These words of a pharaoh to his son suggest that the pharaohs
   a. were mainly interested in their own well-being.
   b. were weak and insincere rulers.
   c. were not interested in strengthening their nation.
   d. were trying to be kind and just rulers.

4. Which of the following statements about Egyptian civilization is true?
   a. The Egyptians made little progress after the Old Kingdom.
   b. The Egyptians had no interest in nearby peoples.
   c. The pyramids required only brute labor to build them.
   d. Egyptian civilization lasted longer than any other.

5. Which of the following was made possible by the discovery of agriculture?
   a. Smaller communities became possible.
   b. It became essential to move from place to place every so often.
   c. A person could be something other than a hunter.
   d. It was now possible to make items out of metal.

DEVELOPING CRITICAL THINKING SKILLS

1. Explain why the Greek historian Herodotus referred to Egypt as "the gift of the Nile."

2. Discuss the reasons for the fall of the New Kingdom.

3. Show how the religions of the Egyptians provided the basis for a strong central government.

4. Describe the role that scribes played in the old Kingdom.

INTERPRETING A MAP

Study the map of ancient Egypt. Using the map and information that you have read in this chapter, answer the following questions.

1. How is the importance of the Nile to ancient Egypt demonstrated by this map?

2. Which parts of Egypt were included in the Old Kingdom? How far to the south and east did Egyptian power extend at the height of the New Kingdom?

3. What does the location of Akhetaton's capital suggest that he might have had in mind when he moved the capital from Thebes?

4. Explain how the location of Axum contributed to its prosperity and, later, to its decline.

ENRICHMENT AND EXPLORATION

1. Working in small groups and using library resources, find out about the nature of the items that ere found in the tomb of Tutankhamon. In a classroom presentation, identify the items, and describe some of the more interesting in detail. Supplement your presentation with pictures and drawings.

2. Consult library resources to find out how the inside of the Great Pyramid or another pyramid was laid out. Prepare a diagram that shows the location of the inner rooms and passageways. Display the diagram on the class bulletin board. Carefully label the various compartments that are shown.

3. In a written and illustrated report, describe the difficult tasks involved in the construction of a large Egyptian pyramid. Describe the process of shaping the stones, moving them to a construction

site, and setting them into position. Consult your library's catalogue system for appropriate references. Present your findings in class.

4. Using information in this chapter and in standard reference sources, prepare a list that will allow you easily to see the progression of important events in ancient Egyptian history. Base your list on the time box on page 52. Identify additional important events that occurred between 3100 B.C. and 31 B.C. Note each date and identify the event. Make your list as thorough as possible. Begin with the information in this chapter, and consult additional sources for more information.

4 African Empires and European Slave Traders

After the decline of Axum, the center of African civilization shifted to the west. There, in the interior of West Africa, a series of wealthy and powerful empire flourished for hundreds of years. Meanwhile other civilizations took shape in eastern and southern Africa.

After about 1500 the European trade in slaves became the most important factor in Africa, disrupting the ways of life of peoples throughout the continent and particularly in West Africa.

LATER AFRICAN CIVILIZATIONS

The following account describes the African city of Kumbi-Salik (KUM-bee-SAH-lik) in the year 800.

> The city consists of two towns lying in a plain. One of these towns is large and has twelve mosques. Around the town are wells of sweet water from which people drink and near which they grow vegetables. The town in which the king lives is six miles [away]. The land between the two towns is covered with houses. The houses of the inhabitants are made of stone and wood.
>
> The king has a palace and a number of dome-shaped dwellings. They are surrounded by an enclosure like the defensive wall of a city. Around the king's town are domed buildings and woods, which contain the tombs of dead kings. These woods are guarded and no unauthorized person can enter them.
>
> When [the king] gives audience to his people, to listen to their complaints and set them to rights, he sits in a pavilion around which stand ten pages holding shields and gold-mounted swords. On his right hand are the sons of the princes of his empire, splendidly clad

AFRICA AND THE WORLD

350–1807

c. A.D. 350	Axum conquers Kush.
c. A.D. 500	Ghana established.
1066	*Norman Conquest of England begins.*
1076	Berbers (Almoravids) conquer Ghana.
c. 1100	Karangas establish Zimbabwe.
1230	Mali displaces Ghana as trade center.
1307–1332	Mansa Musa rules Mali.
1300s	Kitara flourishes in Southern Uganda. Kongo founded.
1440	Mutoto establishes Monomotapa empire.
1441	Portuguese land north of Senegal.
1450	Kitara empire disintegrates.
1464–1492	Sunni Ali rules Songhai.
1468	Gao controls trans-Saharan trade.
1471	Portuguese arrive at Gold Coast.
1482	Diogo Cao arrives at mouth of Congo (Zaire) River.
1485	Changamir established with Zimbabwe as capital.
1488	Bartholomeu Dias reaches southern tip of Africa.
1492	*Columbus lands at San Salvador.*
1493	Askia the Great rules Songhai.
1497	Vasco da Gama circumnavigates Africa.
c. 1500	Africans taken as slaves to Cape Verde.
1526	Kongo King Alfonso protests slave trade.
mid-1600s	British sail to west coast of Africa.
1772	Britain abolishes slave trade.
1776	*U.S. Declaration of Independence*
1807	Britain prohibits slave trade.

and with gold plaited into their hair. The governor of the city is seated on the ground in front of the king, and all around him are his visers [officials] in the same position. The gate of the chamber is guarded by dogs of an excellent breed, who never leave the king's seat. They wear collars of gold and silver, ornamented with the same metals. The beginning of a royal audience is announced by the beating of a kind of drum which they call *deba* (day-BUH), made of a long piece of hollowed wood. The people gather when they hear this sound.

Where was Kumbi-Salik? It was in Ghana, one of many kingdoms that developed in Africa south of the Sahara during the continent's Iron Age. As you have read, Bantu-speaking peoples spread throughout sub-Saharan Africa during this period. Many of these groups eventually formed a huge trading empire ruled by powerful kings. Others established trading **city-states**, that is, self-ruling states made up of a city and its surrounding territory. Still others formed societies with no central authority or formal structure. The material accomplishments of these peoples varied as greatly as their political structures. Among the most elaborate were the kingdoms and states of the region of the Sudan.

Ghana.   The kingdom of Ghana was located in the savanna region of West Africa, to the north and west of the present nation called Ghana. It was established sometime in the sixth century and flourished for hundreds of years until it was conquered by Berbers from northern Africa around 1076. Ghana lay astride the great east-west caravan route across the Sahara. Because of its location, it became a major center of trade and power. Caravans from north of the Sahara came to Kumbi-Salik to exchange salt and other commodities for gold, ivory, and slaves. The king of Ghana exacted a tax on every item bought or sold in his realm. With the wealth gained from taxes, Ghana's kings were able to support a tremendous army and maintain influence over their vast kingdom.

Ghana had many contacts with the outside world. At one time it sent ambassadors to all the kingdoms of Europe. In the eighth century Islam spread to Ghana, and Muslim traders and scholars began settling in cities throughout the empire. They built mosques, introduced Arabic learning and the Arabic alphabet, and converted many of the people to Islam. Most of Ghana's farmers and its ruling classes, however, retained their own religious beliefs.

In government Ghana had no fixed body of laws—only customs, traditions, and systems of fixed loyalties and obligations. Authority rested at two levels. At one level a person was connected to a village

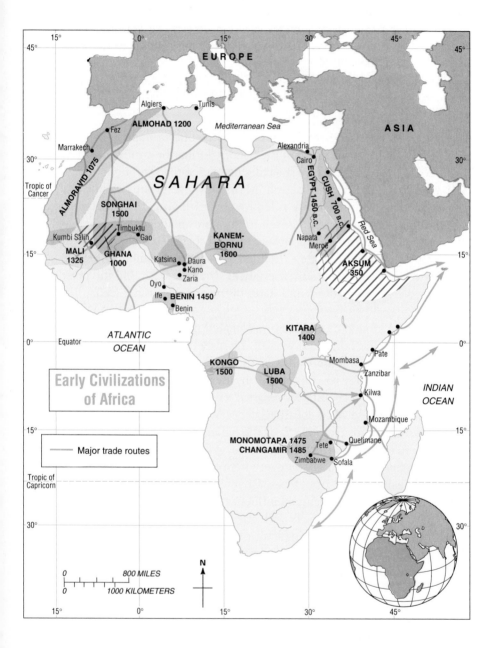

Early Civilizations
of Africa

— Major trade routes

0   800 MILES
0   1000 KILOMETERS

N

ALMOHAD 1200
ALMORAVID 1075
SONGHAI 1500
MALI 1325
GHANA 1000
KANEM-BORNU 1600
EGYPT 1450 B.C.
CUSH 700 B.C.
AKSUM 350
BENIN 1450
KITARA 1400
KONGO 1500
LUBA 1500
MONOMOTAPA 1475
CHANGAMIR 1485

84

community and owed loyalty to it. At another level a person was connected to his or her family or age group and owed loyalty to it. A king came to power by imposing his authority over a growing number of villages and cities. He did not totally dominate these communities, however. Each one retained self-rule but provided services to the king when they were needed.

Following the conquest of Ghana by the Berbers, the kingdom was never able to regain its power. By the thirteenth century it had collapsed. Not much physical evidence of Ghana's great kingdom remains, though the ruins of Kumbi-Salik have been tentatively located by archaeologists. Much of Ghana's culture, however, especially its ideas about government and trade, were passed on to the peoples who succeeded it. Thus Ghana set the pattern of western Sudanic history for some time.

Mali and Songhai. After Ghana's decline various states that had been part of its kingdom tried to gain control over the western Sudan. Out of these struggles a new empire, Mali, gained power in the mid-1200s. With the famed city of Timbuktu at its center, Mali won control over the trans-Sahara trading routes. Eventually it expanded to become the second largest empire in the world, surpassed only by the Mongol Empire in Asia.

In power at the height of Mali's success was the great emperor Mansa Mūsā (MAN-suh moo-SUH), who ruled from 1307 to 1332. Mūsā, a man of intelligence and vision, was a devout Muslim. In 1324 he made the required customary pilgrimage to Mecca, the holy city of Islam. Mūsā's pilgrimage was historic and spectacular. His caravan, consisting of thousands of people and unimaginable amounts of gold, impressed all whom he encountered and did much to establish the reputation of his empire. While on the pilgrimage the king persuaded a number of Islam's finest scholars, architects, jurists, and other professionals to return to Mali with him. Under their direction new buildings were erected, Muslim schools were opened, and Timbuktu became a center of learning and culture as well as a commercial center. Because of Mūsā's influence, several universities arose in Timbuktu. The University of Sankore (SAN-kor-ay) became one of the most important of its time, drawing students from Egypt and the Middle East.

News of Mūsā's wealth and power traveled far. Within 50 years of his pilgrimage, this inscription appeared in a European atlas that also featured his picture: "This [black] Lord is called Mansa Mūsā, Lord of the [blacks] of Guinea. So abundant is the gold which is found in his country that he is the richest and most noble king in the land."

85

While Mūsā ruled Mali, he maintained tight control. Upon his death, however, his successors were not powerful enough to keep the vast Mali Empire intact. Eventually parts of the empire broke away. Around 1468, the small city-state of Gao (GAH-oh) revolted and took control of the trans-Sahara trade.

In time, under a series of powerful kings, Songhai (song-GUY) eclipsed Mali in size, power, and wealth. At its height it was the largest ancient empire in West Africa. It owed much of its success to a trade in slaves. Slaves were taken from the region of Bornu (BOR-noo), led across the Sahara, and sold in North Africa, the Middle East, and Turkey. You will read more about the slave trade in a later section.

Songhai's greatest ruler was Sunni Ali (SOON-ee-AH-lee), who reigned from 1464 to 1492 and was responsible for much of its growth and power. He established a system of government that relied on the loyalty of community leaders throughout the empire. Sunni Ali also set up an efficient civil service.

After Sunni Ali's death, in 1493, Askia (AS-kee-uh) the Great assumed power. Like Mūsā of Mali, Askia made a pilgrimage to Mecca. He also brought back with him scholars and other professionals to act as advisers. Under his reign Timbuktu experienced a revival as a center of learning and culture. Many important books were written by African scholars during this period. Ahmad Baba (AK-mad BAB-uh) wrote books on law and a dictionary of Muslim scholars. Mahmud Kati (ma-MOOD-KAH-tee) and Abdal-Rahman (AB-dal rak-MAN) both wrote important **chronicles**, or histories. Askia was also responsible for further expanding the empire.

The Songhai Empire lasted until 1591, when it was defeated by Moroccan invaders. Thus the era of great empires in the western Sudan drew to a close, but another kingdom in the central Sudan continued to flourish, at least for a while.

Kanem-Bornu. The kingdom of Kanem (KAN-em), located in the central Sudan near Lake Chad, emerged around the ninth century. Gradually it extended its control over a large area that included Bornu. Like the kingdoms of the western Sudan, Kanem-Bornu had a vigorous trans-Saharan trade. It dealt in gold, slaves, and other commodities. By the late 1300s it could boast a large **cavalry**, or army mounted on horseback, which was effectively used to repel attacks and subdue enemies.

Smaller States of West Africa. Existing simultaneously with the great empires of the Sudan were a number of small independent states and kingdoms. Noteworthy were the Hausa city-states of present-day Nigeria—Daura (DAW-rah), Gobir (GOH-beer), Natsina (nat-SEE-nuh), Kano, Zaria (ZAR-ee-uh), and Kebbi (KEB-bee). The Hausa people farmed, crafted fine cotton and leather goods, and kept up an energetic trade with the outside world. One city-state, Kano, eventually surpassed Timbuktu and Gao as a commercial center. Its chief commodities were slaves and kola nuts. Though the Hausa people never formed an empire, they occasionally banded together for mutual defense and to further their mutual interests.

Small city-states also arose in the rain forests of West Africa, especially along the Guinean coast. Essentially, these were self-sufficient urban farming communities carved out of the forest. Typically, intensely cultivated lands surrounded a walled city, where the king lived and commerce took place. The wealth of these states came from their vast deposits of gold, which they traded to merchants of the Sudan region. They also traded kola nuts, ivory, and, later, slaves.

Among the most prominent of these states were the kingdoms of Ife, Oyo (OH-yoh), and Benin in Nigeria. These states are now remembered mainly for their superbly crafted sculpture, considered to be among the finest produced anywhere. Among the material used by these people were terra-cotta, bronze, brass, gold, copper, ivory, and wood. Most of the sculpture was made for religious purposes. Beautifully sculptured heads are believed to have been death masks used to honor important people at their funerals.

A few forest states eventually exerted influence over a large area. Benin was a strong and extensive kingdom at the time of the European arrival in the late 1400s.

City-States of East Africa. While trading empires were developing in the Sudan and West Africa, a series of small trading communities were growing on the East African coast and on the islands off that coast. These were first inhabited by Cushites and later by Bantu-speaking people. Their main trading partners were Arabs who sailed across the Indian Ocean in pursuit of ivory and tortoise shells. The Arabs referred to this African coastal region as the land of Zanj (zanj).

In the tenth century al-Māsʿūdi (al-mas-ou-DEE), a Muslim scholar from North Africa, described the city of Sofala (soh-FAL-uh) in present-day Mozambique:

The sea of the Zanj reaches down to the country of Sofala and of the Wak-Wak (WAK-wak) which produces gold in abundance and other marvels. Its climate is warm and its soil fertile. It is there that the Zanj built their capital. The Zanj use the ox as a beast of burden, for their country has no horses or mules or camels. Snow and hail are unknown to them. Some of their tribes have sharpened teeth and are cannibals. Their settlements extend over an area of about (2,450 miles) in length and in breadth. This country is divided by valleys, mountains, and stony deserts. It abounds in wild elephants.

Although constantly employed in hunting elephants and gathering ivory, the Zanj make no use of the ivory for their own domestic purposes. They wear iron instead of gold and silver.

The Zanj speak elegantly, and they have orators in their own language. These peoples have no code of religion. Their kings follow custom, and conform in their government to a few political rules.

Around the tenth century Muslim Arabs began settling along the East African coast. They intermarried with the local people and converted them to Islam. Eventually the people of coastal Africa developed their own language—Swahili, a mixture of Bantu and Arabic. They also developed their own culture. Commerce expanded, and soon the entire East African coast was linked to the vast trading network of the Indian Ocean. Large sailing ships loaded with cloth, carpets, porcelain, and other goods from Arabia, India, and even China pulled into East African ports. Equally large African ships headed eastward.

In time, the most successful trading communities developed into powerful city-states, each with its own government and sphere of influence. Like the kingdoms of West Africa, these city-states served as marketplaces for gold, copper, ivory, and slaves obtained inland. Among the most prominent of these states were Zanzibar (ZAN-zuh-bar), Geti (get-EE), Pate (pay-TAY), Mombasa (mom-BAH-suh), Sofala, and Kilwa (KIL-wuh).

By the end of the 1100s, Kilwa had become the center of the East African gold trade and its most prominent city-state. Like the ancient Sudanic empires, it exacted a tax on all goods bought and sold. From still-existing ruins and ancient documents we know that Kilwa was a walled city with wide streets, impressive palaces, beautiful mosques, and large houses. There was evidence of luxury and great wealth everywhere. Its people were particularly fond of Chinese porcelain. In 1331, Ibn Battutah (ib-un-bat-TOO-tah), the famous Moroccan scholar and traveler, described Kilwa as "one of the most beautiful and well-constructed towns in the world. The whole of it is elegantly built," he reported.

This carved ivory mask was worn by Benin royalty, along with other elaborate decorations which showed the wealth and importance of the owner.

Empire-Kingdoms of East Africa.   Our present knowledge of the history of eastern Africa indicates that people there tended to live with less centralized political organization during the eras when Ghana, Mali, and Songhai flourished. In the fertile area near Lake Victoria, however, large centralized states did develop. Archaeologists and oral sources point to the existence of a kingdom called Kitara (ki-TAR-uh), located in southern Uganda, which flourished during the 1300s. When the Lwoo and other migrants from the north pushed into the area around 1450, the sprawling Kitara Empire disintegrated. Small, more centralized kingdoms, such as the Buganda (boo-GAN-duh) and Bunyoro (bun-YOR-oh) then emerged. Their people were farmers, cattle herders, ironworkers, and salt extracters. Their iron farming implements, such as hoes, were so well made and the quality of the iron so high, that the tools were valued by farmers all over the lake area.

Salt was obtained from the lakes in the west of the Bunyoro kingdom. It was extracted by women, providing them with not only a profitable occupation but some power in trading matters. The Bunyoro also built canoes. This skill gave them a dominant trade role on the rivers that abound in the region that is present-day southwestern Uganda.

Kingdoms of the Interior. In the Congo region, now Zaire, many powerful states arose. The strongest, the kingdom of Kongo, was founded in the 1300s at the mouth of the Congo (Zaire) River. By the end of the next century, it had become a flourishing state with an elected but powerful king and a regulated monetary system. The king maintained a royal fishery, which provided shells to be used as a medium of exchange.

Linked to the East African city-state of Sofala by a series of well-worn roads and paths was Zimbabwe. It lay in the heart of a rich inland gold- and copper-mining region. It is believed that the city of Zimbabwe was established sometime around 1100 by Bantu-speaking people known as the Karangas (kah-RANG-guhs). Without using mortar or cement these early settlers constructed giant stone buildings throughout the region. Their monumental structures included a great wall and a temple for their king at Zimbabwe. Although the Karanga people farmed and raised animals, most of Zimbabwe's wealth came from the trading of gold and copper with east-coast merchants in Sofala.

The peoples of interior Africa appear to have led a peaceful life for 200 to 300 years. Then, about 1440, an ambitious Karanga king, Mutoto (moo-TOH-toh), set out to take over the gold trade and establish his authority over the Karanga lands. In time, he achieved his goal and created an empire called Monomotapa (mon-oh-moh-TAH-pah).

In 1485 trouble broke out in Monomotapa when one of the chiefs, Changa (chahn-GUH) challenged the authority of Mutoto's successor. Changa established a new empire, with the city of Zimbabwe as the capital, called Changamir (chahn-GUH-meer). Under Changa the wall of the capital was built even higher. These walls of Great Zimbabwe still stand today.

Noncentralized Societies. African societies, from kingdoms and empires to city-states, were as different from one another in their organization as each one was from European societies. We now know that large numbers of noncentralized societies existed in early Africa. In these societies groups of people lived together without a king or central authority and with a democratic political structure. They ruled themselves by **consensus,** that is, according to the wishes of the group as a whole.

90

The Great Enclosure at Zimbabwe is the largest early historical structure in sub-Saharan Africa. The wall contains a variety of designs, including herringbone, chevron, and checkerboard patterns.

A body of elders made decisions. **Age grades** also were often important. An age grade is a group of young people of the same age who pass through various stages of maturity and roles as a group. For example, an age grade of boys will together take the initiation rites to become soldiers.

Because they were based on mutual cooperation and respect, these societies tended to be more stable than Africa's state-building societies. Representative of this type of society were the Ibo of western Africa.

The Ibo were farmers and traders who lived together in thousands of small villages. Each village had a council that included the heads of each family plus any other adult males who chose to participate. Issues were presented to the people, and everyone had a right to speak. There was a strong sense of loyalty to and responsibility for one another among these people.

This sense of responsibility is shown in the way people worked together on ordinary chores. For example, clearing a field for planting was hard work, and friends and family of a farmer usually joined together to perform the task. Each person involved in the effort could then call on the farmer to help clear his fields when the need arose.

ARRIVAL OF THE EUROPEANS

In 1441 an ocean-going vessel from Lisbon, Portugal, set out along the West African coast. Sailing into unknown waters, the vessel made its way to the coast of Rio de Oro (ree-od-ee-OR-oh), north of Senegal. There"the sailors stayed long enough to seize nine captives and some gold dust. Then they headed back to Lisbon. Two years later another Portuguese vessel reached Arguin Island (ar-GWEEN), a little farther south. By 1471 the Portuguese had arrived on what later became known as the Gold Coast. They had sailed around the coast of West Africa. In 1482 a small Portuguese fleet led by Diogo Cão (dee-OH-goh KOW) arrived at the mouth of the Congo River. By this time the Portuguese had explored and set up trading posts at various places along the Guinea coastline. The European arrival in sub-Saharan Africa had begun.

Why had these early Portuguese sailors braved the unknown and the perils of the African coast? The magnet that first attracted them was the riches of Asia and the desire to control European trade with East Asia. At that time Muslims held a monopoly on this trade. It was the aim of the Portuguese to find an all-water route around Africa to the east, and thereby break this monopoly.

Portuguese Success.   The first European explorer to reach the southern tip of Africa was Bartholomeu Dias (DEE-ahsh), in 1488. Then, in 1497, Vasco da Gama (dah-GAH-mah) sailed around, or **circumnavigated,** the southern tip of Africa, reaching India in 1498. On his way he explored the east coast of Africa. At last, the Portuguese dream of reaching Asia by sea had been realized. With this accomplishment the whole course of African history changed.

Da Gama and his men looted and destroyed many of the wealthy trading cities they found on the east coast. When they arrived back in Portugal, they exhibited their booty and described the ravaged cities. Other sailors were eager to follow da Gama's route, for eyewitness reports captured the imagination of explorers and pirates alike.

Other Europeans.   The Portuguese wished to establish sugar plantations on the islands they held off Africa's Atlantic coast. From the end of the 1400s, captured Africans were taken as slave labor to the Cape Verde Islands and from the region around Angola to the islands of Príncipe and São Tomé.

For a half-century Portugal commanded the trade with Africa and Asia. Yet it was not long before other nations of Europe challenged Portugal. By the middle of the 1600s, English ships were sailing to Africa's west coast. Soon after, the French, Dutch, Danes, and Swedes followed. By the end of the 1600s, a lively trade had developed between Africa and the various European nations. Europeans established trading posts and forts at strategic points all along the west coast.

At first, the basis of the African trade was gold, ivory, peppercorns, kola nuts, and other traditional African commodities. Slaves were also sold, but not in great numbers. As the European nations explored and settled North and South America, however, they looked to Africa for laborers for their American colonies. The transatlantic slave trade was about to begin.

The Impact on Africa.   How did the European arrival affect Africa? Initially, it disturbed traditional trading patterns and created new ones. As new trading centers developed along Africa's west coast, the trans-Saharan as well as the Indian Ocean trading networks declined. Furthermore, the presence of the Europeans led to increased warfare and to the decline of some states and kingdoms and the rise of others. Trading states whose wealth depended on the trans-Saharan or the Indian Ocean trade lost power. The formerly weak states along the Atlantic and their inland neighbors became the new masters of trade. Consequently, these coastal and forest states grew and prospered. The arrival of the Europeans thus disrupted traditional social, economic, and political structures.

THE SLAVE TRADE

Slavery and slave trading go back to ancient times. Some scholars believe that the Egyptians sold people from Nubia to the Middle East. The Romans and Greeks bought slaves from Africa. In the tenth century African slaves were being carried to China. But it was the transatlantic slave trade, whose chief participants were Europeans, that had the greatest impact on Africa. It is estimated that this trade, from the sixteenth century to the early nineteenth century, drained Africa of some 50 million of its people.

Growth of the Slave Trade.   Two groups of outsiders participated in expanding the slave trade—the Arabs and the Europeans.

The Arab trade operated mainly from Oman (oh-MAN), on the Arabian Peninsula, and worked along the East African coast. Ivory and gold were the main objects of the trade. Africans captured by the Arabs carried the precious materials out of Africa. They were then sold on the coast or on the island of Zanzibar and sent to Arabia. This trade was heaviest in the 1700s and the 1800s.

European slave traders operated along the west coast of Africa.

A trading center on the West African coast in the 1700s. The area is divided into four parts, each for a different European group—Portugal (left), France (center), England (right), and Holland (right foreground).

Originally the Portuguese dominated the Atlantic slave trade. Then the Dutch entered the market, and finally the English, French, and Americans were also dealing in slaves.

Very few Europeans actually took part in capturing people for slavery. Instead, they built forts along the coast and depended on the African rulers of coastal societies, whom they supplied with guns and ammunition, to obtain people from the interior. Then the rulers sold the captives as slaves and bought more guns and other European manufactured goods.

From many firsthand accounts, we know that slaves captured in the interior were chained together and marched to coastal areas. There they were kept in stockades until they were sold. Finally, they were boarded onto cramped, filthy vessels for the voyage across the ocean. They faced the possibility of death along the way and a potentially brutal life when they reached their destination.

It will never be known exactly how many Africans were sold into slavery. Estimates range from 13 to 50 million people who were captured and sold into slavery over the course of 300 years. Records leave only a few figures. For example, between 1580 and 1680, Portugal took at least 1 million Africans to work in its colony of Brazil. Britain transported no fewer than 2 million to North America and the Caribbean between 1690 and 1790. Experts say that more than 15 million Africans were carried to various Spanish, Portuguese, French, Dutch, and British colonies in North America, South America, and the Caribbean.

Countless other Africans were killed in slave raids and wars, and unknown thousands died or were killed crossing the Atlantic on slave ships in the terrible voyage known as the Middle Passage. This does not take into account the millions who were captured and killed in the Arab trade in eastern Africa.

The overwhelming loss of life in the Atlantic trade depleted West Africa's most important asset: its people. Thus the continent was deprived of many potential leaders and much of its labor force. Moreover, the Atlantic trade encouraged warfare among Africans themselves. Raiders destroyed crops and wiped out entire villages. The slave trade broke down respect for laws and customs as the number of acts punishable by domestic slavery was increased to create more slaves. It fostered a sense of insecurity, fear, and suspicion as the foundations of African life were shaken.

The slave trade as Europeans practiced it weakened West Africa and limited its future growth and development. Many historians argue that the slave trade had a more devastating effect on Africa than did the later colonization by the European powers. The slave trade also left a legacy of racial attitudes that still exist in many places of the world today. The feelings of superiority over blacks that developed among white slave traders and owners degraded both blacks and whites and destroyed any ideas of respect and equality between the two.

The End of the Slave Trade.   Many Africans fought valiantly to resist slavery. Millions died in this resistance. A number of African rulers also tried to end slavery through diplomatic means. As early as 1526, Alfonso, king of the Kongo, wrote a letter to the Portuguese king. In it he asked for an end to the slave trade because it led to "corruption and licentiousness" and was depopulating the country. He said, "It is our will that in these Kingdoms there should not be any trade of slaves nor outlet for them." African resistance to slavery had little effect, however. As long as there was a demand for slaves, Europeans would continue to find and capture Africans.

Fortunately, the demand for slaves eventually declined. Some

CASE STUDY:

A Slave's Account

In 1787 Ottobah Cuguano (ot-TOH-bah coo-GWA-noh) a freed African slave, described his capture and treatment in a book entitled *Thoughts and Sentiments on the Evil of Slavery*. In it he urged the British government and people to outlaw slavery and the slave trade. Cuguano's was the first such appeal by an African to be published in England.

One day we went into the woods as usual. But we had not been more than two hours before our troubles began, when several great ruffians came upon us suddenly. Some of us attempted in vain to run away, but pistols and cutlasses were soon introduced, threatening, that if we offered to stir we should all lie dead on the spot.

I was kept about six days. After I was ordered out. . . I saw many of my miserable countrymen chained two by two, some hand-cuffed, and some with their hands tied behind. When we arrived at the castle, I asked my guide what I was brought there for, he told me to learn the ways of the Browfow, that is the whitefaced people. I saw him take a gun, a piece of cloth, and some lead for me. I was soon conducted to a prison, for three days, where I heard the groans and cries of many, and saw some of my fellow captives.

When a vessel arrived to conduct us away to the ship, it was a most horrible scene. There was nothing to be heard but rattling of chains, smacking of whips, and the groans and cries of our fellow-men. Some would not stir from the ground, when they were lashed and beat in the most horrible manner. When we were put into the ship we saw several black merchants coming on board, but we were not suffered to speak to any of them.

In this situation we continued for several days in sight of our native land. When we found ourselves at last taken away, death was more preferable than life, and a plan was made among us that we might burn and blow up the ship, and to perish all together in the flames.

Adapted and abridged from *Two Centuries of African English*, edited by Lalage Brown (London: Heinemann, 1973), pp. 132-135.

1. Why did Cuguano know so little of the slave trade until he was taken to the ship?

2. How did the slave trade cause instability and warfare among peoples in Africa?

historians argue that this was because of the Industrial Revolution in Britain. Britain in the eighteenth century was the leading slave-trading nation. Much of its economy depended on slave trading and on providing slaves for its colonies in the Caribbean. As Britain became an industrial nation, however, it wanted to expand the world markets for its manufactured goods. By the beginning of the nineteenth century, its West Indian colonies, with their demand for slaves, were less important than was the opening up of new markets for its manufactured goods. Slavery and slave trading were no longer profitable.

Simultaneously, a strong antislavery movement developed in Britain and, later, in the other nations of Europe and in the United States. In 1772 Britain abolished slavery in its home territory. In 1807 it forbade British subjects to take part in the slave trade. In 1833 the slave trade was outlawed throughout the British Empire. Other nations followed suit. The United States outlawed the trade in 1807, although slavery continued to be legal until the Civil War.

Abolishing the slave trade by law did not end it, however. So long as there was a demand for slaves anywhere in the world, traders continued to trade. During the first half of the 1800s, many ships risked capture by European patrol boats for the huge profit in slaves. In vime, however, the patrol boats of various nations gradually reduced and finally ended the infamous slave trade. By the late 1800s slavery had been abolished in most European nations. It persisted in East Africa somewhat longer, though it was illegal. Slavery itself was not ended until 1919 in Tanganyika, when the region was declared a British mandate (see Chapter 5). Thus a shameful chapter in African and world history finally came to a close.

Slaves were yoked together by heavy logs and marched from the interior to the coast. There the African escorts delivered them to slave traders in exchange for cloth, guns, or ammunition.

Chapter 4:
CHECKUP

REVIEWING THE CHAPTER

I. Building Your Vocabulary

In your notebook write the correct term that matches the definition.

consensus   age grade   city-state
cavalry   circumnavigate   Middle Passage

1. a military unit mounted on horseback

2. the crossing of the Atlantic Ocean on a slave ship

3. a group of young people of the same age who pass through various stages and roles as a group

4. to sail completely around

5. agreement about something reached by a group as a whole

6. a self-ruling state made up of a single city and its surrounding area

II. Understanding Facts

In your notebook, write the numbers from 1 to 5. Write the letter of the correct answer to each question next to its number.

1. After the kingdom of Ghana collapsed, what did it pass on to the people who succeeded it?
   a. written laws b. ideas about government and trade
   c. a great mosque

2. What was the capital city of Mali?
   a. Kumbi-Salik b. Sofala c. Timbuktu

3. Who were the first Europeans to reach Africa?
   a. the Portuguese b. the Dutch c. the French

4. What is the minimum number of Africans who were sold into slavery over 300 years?
   a. 6 million b. 13 million c. 19 million

5. What motivated Europeans and Africans to capture and sell slaves?

a. the need for cheap labor b. hatred of Africans c. huge profits

III. Thinking It Through

In your notebook, write the numbers from 1 to 5. Write the letter of the correct answer to each question next to its number.

1. Kingdoms such as Ghana, Mali, and Kanem-Bornu flourished initially because
   a. they had raised large armies.
   b. they had developed written laws.
   c. they controlled large areas for grazing.
   d. they were located on trade routes.

2. The noncentralized societies of early Africa
   a. ruled themselves by consensus.
   b. chose strong kings to guide them.
   c. prized personal independence above all else.
   d. built large cities to house their citizens.

3. The European slave traders generally
   a. obtained slaves for Arabian customers.
   b. depended on African coastal rulers to obtain slaves from the interior.
   c. captured slave during battles with people of the interior.
   d. sold slaves for use in Europe.

4. Mali became a center for learning and culture because
   a. its great wealth enabled it to buy needed goods.
   b. its military power made it possible to obtain slave labor.
   c. its king persuaded many Islamic scholars and professionals to come to his country.
   d. its location attracted peoples from throughout the world.

5. Which of the following statements does *not* describe a result of the slave trade?
   a. The tremendous loss of life depleted West Africa's most important asset: its people.
   b. The slave trade encouraged warfare among Africans themselves.
   c. The feelings of superiority over blacks on the part of the slave traders destroyed ideas of respect and equality between the two.

d. The slave trade was of tremendous importance to the indus
trial development of other countries of the world.

DEVELOPING CRITICAL THINKING SKILLS

1. Discuss the major factor that accounted for the rise of the western
Sudanic kingdoms of Ghana, Mali, and Songhai.

2. Describe how Mali's emperor Mansa Mūsā caused Timbuktu to
become a cultural as well as a commercial center.

3. Explain why the Portuguese first came to Africa.

4. Show how the slave trade dramatically changed the future of Africa.

INTERPRETING A TIME LINE

A time line helps us to understand when different historical events
took place. It shows at a glance how events are related to each
other in time. The time line below shows events in the early history of Africa. Make a copy of the time line in your notebook. Study
it and answer the questions that follow.

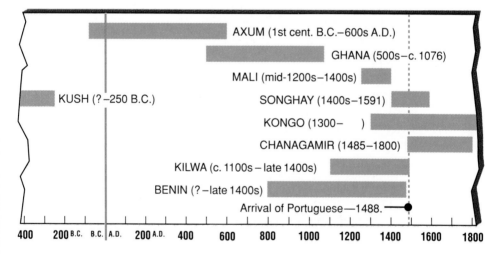

1. What was the earliest kingdom in sub-Saharan Africa?

2. Which kingdom lasted the longest? What does the time line tell
you about when it ended?

100

3. Which kingdoms on the time line were in existence when the Portuguese arrived in Africa?

4. Add the kingdom of Kanem-Bornu to the time line. How would you indicate its beginning and end?

5. According to the time line, which kingdom was the last to fall?

ENRICHMENT AND EXPLORATION

1. Choose one of the great cities of ancient Africa, such as Timbuktu, Zimbabwe, or Sofali. Collect as much information as you can about the city you select, using a variety of reference sources. Present your findings in the form of an illustrated booklet.

2. Research the slave trade in Africa. When you complete your research, present your finding to the class in the form of an oral report. Use a map to illustrate the major routes that the slave ships followed in delivering their human cargoes. Be sure to explain where the slaves were delivered and how they were used after they reached their destinations.

3. Find out as much as you can about how slaves were captured and how they were transported. In addition to standard reference works, consult the cataloging system in your library under such headings as "Slave Trade—Africa" and "Slavery—Africa." Try to reconstruct a clear picture of life on the slave ships. Present your findings in the form of an oral or written report.

AFRICA AND THE WORLD

1770–1945

1770	James Bruce traces Blue Nile.
1776	*U.S. Declaration of Independence*
1788	African Association founded.
1795	Mungo Park seeks source of Niger.
1831	David Livingstone establishes missions.
mid-1800s	Atlantic slave trade ends.
1851	British take Lagos.
1859	Livingstone becomes first European to cross African continent.
1861–1865	*U.S. Civil War*
1873	British and allies overwhelm Ashanti.
1877	Missionaries enter Buganda.
1884–1885	Berlin West African Conference
1884–1914	All of Africa, excepting Ethiopia and Liberia, comes under European rule.
1887, 1896	Ethiopian army defeats Italians.
1897	Aborigines' Rights Protection Society formed.
1900	Ashanti rise up against British.
1905–1907	Maji Maji Rebellion in Tanganyika
1914–1918	*World War I*
1919	First Pan African Conference
1921	Thuku founds Young Kikuyu Association.
1930s	Mussolini's Italy invades Ethiopia.
1935	Nnamdi Azikewe begins *Africa Morning Post*.
1936	Nigerian Youth Movement founded.
1937	Azikewe convicted of sedition.
1938	West African Youth League formed.
1939–1945	*World War II*
1945	Fifth Pan African Congress

5 *Colonization to the Eve of Independence*

During the nineteenth century Europeans reached the interior of Africa. They arrived as traders, explorers, missionaries and, finally, as colonizers. By the end of that century nearly all of Africa was under foreign domination. This European **imperialism**—the extension of a nation's power over other areas—was motivated by economic and nationalist interests. **Nationalist** competition in Europe, competition between nations eager to enhance their power, wealth, and prestige, resulted in intense competition for colonies in Africa and other parts of the world. The major imperialist nations that invaded Africa in the late 1800s were Great Britain, France, Germany, Belgium, and Italy. As these nations used Africa for their own purposes, they left a political, economic, and social impact that survives to this day. With their ideas of white superiority and their notion that Africans needed to be "civilized," the colonial powers undermined traditional African political institutions and turned Africa's economy to their own use. Many Africans resisted, while others accommodated the Europeans. But whether Africans fought back or cooperated, Europeans were unable to maintain their hold. African resistance, African nationalist movements, the impact of World War II, and, finally, the struggle of the African people to regain their independence, drove the European powers from Africa.

OPENING THE INTERIOR

In the early 1800s nearly all of sub-Saharan Africa was ruled by Africans. The exceptions were the British Cape Colony (later called

Cape Province) in Southern Africa and Portuguese-ruled Angola in West Africa. Throughout the western Sudan numerous trading cities had developed. In the region of Lake Chad, the kingdom of Bornu still held sway. In the forest areas of West Africa (in present-day Ghana) lay the powerful state of Ashanti. Dahomey (duh-HOH-mee), Oyo, and Benin (in modern Nigeria) were other chief states.

Among the kingdoms that ruled in the lake regions of East Africa were Bunyoro, Buganda, Ankole (an-KOH-lay), Rwanda, and Burundi. To the northeast was the ancient Christian empire of Ethiopia and, off the coast, the sultanate of Zanzibar. These states were highly centralized and often militarily strong.

Shifting Patterns of Trade.   As you have read, by the mid-1800s the Atlantic slave trade was coming to an end because the Europeans no longer found it profitable. Europeans did not abandon their interest in Africa, however. Rather, they turned their attention to "legitimate" commerce.

The British led the way in seeking control of trade in Africa. To make up for the lost slave trade, they began a profitable trade in palm oil. This enterprise was concentrated along the delta of the Niger River on the continent's west coast. Palm oil was one of the chief products of the region and was in heavy demand for England's soap factories. By the 1830s Africans and British merchants were carrying on a thriving business in the region, which was known as the Oil Rivers of Nigeria. At the same time, the French were moving into the area of Senegal farther north, where they hoped to gain control of some of that region's profitable trade.

In spite of European naval patrols along Africa's west coast, an illegal slave trade continued. To end this trade and protect their new commercial interests, Europeans began to exert more influence. Spurred on by what they believed was the great potential wealth of Africa, especially in minerals, Europeans were eager to move into the interior and expand their trade. They realized that to do this, they would have to take control of trade away from African middlemen. European governments began to send official representatives, sometimes backed up by gunboats, to make treaties. Often they gave money to African rulers and in turn won rights to the land.

Sometimes through treaties, sometimes through force, European powers, especially Great Britain, began to make West Africa their own. In 1851, for instance, the British took Lagos (LAH-gohs) by force. They deposed the king and replaced him with a ruler who would not oppose them. The new ruler signed a treaty giving Great Britain control of all trade in the area and accepting British protection. In 1861 Great Britain annexed Lagos as a colony.

Explorers and Missionaries.   Initially economic interests lured Europeans into the interior of Africa. Another motive, however, was scientific curiosity. The early 1800s was a time of great interest in science, and many advances were taking place in both Europe and America. New research in geography, botany, astronomy, and archaeology encouraged scientists to gather information about places unknown to them—especially Africa. Geographers were particularly interested in locating the sources of Africa's great waterways. These rivers had fired the imaginations of Westerners from the time of the Greek historian Herodotus in the fifth century B.C.

From the last part of the eighteenth century and well into the nineteenth, explorers investigated the interior of Africa. In the process, they gathered information on African geography, history, and cultures. In West Africa the challenge was to locate the source of the Niger River and trace its course. In East Africa explorers searched for the source of the Nile. This exploration coincided with the interests of merchants and traders. Knowledge of Africa's waterways would open them up as avenues of trade and further expand Europe's commerce in the interior.

A third motive for European interest in Africa was to extend Christianity throughout the continent. In both Great Britain and the United States the early 1800s saw a remarkable growth of missionary zeal, especially among the Protestant churches. Religious societies dispatched missionaries around the world to carry the Christian message. Africa, long thought by Westerners to be the Dark Continent, was of special interest.

Most missionaries were prompted by **humanitarianism**—a belief in improving society—as well as by the desire to spread their religion. A major concern was to stop the still-lingering slave trade. Missionaries began schools and hospitals and encouraged their converts to spread Christianity among neighboring peoples. In a few cases, European missionaries shared leadership positions in the churches with Africans. Some missionaries, such as the Scottish doctor David Livingstone, were also explorers. Livingstone, as well as others, gathered information about the African peoples' customs, languages, and ways of life. A number of them compiled dictionaries, grammars, and textbooks of African languages. Putting African languages into writing and translating the Bible into African languages helped lay the basis for written

Mungo Park often illustrated his reports of his travels in West Africa. Here is a sketch he drew of a village near the southern course of the Niger River.

African literature. The Christian missionizing was limited in scope, however, through most of the 1800s. Not until the twentieth century, when the colonial system was well in place, were great numbers of Africans converted to Christianity. Scholars point out that in educating Africans and in spreading ideas about Christian brotherhood, missionaries were indirectly establishing the groundwork for the future overthrow of European colonialism.

The Exploration of West Africa. In 1788 a group of British scholars and scientists founded the African Association. Its purpose was to promote the scientific study of Africa and to turn whatever discoveries were made there to commercial use. The founding of the association marked the beginning of an era of purposeful exploration of the continent.

The African Association believed that the Niger River was the place to begin exploring Africa for its inland trade potential. In 1795 the association commissioned a young Scottish doctor, Mungo Park, to locate the source of the Niger and trace its course. The next year Park reached the Niger at the city of Ségou (say-GOO) and found that it flowed northeastward. In a second trip, in 1805, Park explored the river along its southward route. He died before he could find the river's outlet on the west coast. Yet Park's descriptions of the river and of the geography of the region spurred others to explore further. Finally, in 1830, using

Park's information, the British explorers Richard and John Landers traveled southward down the Niger and found the delta of this great river.

Further exploration in West Africa included the travels of the German explorer Heinrich Barth, who was employed by the British in 1855. Barth traveled from Lake Chad west to the Niger and then north to Timbuktu. For ten months his expedition moved down the Niger and then crossed overland back to Lake Chad. Barth's account of his travels became a valuable guide for other explorers as well as for traders and future colonial officials. Barth's journal described in great detail the geography and peoples of the region.

The Exploration of East Africa.   European motives in exploring East Africa were the same as those in West Africa—economic and political interests, a quest for scientific knowledge, and the desire to spread Christianity. During the 1700s and early 1800s Muslim Arabs and Swahili controlled most of the city-states of coastal East Africa. Swahili caravans moved back and forth from the coast to the interior, trading for slaves, gold, and ivory. British and French trading ships called regularly at Mombasa (in present-day Kenya) and at the island of Zanzibar. Although most Europeans had abandoned the slave trade, gold and ivory were precious commodities in Europe. It was not until the early 1800s, however, that Europeans, and especially the British, became interested in the interior of East Africa. That interest focused on locating the source of the Nile.

As early as 1770, the Scottish explorer James Bruce had come upon the source of the Blue Nile at Lake Tana (TAN-uh) in Ethiopia. Bruce followed the course of the river until he saw it flow into the White Nile at Khartoum in the Sudan. When he published an account of his journey, it was rejected by many Europeans. They found the wonders he described difficult to believe, and, for a time, Bruce's exploits were forgotten.

Then, in the 1840s, two German missionaries, Johann Krapf and Johannes Rebmann, journeyed into the interior, across what is now Kenya, searching for the headwaters of the White Nile. Instead they came upon the Ruwenzori Mountains, the fabled Mountains of the Moon. They were also the first Europeans to see Mount Kilimanjaro and Mount Kenya. Their reports of snow-capped mountains in the interior of "tropical" Africa also seemed unbelievable to many.

Over the next twenty years Great Britain sponsored several expeditions into the interior to search for the source of the White Nile. By

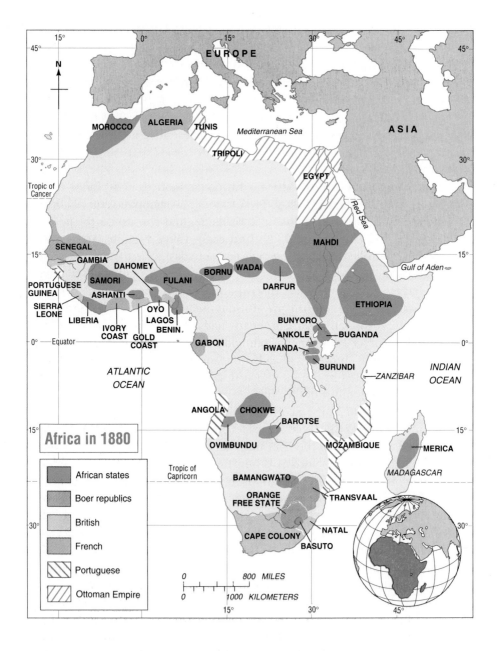

Africa in 1880

MOROCCO
ALGERIA
TUNIS
TRIPOLI
EGYPT

SENEGAL
GAMBIA
DAHOMEY
WADAI
BORNU
MAHDI
PORTUGUESE GUINEA
SAMORI
FULANI
DARFUR
SIERRA LEONE
ASHANTI
ETHIOPIA
LIBERIA
OYO
LAGOS
BENIN
IVORY COAST
GOLD COAST
BUNYORO
GABON
ANKOLE
BUGANDA
RWANDA
BURUNDI
ZANZIBAR

ATLANTIC OCEAN
INDIAN OCEAN

ANGOLA
CHOKWE
BAROTSE
OVIMBUNDU
MOZAMBIQUE
MERICA
MADAGASCAR

BAMANGWATO
ORANGE FREE STATE
TRANSVAAL
CAPE COLONY
NATAL
BASUTO

EUROPE
Mediterranean Sea
ASIA
Red Sea
Gulf of Aden

Tropic of Cancer
Equator
Tropic of Capricorn

- African states
- Boer republics
- British
- French
- Portuguese
- Ottoman Empire

0   800 MILES
0   1000 KILOMETERS

1862, through the efforts of the English explorers Sir Richard Burton and John Speke, Lake Victoria was finally identified as the White Nile's source. Armed with this knowledge, explorers and missionaries began in earnest to probe deeper into the interior of East Africa.

David Livingstone. One of the greatest explorers of Africa, and certainly the best known, was a rugged Scottish missionary, David Livingstone. In 1831 Livingstone made his first trip to Africa to establish Christian missions there. This marked the beginning of a remarkable career that was to include exploration as well as missionary work.

After witnessing the horrors of the slave trade, which still continued in East Africa, Livingstone took on another goal—to abolish slavery once and for all. He strongly believed this could be accomplished by bringing new forms of commerce to the interior of Africa. He reasoned that if new trading opportunities were open to Africans, they would have no need to continue the trade in human beings. In his desire for a new kind of trade, Livingstone was in accord with the commercial interests of Great Britain.

Livingstone made several trips into the interior of Africa. In 1849 he guided the first European crossing of the Kalahari Desert and came upon Lake Ngami (en-GAM-ee). He reached the Zambezi River in 1851. Thinking it well might be the key to opening up the region, he spent several years exploring this river. In 1859 he completed the course of the river to its source and came upon Lake Malawi and the Shire Highlands. Livingstone could claim to be the first European to cross the African continent.

Five years later Livingstone turned his attention to the lakes region. He wanted to find for himself the source of the White Nile. During the course of this journey, Livingstone disappeared. He was found in 1871 by the expedition of Henry Morton Stanley.

More than any other single person, Livingstone kindled European interest in Africa. Through his eyes people became sensitized to the inhumanity of slavery. In addition, he expanded Europe's knowledge of Africa. Livingstone also encouraged commercial pursuits in Africa.

Henry Morton Stanley. Sir Henry Morton Stanley, a journalist and adventurer, had originally been hired by a New York City newspaper to find Livingstone. Once he accomplished this, he returned to Africa to begin his own exploration. In the 1870s Stanley followed the course of the Congo River and explored the lakes region. Later he came upon the Ruwenzori Mountains. Besides adding to Europe's geographic knowledge of Africa, Stanley played a significant role in opening Africa to commerce. He also lobbied to have Christian missionaries sent to East Africa.

African Assistance in Exploration.　For the most part, European explorers were only "discovering" what Africans already knew about Africa. No group of Africans had acquired a body of knowledge about the whole continent. But each group of people was familiar with its own area and the areas in which it traded. In fact, explorers usually followed trade routes well known to Africans. On most of the great trips of exploration, Africans assisted Europeans, giving them information and supplies. Africans acted as guides and interpreters and in great numbers served as porters. Without the good will, supplies, and assistance of Africans, Europeans would not have been able to penetrate the continent.

European Attitudes toward Africans.　How did Europeans view Africans? The German explorer Heinrich Barth once advised that "the best weapon for the Christian traveler in Africa is decency—impeccable decency—toward the natives." Unfortunately, Barth's view was not shared by most Europeans. In general, they believed in white superiority and black inferiority. For the most part, they looked upon Africans as a people to be exploited and civilized through the influence of Christianity and Western education.

The notion that Africans were inferior was reflected in the phrase "the white man's burden." First coined by the English writer Rudyard Kipling, these words expressed the idea that it was the duty, and the right, of "high" civilizations to dominate what they perceived as "lower" civilizations. In the process, Europeans reasoned, progress would come to all.

The attitude of Henry Morton Stanley toward Africans typified the ideas of most Europeans. Although Stanley claimed to accept Africans as his brothers, he characterized Africans as childlike, idle, ignorant, cruel, and superstitious.

Stanley's racist views may seem extreme, but they were not uncommon. Accepting the idea of white superiority, Europeans believed they had the duty to "civilize" people they regarded as **pagan**, that is, followers of traditional religions, which many Westerners considered inferior to their own. Not incidentally, the Europeans believed they had the right to the commercial benefits that would come to them. These ideas were used to justify exploitation of the Africans. Armed with their beliefs and their superior technology, Europeans proceeded to colonize all of Africa.

EUROPEAN COLONIZATION

Before 1885 European countries had minimal presence in Africa. The Portuguese had footholds in Angola, Mozambique, Guinea, São Tomé, and Príncipe. The Cape Colony in Southern Africa was under British rule, as were Gambia and Sierra Leone. The French were active in Senegal, and a few coastal strips, such as Lagos, Gabon, and the Gold

Germans claiming Cameroon in 1881. After World War I Cameroon was divided between the British and French. Thus Cameroonians had experiences with three different colonial powers.

CASE STUDY:
Africans Meet Europeans

Here is an African view of the European encounter. It describes Henry
Morton Stanley's trip across the interior of Africa to meet with Mutesa,
the king of Buganda, on the shore of Lake Victoria. (Nyanza is the
Ganda name for the great lake.)

> Such a time of it they had;
> The heat of the day
> The chill of the night
> And the mosquitoes that followed.
> Such was the time and
> They bound for a kingdom.
>
> The thin weary line of carriers
> With tattered dirty rags to cover their backs;
> The battered bulky chests
> That kept on falling off their shaven heads.
> Their tempers high and hot
> The sun fierce and scorching
> With it rose their spirits
> With its fall their hopes. . . .
>
> Then came the afternoon of a hungry march,
> A hot and hungry march it was;
> The Nile and the Nyanza
> Lay like two twins
> Azure across the green countryside . . .
> Hearts beat faster
> Loads felt lighter
> As the cool water lapped their sore soft feet. . . .
>
> The village looks on behind banana groves,
> Children peer behind reed fences.
> Such was the welcome
> No singing women to chant a welcome
> Or drums to greet the white ambassador;
> Only a few silent nods from aged faces
> and one rumbling drum roll
> To summon Mutesa's court to parley
> For the country was not sure.

Steered by a crew of Africans, Henry Morton Stanley and his party "shoot" the Congo River rapids.

The gate of reeds is flung open,
There is silence
But only a moment's silence—
A silence of assessment.
The tall black king steps forward,
He towers over the thin bearded white man
Then grabbing his lean white hand
Manages to whisper
"Mtu mweupe karibu" [mm-TOO-mway oo-PAY-
    kuh-ree-BOO]
White man you are welcome.
The gate of polished reed closes behind them
And the west is let in.

James D. Rubadiri, "Stanley Meets Mutesa." In *African Voices*, edited by Peggy Rutherfoord (New York: Vanguard Press, 1960), pp. 90-91.

1. Describe the feelings of the Africans in Stanley's party.

2. What were the reactions of Mutesa and the Ganda to Stanley's arrival?

3. Compare and contrast the attitudes of the two groups of Africans in this poem.

Coast, were colonial states. But none of these areas was as extensive as those that bear these names today. Indeed, the majority of Africa was still self-governing. Fifteen years later, however, virtually the whole of the continent was under European colonial rule.

The Scramble for Africa.   Fueling what the London *Times* described as "the scramble for Africa" were the growing feelings of nationalism that marked the late 1800s in Europe. Each nation looked for ways to boost its prestige in the world. It was believed that world empires, bringing millions of people under one rule, were the marks of a powerful nation. It was also the view of European nations that Africa was an economic prize. Africa, they reasoned, would bring valuable raw materials, especially minerals, to the steadily growing factories of the industrial nations. On the other hand, Europeans saw Africa as a market that would be opened up for their industrial goods.

The Berlin Conference.   As the scramble intensified and European nations found themselves competing for the same territory, it became clear that some kind of formal agreement concerning Africa needed to be worked out. In 1884-85 the major powers met in Berlin to draw up rules for dividing the African continent.

At the Berlin Conference it was agreed that to lay claim to a territory in Africa, a nation had to

1. make a formal, public announcement of the claim
2. effectively occupy the territory (which might be accomplished by building roads or a railroad into the region)
3. extend control from the coast to the interior
4. negotiate a treaty with local peoples that would constitute a claim to sovereignty.

The powers also agreed that traders and missionaries of all nations should have free access to the African interior and that the Niger and Congo rivers should remain international waterways. Furthermore, they agreed that Christianity should be brought to Africans and that what was left of the slave trade should be destroyed.

After the Berlin Conference each nation worked furiously to establish its claims. In the years between 1884 and 1914, all of Africa, except Ethiopia and Liberia, was under some form of European rule. Great Britain and France ended up with the largest holdings on the continent.

The map on page 116 shows how Africa was **partitioned** or divided. You can see the effect was that of crazy quilt. Africa was divided with scant regard for African peoples and their traditional lands. As one expert put it, "Africa was divided by Europeans for Europeans." Often occupation was carried out brutally by greedy mercenaries with the support of their governments. Boundaries in many cases were drawn right through traditional territories, separating closely knit groups of people. Under the control of colonial powers, West Africa was the most fragmented region on the continent.

AFRICAN REACTIONS TO COLONIZATION

How did Africans react to the European takeover of the continent? Generally, there were three responses. Some resisted violently, and immediately, with all their might. Among this group were the Ashanti, the Malinke (muh-LING-kay), and the Mende (MEN-dee) of West Africa. The Ethiopians, the Hehe (HAY-hay), and the coastal people of East Africa also resisted. In Southern Africa the Zulu and the Herero (huh-RAIR-oh) peoples fought the invaders. Others, however, including the Fante (FAN-tee) of West Africa and the Ganda of East Africa, cooperated with the Europeans and tried to work out favorable agreements with them. Still others at first tolerated the Europeans and then later rebelled. Among this group were the people of Tanganyika, who rose against the Germans in the Maji-Maji (MAH-jee MAH jee) Rebellion of 1905-7.

The reasons for each response were complex. In general, it was a questions of a means, not an end. No African group intended to give up its **sovereignty**—its freedom from outside control—or its way of life. Even those who cooperated with the Europeans did so only because they thought that that choice was the lesser of two evils or in their own interest. All were seeking to protect their trading position, their way of life, their land, and their sovereignty.

Resistance.   Resistance to colonial rule arose among those Africans who saw no advantage in submitting to the Europeans. These words written in 1890 to a German officer by Chief Macemba (mah-CHEM-bah), head of the Yao (yow) people in southern Tanganyika, reflect this point of view:

> I have listened to your words but can find no reason why I should
> obey you—I would rather die first. I have no relations with you and

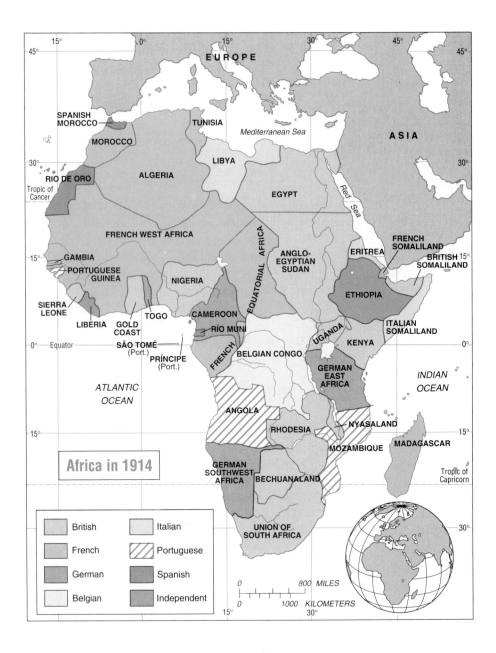

Africa in 1914

EUROPE

SPANISH MOROCCO
TUNISIA
Mediterranean Sea
ASIA
MOROCCO
LIBYA
RIO DE ORO
ALGERIA
Tropic of Cancer
EGYPT
Red Sea
FRENCH WEST AFRICA
FRENCH SOMALILAND
GAMBIA
EQUATORIAL AFRICA
ANGLO-EGYPTIAN SUDAN
ERITREA
BRITISH SOMALILAND
PORTUGUESE GUINEA
NIGERIA
SIERRA LEONE
ETHIOPIA
LIBERIA
GOLD COAST
TOGO
CAMEROON
ITALIAN SOMALILAND
RÍO MUNI
SÃO TOMÉ (Port.)
FRENCH
BELGIAN CONGO
UGANDA
KENYA
Equator
PRÍNCIPE (Port.)
ATLANTIC OCEAN
GERMAN EAST AFRICA
INDIAN OCEAN
ANGOLA
RHODESIA
NYASALAND
MADAGASCAR
MOZAMBIQUE
GERMAN SOUTHWEST AFRICA
BECHUANALAND
Tropic of Capricorn
UNION OF SOUTH AFRICA

British
French
German
Belgian
Italian
Portuguese
Spanish
Independent

0   800 MILES
0   1000 KILOMETERS

116

cannot bring it to my mind that you have given me so much as a pesa [a small amount of money] or the quarter of a pesa or a needle or a thread. I look for some reason why I should obey you and find not the smallest. If it should be friendship that you desire, then I am ready for it, today and always. But to be your subject, that I cannot be. . . . If it should be war you desire, then I am ready, but never to be your subject.

Other Africans responded differently. When Europeans began invading the continent in large numbers in the late 1800s, they had several advantages. They had better weapons—an abundance of them— and greater technical know-how. A number of African peoples saw the potential of this strength. In exchange for cooperation, they won promises of European friendship and protection, arms, and con-sumer goods. African leaders saw **collaboration,** or cooperation with an enemy, especially an occupying force, as a way of gaining greater wealth and ensuring their own power. Some even assisted the Europeans in conquering other Africans. They hoped in this way to expand their own authority over the conquered people.

Whether a group fought the Europeans or accommodated them, the result was much the same. In the end the Europeans exerted control over most of the peoples of Africa and subjected them to colonial rule.

Ethiopian Resistance.   An exception to European domination oc- curred in Ethiopia. There in 1887 and again in 1896, the Ethiopian army defeated the Italians, who were attempting to gain a foothold on the Red Sea and make a claim on northeastern Africa. The Ethiopian resistance was later to spur other Africans as they organized to regain their independence.

The Ethiopian emperor, Menelik II (MAY-nuh-lik), whose army was responsible for routing the Italians, went on to create the modern state of Ethiopia. His strategy was to incorporate a number of previously independent neighboring kingdoms. Menelik's objective in these wars was to build an expanded empire, one capable of countering the Italians as they extended their control in the nearby Somali territories. This strategy worked for many years. Ethiopia remained independent until the 1930s, when the Italian dictator, Benito Mussolini, urged his people to revenge their earlier defeats and sent an army to occupy Ethiopia.

The Ashanti Resistance.   One group who vigorously fought the Euro- pean invasion of Africa was the Ashanti. In the late 1600s the Ashanti

Ethiopian soldiers in the 1930s. The League of Nations refused to support the Ethiopian king against Italian invaders and the country fell to European rule for the first time.

began to build an empire in the densely forested hill region of West Africa's Gold Coast (modern-day Ghana). At the time the region consisted mostly of small independent states of Akan-speaking people. Under a powerful Akan (AH-kan) ruler, Osei Tutu (OH-say TOO-too), the small states were united into one kingdom. Osei Tutu established himself as king. He founded Kumasi (koo-MAH-see) as his kingdom's capital and set about centralizing his authority. Over the course of many years, Osei Tutu fought many battles to extend his power and his control of trade in the region. At his death, in 1712, the Ashanti Empire was one of the richest and most powerful in all of West Africa.

Later kings continued to add to the empire's greatness and wealth. Believed to be divinely appointed, they were able to unify and command respect from all the people in the empire. By the early 1800s the Ashanti Empire covered some 150,000 square miles and included between three million and five million people. It had a strong political organization under the king, with civil servants appointed and promoted on merit. The splendor of the Ashanti court was legendary. A European visitor to Osei Tutu Kawanmena's court was amazed at "the extent and display" there. As he reported, it was an area of nearly a mile in circumference . . . crowded with magnificence and novelty. The king, his tributaries, and captains, were resplendent in the distance, surrounded by attendants of every description, fronted by a mass of warriors which seemed to make our approach [impossible]. The sun was reflected, with a glare scarcely more supportable than the heat, from the massive gold ornaments, which glistened in every direction. More than a hundred bands burst at once on our arrival . . . the horns flourished their [challenge], with the beating of innumerable drums and metal instruments, and then yielded for awhile to the soft breathings of their long flutes, which were truly harmonious.

Not only was the king's court spectacular, but Kumasi, the capital, had grown into a bustling commercial center. It attracted merchants, political and religious leaders, and learned Muslims from throughout West Africa. It was a sprawling city, where some 40,000 people lived comfortably. One European was struck by the city's cleanliness. "The rubble of each house," he said, "was burnt every morning at the back of the streets, and the inhabitants were as nice and cleanly in their dwellings as in their persons."

The Ashanti had become wealthy by working the fertile land and trading in gold and slaves. The gold came from the rich mines of the region and was the cornerstone of their economy. The kingdom was also renowned for its artisans. Many of them worked the gold into intricate, elaborate decorations and jewelry, such as that described above.

Throughout their history, the Ashanti were involved in struggles to retain their power. Often they warred with neighboring peoples over trading rights. When the British moved in to take control of the gold trade from the Ashanti, the people resisted with force and stubbornness.

Over the course of some 75 years, the Ashanti clashed with the British in the region several times. In 1824 they won a major victory when they defeated a well-trained British army outside of Dunkwa (DUN-kwuh) and killed the British governor. Finally, the British grew tired of being beaten by the Ashanti. In 1873 they launched a full-scale attack. A combined force of British soldiers and African allies overwhelmed the Ashanti with superior weapons.

For the next 20 years the empire was in disarray. Nevertheless, the Ashanti tried to rebuild some of what they had lost. In 1896 the British, fearing the Ashanti would succeed, again marched against them. For the first time the British succeeded in entering Kumasi. Clearly outnumbered and outgunned, the Ashanti refused to fight. Even then, however, the Ashanti would not consider themselves under British rule. In 1900 they once more rose up against the colonials in bitter combat. This time their armed opposition was successfully broken. The Ashanti people were finally incorporated into the British colony of the Gold Coast.

The Ganda Accommodation. In his travels through the lakes region of East Africa, the explorer Henry Stanley came upon a place he described as a garden of Eden. This was the kingdom of Buganda on the north side of Lake Victoria. Here, on a partly forested plateau, the Ganda people had developed a rich and powerful trading state. With a strong central government and a system of **tribute**, or payments by neighboring rulers in exchange for protection, Buganda exerted influence over a large area of diverse peoples.

When Stanley arrived in Buganda in the 1870s, the king, Mutesa (moo-TAY-suh), enjoyed great power and wealth. The basis of the Ganda economy was farming and cattle herding. Food abounded in the central part of the kingdom because the land was so fertile. Many people fished in Lake Victoria's waters. Others used large dugout canoes to trade Ganda goods to peoples living around the lake.

Notables, or dist' guished persons, from all over Buganda attended the king's court to offer him advice about the areas in which they lived. If war against an uncooperative neighbor was decided on, these notables were responsible for raising armies in their areas. In addition, they had to collect tribute from the king's subjects. Also in attendance at the court were religious leaders, often women, who advised the king on spiritual matters. And anyone wishing to travel through the kingdom or to trade with it had to obtain permission from the Ganda king. This often meant that traders and travelers had to spend months living at court while they negotiated the terms of their agreements.

The king was also served by hundreds of page boys for whom the court was a school. A promising boy from any section of Buganda hoped to find a **patron**, someone to support him while he was at court. There, with boys his own age, he would learn about the kingdom's history and economy. He would also observe its politics firsthand.

With all this activity at the king's court, it is no wonder that Stanley was impressed by Buganda. Observing its fertile farm land, its well-developed political organization, and its great wealth, Stanley believed that Buganda could become a model Christian enclave. Besides, the Ganda had already demonstrated that they were open to new ideas and people. Earlier in the century they had allowed Muslims to settle and set up schools there.

120

In 1877 Roman Catholic and Protestant missionaries arrived in Buganda. Mutesa welcomed them enthusiastically. Some of the Muslims in Mutesa's court were challenging his authority. Mutesa saw the establishment of mission schools as a way of cultivating another body of young men more loyal to him. He agreed to allow his page boys to be taught the Bible.

Here, then, was a case of an African king cooperating with European intruders to accomplish his own ends. Mutesa allowed the missionaries to establish themselves in his land because he saw the benefits that might come to him. With this act of accommodation, Mutesa set a pattern in Buganda that was followed elsewhere on the continent by Africans and Europeans.

In the years that followed, Great Britain and Germany vied for superiority in East Africa. Great Britain considered Buganda and the rest of Uganda vital to its interests in Northeast Africa. Specifically, it was concerned about acquiring control of the Nile, from its source at Lake Victoria to the Mediterranean Sea.

Throughout this period Great Britain intensified its ties with Buganda. From time to time, various Ganda factions made use of the British presence to improve their own positions in the empire. For instance, in 1884 Mutesa died and was succeeded by another king, Mwanga (mwan-GUH). Mwanga was unable to keep control of the rival factions in his kingdom. A three-sided civil war developed among Muslims, Catholics, and Protestants, with the British supporting the Protestants. Eventually, with the aid of British imperial forces, the Protestants won the war, and Mwanga was exiled.

In 1900, to ensure the loyalty of the Ganda chiefs, the British gave them powers they had never had before. For instance, until then much of the area that the notables administered could be taken away from them by the king if they abused their power. Now the British granted the notables these areas as their own private land. The Ganda king no longer controlled a major resource of the kingdom—land for farming. The British government, on the other hand, gained the right to levy taxes and won rights to the forests and mineral deposits. The British also declared certain parcels of land to be theirs and, in general, took control of Buganda as part of Britain's Uganda **protectorate**. In the terms of colonial government, a protectorate is a political unit that is dependent on a more powerful state for its protection. The Ganda did not suffer the devastation to their way of life that the Ashanti did when they resisted colonial rule. However, Buganda's politics and economy were drastically altered as a result of the Ganda's cooperation with the European intruders.

The young king of Buganda and his advisers in the early 1900s. Under colonial rule, the king's powers were limited and he received a set monthly salary from the government.

COLONIAL RULE

The various European nations ruled their colonies in different ways. Furthermore, the same nation sometimes controlled one of its possessions quite differently from another, depending on circumstances. Certain patterns emerged, however.

Basically, all governments exploited their colonial territories. With few exceptions, the well-being of the Africans was barely considered. Europeans generally looked down on Africans and their culture. In addition, most nations were **paternalistic** in their treatment of the colonies. That is, they regulated their colonial governments very closely, as though the Africans were not capable of governing themselves.

All the governments imposed taxes on their colonial subjects. These taxes were used to pay for the administration of the colony plus projects for development, such as irrigation or transportation systems, and for any services supplied. Whether government was by direct rule or indirect rule, it was always **autocratic**—having total control—and repressive. With few exceptions, Africans were denied political or civil rights. All governments took land from African groups, generally allowing them only to retain land actually under cultivation. Then the Europeans dictated to the Africans what they should grow. Europeans looked on their colonies as pools of labor. Most required Africans to take part in public works projects and serve as soldiers. Further, because the government determined what crops could be grown, families could not provide for their own needs in the traditional way—through farming. Instead, they needed cash for basic necessities and to pay the colonial taxes. Often the male head of the family was compelled to travel far from his family, seeking work at wages much lower than those earned by Europeans. In this way the independence and stability of African families was undermined.

Generally, the governments provided little for their colonies. The few services that were supplied, such as health clinics and schools, were usually established by missionary or other private groups, using African labor and financial contributions for their construction and maintenance.

Direct Rule. Under direct rule a European nation controlled the government of its colony at all levels. It appointed its own officials to replace local African leaders. It initiated all laws, rules, and regulations. It usually cast aside traditional African institutions in favor of its own. Direct rule was practiced by the French, Belgians, Portuguese, Germans, and Italians.

In the French colonies power was highly centralized. Ultimately the power rested in the French legislature in Paris. France practiced a policy that has been described as **assimilation**. Its aim was to mold a colony, politically and culturally, so that it became as much like France as possible. Africans were expected to exchange their customs and beliefs, their cultural heritage, for French ways. In the few schools established in its colonies, French language, religion, customs, and ideas were taught.

Belgian rule was the most repressive. Under King Leopold II the government ruled directly and brutally. The Congolese people were treated as slaves in their own land. They were required to work at whatever jobs the Belgians delegated to them. If they objected, they were cruelly punished. Later, after Leopold, the Belgian policy toward the Congolese softened somewhat, but it continued to be harsh and exploitive.

Portugal by the late 1800s had become a nation of little prestige, power, or wealth. Looking at its colonies as a way of restoring some of its past grandeur, Portugal also ruled its territories with stern control.

Indirect Rule. Under indirect rule traditional African leaders were given a role in the colonial government. The colonial power created laws and installed a governing body over the colony. But, especially at the local level, traditional rulers retained some authority. In fact, some rulers often gained more power than they had before. In some instances the British, for their own advantage, even created African leaders where none had existed. Generally, traditional leaders conducted the day-to-day administration of their people under the supervision of the European authorities. Some of their duties included maintaining order, collecting taxes, organizing cash-crop production, and providing labor, forced and otherwise, for road building, other public-works projects, and plantations.

Under indirect rule, however, these African leaders were responsible to the colonial government, not to their own people, as they had been in the past. Thus the very tradition that made them leaders of their people was undermined.

For the most part, British rule in Africa was indirect. The reasons for this were wholly practical. Great Britain, a small nation, had more colonies than any other major power. With a limited number of officials to manage its far-flung empire, it had to rely to some extent on local leaders. Furthermore, indirect rule was less expensive, requiring the services of fewer British officials.

In the end, however, the effect of indirect rule on the average African was little different from that of direct rule. The domination of Africa by the colonial powers served to weaken all existing African political institutions. Colonization imposed upon Africans a Western

During the colonial era, Freetown, on the Sierra Leone coast, was a bustling port. Many Africans moved there from the interior to find work. Others came to the town to sell their produce or buy imported goods.

system of administration and organization. Whether direct or indirect, the authority of traditional African leaders was ultimately replaced by Western administrators. African leaders were required to carry out the regulations of the colonial authorities, whether or not they were to benefit the African people.

African leaders did not have the power to challenge colonial authorities and hence in many cases lost the respect of their people. Overall, the major impact of colonialism was the loss of sovereignty by nearly all African people.

EFFORTS TOWARD INDEPENDENCE

Once colonial rule was established in Africa, the people's resistance to it did not disappear. During the early 1900s there were frequent uprisings throughout the continent. These were somewhat different from the Ashanti resistance because they often involved people from more than one ethnic group. Sometimes resistance involved the participation of members of African Christian churches.

The Maji-Maji Rebellion.   The Maji-Maji rebellion in Tanganyika (1905-7), was one of many uprisings in the early 1900s in East Africa. In the Maji-Maji rebellion people from a number of groups across the territory rose up against the severity of German rule. The word *Maji* means "water" in Swahili. The people who revolted often sprinkled themselves with a holy water, which they thought would ward off bullets. It did not, and tens of thousands of Africans were killed in this effort to overthrow German colonials.

Some historians point to this uprising as an example of how the colonial experience, early on, had begun to undermine traditional African social groupings. At the same time, it encouraged Africans of different ethnic groups to cooperate against a common enemy, the colonial powers.

Early Nationalist Organizations.   As early as 1897, another kind of resistance had also begun. Usually led by men and women who had been educated in the colonial schools, this resistance took the form of nationalist associations. These early organizations were the forerunners of the movements for independence that followed World War II.

One such organization was the Aborigines' Rights Protection Society. It was formed in 1897 by African leaders in the British colony of the Gold Coast. Its object was the protection of its own rulers and peoples. In a protest to Britain, members of the organization were successful in persuading the government to withdraw a bill that would have undermined the authority of their rulers. This was the beginning of several West African organizations that were formed to protest colonial rule.

The National Congress of British West Africa was formed in 1919. Begun by leaders of the Gold Coast, its major goal was to unite all the people of West Africa in a nationalist movement. The congress demanded **universal adult suffrage** (the right of every adult person to vote), opportunities for higher education and equal job opportunities for all Africans, and a system of free education for all children. The congress pressed Britain to meet its demand and was able to gain some voting power for major towns along the Gold Coast. Ultimately the congress was unsuccessful, however. Partly because of British resistance and partly because its own members quarrelled among themselves, the congress failed. Some experts point out that its main fault was that it depended on the educated few and ignored the great masses of people. Nevertheless, the National Congress of British West Africa helped lay the groundwork for future independence movements.

Negritude.   Under French rule, another form of opposition to colonial rule emerged. It began in the 1930s, when Léopold Senghor (lay-oh POLD san-GOR), later to become the first president of Senegal, went to Paris to study. There he met Aimé Césaire (eh-MAY say-ZAIR), a student from the French Caribbean colony of Martinique (mar-tin-EEK). From Césaire, Senghor learned that the French policy of assimilating native culture, making it like French culture, was also practiced in the Caribbean islands that the French controlled.

In the first issue of a student publication that Senghor and Césaire put together, they coined the word *Negritude* to describe their reaction to assimilation. Both men were poets and became the leaders of a group who became known as the Negritude poets.

Senghor, Césaire, and others looked to their black cultures for inspiration. Instead of rejecting their African heritage, the Negritude poets praised it. They wrote about their own customs, dances, people and beliefs. Often they noted that their poems should be recited to the accompaniment of traditional instruments. Among French-speaking peoples in Africa and the Caribbean especially, Negritude became a powerful means of expressing opposition to colonial rule. "Africa," by the Sengalese poet David Diop (dyawp), is just one example of this literature:

> Africa my Africa
> Africa of proud warriors in ancestral savannas
> Africa of whom my grandmother sings
> On the banks of the distant river
> I have never known you
> But your blood flows in my veins
> Your beautiful black blood that irrigates the fields
> The blood of our sweat
> The sweat of your work
> The work of your slavery
> The slavery of your children
> Africa tell me Africa
> Is this you this back that is bent
> This back that breaks under the weight of humiliation
> This back trembling with red scars
> And saying yes to the whip under the midday sun
> But a grave voice answers me
> Impetuous son that tree young and strong
> That tree there
> In splendid loneliness amidst white and faded flowers

That is Africa your Africa
That grows again patiently obstinately
And its fruit gradually acquire
The bitter taste of liberty.

The East African Association.   In Kenya in 1921, Harry Thuku (THOO-koo), a young man who worked for the colonial government, formed a movement called the Young Kikuyu Association. The association was clearly meant to appeal to the Kikuyu, Thuku's ethnic group. Its aims also appealed to a wider audience of Africans in Kenya, however, and many joined him. Later Thuku changed the movement's name to reflect this—the East African Association.

Thuku at first demanded that a law requiring Africans to carry identity passes be repealed. By the time of a mass meeting in Thika (THEE-kuh), Kenya, in November 1921, his aims had expanded. Thuku announced the following resolutions:

> That the Government is respectfully requested to repeal the Native Registration Ordinance or to suspend its operation for a period of five years.
> That the Government is requested to issue instructions to district officers to treat native chiefs with due respect and dignity and not compel them to carry loads like porters.
> That the Government is requested to repeal the Hut Tax and to charge only Poll Taxes as done in the case of Europeans and Asiatics.
> That the Government is requested to allow natives to purchase land throughout their country.
> That if no satisfaction is obtained from the local Government the Chairman is authorized to make further representations to the Secretary of State for the Colonies.

In early 1922, when Thuku's causes were gaining a great deal of public support, the colonial governor arrested him. Workers in Nairobi, where he was jailed, immediately went on strike, calling for his release. People gathered at the prison where he was being held. By noon the next day, there was estimated to be between 7,000 and 8,000 people in the crowd. When a delegation of Thuku's colleagues came to tell the people that the government would not release Thuku but would give him a fair trial, many people became so angry that they accused the colleagues of having been bribed. One woman, Mary Muthoni (moo-THOH-nee), was so incensed that she taunted the men with these words: "You take my dress and give me your trousers. You men are

Nairobi Railroad Station, 1925. The railroad was originally built across Kenya to allow farmers to export their goods to Britain. The railroad, and this station, are still major links in Kenya's transportation system.

cowards. What are you waiting for? Our leader is in there. Let's get him." She and hundreds of unarmed men and women then rushed the prison. Government officials, taken by surprise, fired their guns into the crowd. After the shooting some 50 people, including Mary Muthoni, were dead. Thuku himself was deported. Without its leader the power of the East African Association declined. Colonial authorities had once again asserted their authority.

The Role of African Churches.   As Africans learned that their political associations would be banned by colonial authorities, they found other ways to voice their discontent. Some turned to their Christian churches for help. Christian doctrine taught that all are equal in God's eyes. Within the missionary-established churches, however, Africans found that this doctrine was not always practiced. In most churches European missionaries did not encourage men to become priests or ministers. The few Africans who did become members of the clergy were still not equal members of the church council.

In some areas, too, the European churches tried to outlaw African traditions that they saw as un-Christian. For example, in the late 1920s in Kenya, Protestant missionaries forbade African Kikuyu Christians to

129

participate in their people's **initiation rites,** ceremonies that made them full members of the group. For the Kikuyu this was unreasonable, since they believed that only fully initiated men and women could be considered mature adults. Their response was swift and decisive. They broke with the missions, establishing their own church, which allowed the initiation ceremonies.

Thousands of new Christian churches were formed all over the continent in a similar manner. In South Africa alone, more than 2,000 independent Christian churches were founded.

Youth Organizations and the Rise of Political Parties. Partly as a reaction against the older, more conservative and more elite leaders, several African youth organizations were formed in the 1930s. The Nigerian Youth Movement, founded in 1936, attempted to unite all ethnic groups in Nigeria. Its goal, however, was not complete independence for Nigeria but, rather, political freedom to run its own affairs as well as to gain economic and social reforms. The movement helped to give Nigerians a stronger political awareness, but in the end it failed because of ethnic rivalries.

In 1938 the West African Youth League was formed to unite the young people of the Gold Coast. The league attracted support from all members of the colony, not just the young. Its object was to give people a chance to meet and discuss political, social, and economic problems. The league held mass meetings, organized trade unions, and published its own newspaper. Eventually it developed into a political party. It received enthusiastic mass support, but, like the Nigerian Youth Movement, it did not demand full independence from colonial domination.

The years between the two world wars saw an expansion of both educational opportunities and the popular press. For example, in Ghana the number of children attending primary school rose from 15,000 in 1902 to about 50,000 in 1924 and 65,000 in 1935. This growth was also evident in other colonial territories. What it meant was that more people all over Africa were able to read and write, and they could use these tools to complain about the abuses of colonial rule.

Newspapers began to give a voice to these newly educated people. Often the colonial government shut down the papers and jailed the editors for **sedition,** action directed against the authority of the government. But as quickly as the papers were closed, new ones opened. Moreover, the jailed newspaper editors and writers often started new papers as soon as they were released from prison.

Dr. Nnamdi Azikewe (en-nam-dee ah-zee-KAY-way), who would

later become a Nigerian head of state, was one such editor. In 1935 he began the *African Morning Post* in Accra, Ghana. Azikewe was jailed in 1937, convicted by the British of sedition for an article he wrote for the Post. When he was released, he returned to Nigeria. There in 1938 he founded the *West African Pilot*. This became the central newspaper in a chain of Nigerian papers.

The popular press did more than just provide an outlet for people's dissatisfaction. It also let readers realize that they were not alone in having complaints against their government. In addition, popular papers contributed to the development of political parties. Those who worked on a newspaper and those who read it frequently shared similar points of view. Thus newspapers prepared the way for people to join together in political parties to oppose the government and demand independence. Azikewe's *West African Pilot*, for example, paved the way for the National Council for Nigeria and the Cameroons (NCNC). Azikewe was the NCNC's first general secretary and, later its party leader. This organization became a major force in Nigeria's drive for independence.

World War II. Throughout World War II (1939-1945) Europeans clung to their colonies in Africa. France and Great Britain, especially, relied on African troops as well as African workers. The Africans built airfields and roads and produced vital raw materials for the colonial powers.

Africans were well aware of the contributions they made to the war and of the hardships they suffered. Food and other goods were scarce, trade was disrupted, inflation soared, and thousands of African men were taken from the countryside to serve in the colonial armies. Africans were also aware of the declarations made by Great Britain and the United States. These powers claimed that the war's goal was freedom for all peoples and their right to determine their own destiny. The United Nations' charter spelled out the world's opposition to colonialism and racism.

Pan-Africanism. While individual nationalist parties were formed in different colonies, party leaders saw their countries' independence linked with the independence of their neighbors. They understood that each colony's claims would be strengthened if they were combined with the demands of others. Thus in 1945 Africans from all over the continent attended the Fifth Pan-African Congress in Manchester, England.

The First Pan-African Congress had taken place in 1919, at the peace conference set up to end World War I. It was organized by an American, W.E.B. Du Bois. Du Bois believed that black people, especially those in the Caribbean and the United States, could gain racial equality faster if they worked together. At the 1945 conference, however, the emphasis shifted. Pan-Africanism then focused more on helping African countries to win their independence. Prominent among the leaders setting this direction were Kwame Nkrumah (KWAH-mee en-KROO-mah) of Ghana and Jomo Kenyatta (JOH-moh ken-YAH-tuh) of Kenya.

Later, as more and more African countries gained their independence, Pan-Africanism took on yet another meaning. It became a movement in search for ways of unifying the independent African countries. Africans had seen how they were able to achieve independence when masses of people rallied to the cause. If all Africans could be united, they reasoned, they would become a major force on the world political scene. You will read more in the next chapters about the measures Africans took to achieve this goal.

Chapter 5:
CHECKUP

REVIEWING THE CHAPTER

I. Building Your Vocabulary

In your notebook write the correct term that matches the definition

assimilation   imperialism   protectorate
collaboration   sedition   sovereignty

1. the extension of a nation's power over other areas
2. a nation's freedom from outside control
3. cooperating with an enemy in order to ensure one's own power
4. action directed against the authority of a government
5. absorbing a group into a larger group
6. a political unit that is dependent upon a more powerful state for protection

II. Understanding The Facts

In your notebook, write the numbers from 1 to 5. Write the letter of the correct answer next to the number.

1. In 1914, how many nations in Africa were independent?
   a. 8 b. 6 c. 2

2. Which of the following fought most strongly against accepting colonial rule?
   a. the Ashanti b. the Congolese c. the Kikuyu

3. What did the early European explorers focus on?
   a. mineral wealth b. ethnic groups c. sources of rivers

4. Which of the following nations did *not* have an African colony?
   a. Russia b. Portugal c. France

5. Which of the following nations ruled its colonies most harshly?
   a. Great Britain b. Italy c. Belgium

III. Thinking It Through

In your notebook, write the numbers from 1 to 5. Write the letter of the correct answer to each question next to its number.

1. Europeans were very skeptical about the reports of early African explorers that
   a. the continent had both rain forests and deserts.
   b. mighty rivers flowed through the continent.
   c. snow-capped mountains existed in tropical Africa.
   d. Africans extended good will to explorers.

2. David Livingstone was both a explorer and a
   a. scientist
   b. business person
   c. political leader
   d. missionary

3. The statement "These childlike people need a fatherly government to look after their interests" is an example of
   a. collaboration
   b. sedition
   c. paternalism
   d. autocracy

4. Which of the following statements sums up the goal of Pan-Africanism?
   a. The just claims of each group will be stronger if they are all linked together.
   b. Colonial governments have no right to tax Africans.
   c. Christian missionaries have no sincere interest in Africans.
   d. Africans must be equal partners with Europeans.

5. Which of the following would be an appropriate topic for the Negritude poets?
   a. the injustice of colonization
   b. economic fairness
   c. dances associated with the harvest
   d. Africa of the future

DEVELOPING CRITICAL THINKING SKILLS

1. Explain the three motives that lured Europeans to the African continent.

2. Show how the Negritude movement was an effective form of opposition to colonial rule and how it is consistent with what you already know about the peoples of Africa.

3. Describe the differences between direct and indirect rule.

4. Discuss how both resistance and collaboration on the part of African peoples yielded the same results.

INTERPRETING A MAP

The map on page 137 shows the current national boundaries in Africa. It also indicates when each country gained its independence. Using the map and information you have gained in this chapter, answer the following questions.

1. Which two countries never experienced colonial rule during the first three decades of the twentieth century?

2. Which country was the first to gain its independence?

3. Which areas of Africa achieved independence first?

4. The Gold Coast was the first black African nation to gain its independence, becoming Ghana in 1957. Why might that have been expected?

5. Why is it important for Lesotho and Swaziland to maintain good relations with South Africa?

ENRICHMENT AND EXPLORATION

1. Find out more about one of the early African nationalist movements that you read about in this chapter. Report on your findings in writing or orally in class. Be sure to include information on the goals of the movement you have chosen. Point out how successful the move-

ment was in reaching those goals. Describe what eventually happened to the movement.

2. Choose one of the European powers that established colonies in Africa. Draw a time line that traces that power's initial interest in Africa to the point of its colonies' independence. Use appropriate library resources to gather information for your time line.

3. Using a variety of sources, find out about the current status of Namibia, the former colony of German South West Africa. In writing or orally in class, report on the area's history from World War I to the present.

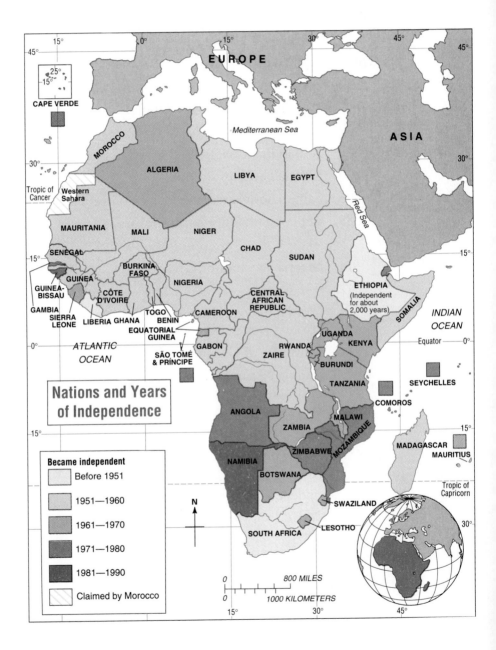

Nations and Years of Independence

Became independent
- Before 1951
- 1951—1960
- 1961—1970
- 1971—1980
- 1981—1990
- Claimed by Morocco

N

0   800 MILES
0   1000 KILOMETERS

EUROPE

ASIA

Mediterranean Sea

Red Sea

INDIAN OCEAN

ATLANTIC OCEAN

Tropic of Cancer

Tropic of Capricorn

Equator

CAPE VERDE

MOROCCO

Western Sahara

ALGERIA

LIBYA

EGYPT

MAURITANIA

MALI

NIGER

CHAD

SUDAN

SENEGAL

GUINEA-BISSAU

GUINEA

GAMBIA

SIERRA LEONE

LIBERIA

BURKINA FASO

CÔTE D'IVOIRE

GHANA

TOGO

BENIN

NIGERIA

CAMEROON

CENTRAL AFRICAN REPUBLIC

ETHIOPIA
(Independent for about 2,000 years)

SOMALIA

EQUATORIAL GUINEA

SÃO TOMÉ & PRÍNCIPE

GABON

ZAIRE

RWANDA

BURUNDI

UGANDA

KENYA

TANZANIA

SEYCHELLES

COMOROS

ANGOLA

ZAMBIA

MALAWI

MOZAMBIQUE

MADAGASCAR

MAURITIUS

NAMIBIA

ZIMBABWE

BOTSWANA

SWAZILAND

SOUTH AFRICA

LESOTHO

137

WEST AFRICA AND THE WORLD

1100–*Today*

1100s	Hausa and Bornu empires prosper.
1471	Portuguese first visit Gold Coast.
1482	Portuguese build fort at Elmina.
1492	*Columbus lands at San Salvador.*
1827	Fourah Bay College established in Sierra Leone.
1847	Liberia becomes a republic.
1882–1898	Samori Touré resists French colonization.
1884–1885	Berlin Conference partitions Africa.
1914–1918	*World War I*
1914	Nigeria becomes British colony.
1939–1945	*World War II*
1945–1950s	Felix Houphouet-Boigny represents Côte d'Ivoire at French Assembly.
1948	University of Ghana founded.
1949	Kwame Nkrumah founds Ghana's Convention People's Party.
1952	Nkrumah becomes Prime Minister of colonial government in Ghana.
1957	Ghana proclaimed independent.
1957–1965	Most West African countries become independent from colonial rule.
1960	Côte d'Ivoire and Nigeria gain independence.
1965	*U.S. combat troops sent to Vietnam.*
1966–1970	Civil war in Nigeria
1972	Ghanaian army overthrows elected civilian government.
1975	Nigerian General Gowon overthrown.
1980	Côte d'Ivoire begins to produce oil.
1990	Opposition parties legalized in Côte d'Ivoire.

6 *West Africa*

West Africa is a region with a particularly rich history. For over a thousand years many powerful kingdoms flourished there. These were prosperous, well-organized communities that promoted commerce and learning. Their peoples created beautiful crafts and art and built elaborate palaces. A Dutch visitor to the capital of the kingdom of Benin in the early 1600s described what he saw:

> The town seemeth to be very great, when you enter it, you go into a great broad street. . . . In this great street, you see many streets on the sides thereof, which also go right forth, but you cannot see the end of them, by reason of their great length. . . . Their houses have two or three steps to go up. . . . Their rooms within are four-square . . . and therein they lie and eat their meat, but they have other places besides, as kitchens and other rooms.

Europeans first arrived in West Africa in the 1400s. They knew little or nothing of the region. By the late 1800s, however, most of West Africa's great empires were under the control of European powers. Today, the Europeans are gone, and West Africa is once more a land of independent nations. The region is struggling to overcome its colonial past and the effects of drought, desertification, overpopulation, and political upheaval. With its exceptional resources, West Africa has the potential to become great again.

THE REGION

West Africa consists of 16 countries: Benin, Burkina Faso, Cape Verde, Gambia, Ghana, Guinea, Guinea-Bissau, Côte d'Ivoire, Liberia, Mali, Mauritania, Niger, Nigeria, Senegal, Sierra Leone, and Togo (see chart on page 141). The region covers nearly one-quarter of the African continent and has a land area of about 3 million square miles. This makes it roughly the size of the continental United States.

The Land.   Most of West Africa is grassland. A small part of the region, along the Atlantic coast, is rain forest. The rest, bordering on the Sahara, is rather dry. Parts of Mali and Niger are in the Sahara and can barely support human activity. Most of West Africa is less than 1,200 feet above sea level.

The grasslands of West Africa have a tropical wet-dry climate. This means that there is a distinct rainy season (from April to October) and a distinct dry season (from October to March). In areas near the rain forest, there may be over 80 inches of rainfall per year. Nearer the desert, there may be as little as 20 inches. In the Sahel, just south of the desert, only 10 to 20 inches of rain falls in an average year.

West Africa's major rivers are the Niger, the Senegal, the Volta, and the Gambia. The Niger, which flows for 2,600 miles, is the longest. Because their flow is frequently interrupted by **cataracts**, or great rapids, none of the rivers is navigable for its entire length. Centuries ago market towns grew up along the rivers, allowing some trade among local people. But the use of these rivers for transporting goods and people to the coast or for export is limited. Lacking good waterways, West Africans must rely on more expensive alternatives, such as railroads, roads, or—most expensive of all—airplanes.

In general, soil fertility in West Africa is "fragile." This means that although the land will be productive for a few years, the soil is unable to support the raising of crops over a long period of time. Increasing the productivity of the farmland in West Africa has proved difficult. Deep plowing threatens soil fertility in most areas. And chemical fertilizers are too expensive. Animal manure, a possible alternative, is available only where there are large animals, generally in the northern areas of West Africa. There, however, the lack of rain makes agriculture difficult. Where rainfall is adequate, West African farmers must plant and harvest their crops between April and October. During the rest of the year, the land is too dry to support agriculture.

Population.   There are an estimated 206 million people in West Africa, nearly half the population of the continent south of the Sahara. Most live along the Atlantic coast, from Ghana to Nigeria, and south of the Sahel, in northern Nigeria and Burkina Faso.

Population growth in the region is among the highest in the world—

COUNTRY	CAPITAL CITY	POPULATION (millions)	AREA (square miles)	PER CAPITA INCOME (U.S. dollars)	LITERACY RATE (percentage)
		Some Facts About West African Countries			
Benin	Porto-Novo (POR·toh NOH·VOH)	4.7	43,483	$ 374	26%
Burkina Faso	Ouagadougou (wah·guh·DOO·goo)	9.0	105,869	170	13
Cape Verde	Praia (PRY·ah)	.4	1,557	500	48
Côte d'Ivoire	Yamoussoukro (yah·muh·SOO·kroh)	12.5	124,503	921	43
Gambia	Banjul (BAN·jool)	.8	4,361	255	25
Ghana	Accra (AK·ruh)	15.2	92,099	390	53
Guinea	Conakry (koh·nah·KREE)	7.2	94,964	305	48
Guinea-Bissau	Bissau (bi·SOU)	1.0	13,948	170	34
Liberia	Monrovia (mun·ROH·vee·ah)	2.6	43,000	410	35
Mali	Bamako (bah·mah·KOH)	8.1	478,764	200	18
Mauritania	Nouakchott (nwak·SHOT)	1.9	397,954	450	17
Niger	Niamey (nya·MAY)	7.9	489,189	310	14
Nigeria	Lagos (LAY·gos)	118.8	356,667	790	42
Senegal	Dakar (dah·KAR)	7.7	75,750	380	28
Sierra Leone	Freetown (FREE·town)	4.2	27,699	320	21
Togo	Lomé (loh·MAY)	3.7	21,622	240	41

about 3.1 percent per year. In ten West African countries the rate is even higher. Because of this high rate of growth, a substantial proportion of the population of most West African countries is under the age of 16.

At the same time, West Africa also has a very high infant mortality rate. More than 10 percent of infants die between birth and the age of one year. There are so many infant deaths largely because lack of clean drinking water and inadequate medical care result in widespread disease.

Cities.   About 25 percent of West Africa's population lives in cities. The urban population is growing rapidly. The largest city in West Africa is Dakar, the capital of Senegal, with an estimated population of 1.4

A busy street scene in Lagos, Nigeria. The vendor is selling newspapers in English and in African languages.

million. Other major cities are Lagos and Ibadan in Nigeria, Abidjan in Côte d'Ivoire, and Accra in Ghana.

Economic Activities. The economies of West African countries vary greatly. Burkina Faso, Guinea-Bissau, Mali, and Togo have average **per capita incomes** (the average annual incomes for each person) of less than $250. Thus they are among the poorest nations in the world. On the other end of the scale is Côte d'Ivoire. This nation has been among the most successful in Africa in developing its economy and improving the standard of living of its people. In some years its per capita income has reached $1,000. In between are Ghana and Nigeria, two nations with tremendous economic potential.

One source of income for West Africa is its mineral resources. A few West African countries already export minerals to Europe and the United States. Ghana exports gold, diamonds, and manganese. Liberia and Mauritania export ores; Sierra Leone and Ghana export diamonds; and Nigeria exports oil. Other income is earned from the export of certain crops—cocoa, coffee, yams, cassava, peanuts, millet, and cotton.

In many West African countries the government is the largest employer. It hires people to administer policies and programs, run hospitals, build roads, collect garbage, and serve in the army. The schools and universities are also run by the government, as are the airlines, buslines, railroads, and utilities. In Ghana the army takes part in road construction and other public works projects. Many Africans seek government jobs, since there is little cash to finance private businesses.

HISTORY

Most early West Africans were farmers. Some people along the coast engaged in fishing. There were also skilled crafts workers who produced delicate metalwork and carvings in wood and stone. Weavers produced fine cotton cloth. A visitor to Mali during the 1500s reported that "their cloth is white and made of cotton which they cultivate and weave in the most excellent fashion."

Early History. As early as the seventh century, West Africans had begun to trade with the North Africans who lived along the Mediterranean Sea. Crossing the Sahara on camels, they exchanged gold, kola nuts, ivory, and slaves for salt, cloth, metal goods (pots, pans, knives, and swords), and horses. They also brought back books, purchased from Muslim scholars in the great city of Timbuktu.

Between about 1000 and the late 1800s, West Africa was a land of many kingdoms. As you have read in Chapter 4, the greatest were Ghana, Mali, Songhai, Benin, and Ashanti. In 1352 a traveler to the powerful kingdom of Mali wrote of the Africans he met there:

> One of their good features is their lack of oppression [unjust or cruel use of power]. They are the farthest removed people from it and their [king] does not permit anyone to practice it. Another is the security embracing the whole country, so that neither traveler there nor dweller has anything to fear from thief or usurper [challenger].

The Slave Trade.   The transatlantic slave trade began in the 1500s, reached its height in the 1700s, and ended in the 1800s. One Ghanaian historian has pointed out that the growth of kingdoms on the West African coast closely followed the rise of the transatlantic slave trade.

In these coastal regions slaves captured in war were usually given to the king and his nobles. When the Portuguese observed this, they decided not to attempt to capture slaves themselves. Instead, they set up trade with the African rulers, exchanging weapons and other valuables for their slaves. African leaders organized raids on their neighbors and also took convicted criminals and debtors. They marched their captives to the so-called Slave Coast—the area along the Atlantic Ocean in today's countries of Togo, Benin, and Nigeria. There, in return for firearms and other goods, they sold the unfortunate Africans to the Europeans.

As you have read, during the eighteenth century industrial development in Europe and the United States began to make the slave trade less profitable. In addition, more and more people in West Africa, Europe, and the United States were loudly condemning the dehumanizing slave trade. When Britain and France abolished such trade, they encouraged cash crops into West Africa. These crops were essential for new industries they were developing at home. In fact, by the middle of the 1800s, the Niger River and its outlets became known as the Oil Rivers because the area was producing so much palm oil for use in Europe.

The introduction of cash crops resulted in more than just the abolition of the slave trade, however. The Europeans needed both large-scale cash-crop production and new markets for their industrial goods.

When the Africans did not organize these activities themselves, the French and the British used this as an excuse to partition West Africa.

European Colonization. The colonization of West Africa—indeed, of all of Africa—was also a result of the European nations' rivalries among themselves. After they had partitioned the continent at the Berlin Conference in 1884-85 (see Chapter 5), the European powers attempted to occupy the territories that they had claimed.

In West Africa large numbers of Africans resisted the colonial intrusion. In Chapter 5 you read about the British struggle with the Ashanti. The French also had to fight to impose their rule. For example, Samori Touré (suh-MOR-ee too-RAY), an African trader, joined the army of a neighboring kingdom in order to secure his captive mother's release. Touré rose through the ranks to command an army in the upper Niger region. From 1882 to 1898, he fought French troops who were attempting to turn large areas of the interior into French West Africa. Eventually, however, the superiority of French weapons forced him to submit to the colonial ruler.

Armed resistance to colonialism in West Africa ended early in the 1900s. Africans, nevertheless, did not end their opposition. Instead, they looked for new ways to express it. Several Africans who had received a Western-style education turned their attention to the press. There had been African newspapers in Liberia and Sierra Leone since the mid-1800s, and African journalists often wrote in these and other papers about the needs of their countries. Other Africans became lawyers, arguing for greater equality under the law. Still others became teachers, ministers, and doctors.

Independence. After World War II the movement for gradual economic development and independence, which many of the early professionals encouraged, was overcome by a trend of militant nationalism. Many West Africans had served with the Allied forces in World War II. They had fought for European freedom. Now they began to demand their own. Often these were men who had little formal education but were respected members of their villages and towns. Their stories and experiences awoke in their relatives, friends, and co-workers the desire to be citizens of an independent country.

One way in which West Africans showed their feelings was by mounting strikes against foreign-owned shops. Others refused to pay taxes. The British and French governments, weary of war and facing massive redevelopment programs at home, eventually realized that they could no longer hold on to their African possessions.

The Political Organization of the New Nations.   Except for Liberia, which was settled by blacks from the United States and became a republic in 1847, all of the countries of West Africa became independent after World War II. Most gained independence from colonial rule between 1957 and 1965. At the time of independence, a democratic system of government was established in each of these countries except Guinea-Bissau. The governments were modeled on the systems of either Great Britain or France. Constitutions were written before the colonial governments gave up control.

Adult men and women in each nation voted to elect a prime minister or president. They also elected representatives to serve in their country's legislature. Each country had a modern court system, presided over by judges who were trained lawyers.

After independence was achieved, many West African political leaders began to make changes that undermined the democratic governments that had been established. In most countries constitutions were changed to give greater power to the president and the executive branch. Politicians in power eliminated the political parties that were in opposition to their own party. Elections were no longer held, or, if they were, often only one candidate ran for each office. Freedom of the press was curbed in many countries, to prevent criticism of the regime in power.

In many countries the leaders of the armed forces have staged a **coup d'état** (koo-day-TAH), a sudden, violent overthrow of the government by a small group. They have suspended their constitutions and banned all political parties. Thus the legislative branch no longer functions, and the military rulers make all of the laws. They also control the courts, which no longer protect the citizens from the abuse of power by government officials.

About half of the countries in West Africa are at present ruled by military governments. Multiparty, democratic governments exist only in Senegal and Gambia. The remaining countries are ruled by civilian leaders who control their nations' politics and governmental systems.

THE PEOPLE AND CULTURE

The boundaries of today's West African nations are the same as those drawn by the Europeans for their colonies in the 1800s. As you read in

This mosque is in Djenné, one of Africa's earliest and most famous centers of Muslim learning. It is made out of local cement and is the same color as the ground on which it stands.

Chapter 2, these boundaries were established without regard to ethnic divisions. As a result, many West Africans countries have within their borders peoples with different languages, religions, and customs. With deep differences among their peoples, it is difficult for the nations of West Africa to achieve unity.

Language. In order to ease communication among the many different peoples, each nation of West Africa has adopted an official language.

147

This is usually the language of the nation's former colonial ruler. Thus, in Benin, Burkina Faso, Guinea, Côte d'Ivoire, Mali, Mauritania, Niger, Senegal, and Togo, French is the official language. English is the official language of Gambia, Ghana, Liberia, Nigeria, and Sierra Leone. The official language of Guinea-Bissau is Portuguese.

Religion. As in the rest of Africa, many local traditional religions are practiced in West Africa. Each group has its own set of beliefs and practices. The members of one group do not try to spread their ideas to other people.

Traditional religions do have a number of beliefs in common, including a belief in a single high god, who is the creator of the universe. In addition, there are many lesser gods and spirits, including spirits of dead ancestors. The role that traditional religions play in people's lives has changed in response to the modern world, but these religions remain important. West African countries in which traditional religions are dominant today include Benin, Côte d'Ivoire, Sierra Leone, and Togo.

Islam and Christianity are gaining strength in West Africa. West African people began converting to Islam shortly after the arrival of the Muslims in the eighth century. Conversion to Christianity did not occur on a large scale until the early twentieth century.

The largest Muslim populations are in Nigeria (about 47 percent of the total) and the countries just south of the Sahara—Gambia, Guinea, Mali, Mauritania, Niger, and Senegal. A large part of Ghana's population is Christian (about 42 percent of the total). In other West African nations Christians account for between 1 and 30 percent of the population. A small number of West Africans belong to independent churches that are based on Christian beliefs and often blend traditional or Islamic religious practices.

Rural Life. The majority of West Africans live in rural areas. Most are farmers, and people who live near water often fish as well. Many farmers grow food crops, both for themselves and to sell to feed the people living in the cities. Major grain crops are maize, sorghum, and millet. Important root crops are cassava and yams. A small number of farmers raise cash crops for export to Europe and America.

The root crops provide the West African diet with a plentiful supply of carbohydrates. Many West Africans, however, do not get enough protein.

Many farmers in West Africa clear the land by the **slash-and-burn**

method. That is, some of the brush is cut down and set on fire. The fire spreads, burning the remaining brush and grasses, and the ash that results fertilizes the soil. The most important tools for the West African farmer are the short-handled hoe and the **machete,** a large, heavy knife. West Africans rarely use modern technology on their farms because it is expensive and not readily available. Moreover, tractor parts and other machinery parts quickly rust or rot and are very difficult to replace.

Urban Life.   In the cities men and women work in a variety of occupations. Some work in factories that produce beer, cloth, furniture, canned goods, shoes, or household utensils. Others work for businesses in such fields as photography, electronics, dry cleaning, construction, and machine repair. A few own their own businesses. As you read earlier, many West Africans are employed by their government. African professionals, such as doctors and lawyers, usually live in the major cities.

The Family.   African families are extended families. Often, especially in rural areas, many relatives live near one another in the same village. Because of close family relationships, someone is always nearby to care for the children. The elderly are also cared for by the family group.

Family members help one another in many ways. The larger family group may offer financial support to enable a child to stay in school or attend a university. Family groups may provide a loan to help an enterprising family member start a business. And it is to the family group that individuals turn if they lose a job, are mourning a death, or get divorced. When personal problems arise, one can always return to the family group and be cared for.

The Role of Women.   The Ashanti say, "It is a woman who gave birth to a man. It is a woman who gave birth to a chief." This saying indicates the way in which many West Africans have viewed the vital roles of women in their society.

Women in West Africa have always been active in agriculture, arts and crafts, and trade. In precolonial times these occupations often gave women a political role as well. For example, in southeastern Nigeria, women had their own courts, group advisers who were specifically interested in women's issues, and market managers. Since women managed trade in the local market, they set prices, settled quarrels among the settlers, and fined those who disobeyed the rules.

In many early West African kingdoms the queen mother's role was quite important. She had a great deal of authority in advising the king and other royal family members. During the colonial period, however, the roles of African women were often downgraded. European administrators, mostly men, looked to African men to interpret their peoples' laws, collect and pay taxes, and become active in new businesses. Women continued to farm, but their work was not valued in the colonial economic system as much as the men's work was. It was the men who were encouraged to become wage earners and cash-crop farmers.

In much of West Africa, women are in charge of the markets. Almost anything can be bought, especially food items, in this market in Abidjan, Côte d'Ivoire.

During the drive for independence in West Africa, women asserted themselves, actively opposing the colonial governments. In a strike in Guinea in 1953, women traders refused to sell dairy products to the French, and women farmers collected and distributed food to strikers in the towns. In Côte d'Ivoire, women invaded a prison in the middle of the night, frightening both the prison wardens and the French government. Their leaders, whom they were seeking to free, were let go within a few days.

After independence most West African governments set up organizations to look after women's interests. But as the governments failed, so have many of these women's groups. On the whole, women in West Africa have become most concerned with looking after their immediate economic concerns. They still dominate the markets in many areas. They also continue to carry the burden of farming and looking after the children. When they are able to, they join and support organizations that address these economic issues.

Today many West African women have begun to work outside the home. In Senegal, for example, a number of women have become quite prosperous as owners and managers of retail businesses. In other countries women own real estate, taxis, small buses, and even fishing boats and fishing nets. In 1985, 15 percent of the home owners in metropolitan Lagos were women.

Other women, particularly those who are educated, have moved into the professions, mainly nursing and teaching, but also medicine and law. Recently women have served as government ministers and members of parliament. One lawyer, Angie Brooks of Liberia, represented her country as ambassador to the United Nations.

Education.   During the 1800s the Europeans started schools in West Africa, and eventually they began to employ Africans as teachers. In order to provide the necessary teacher training, a school called Fourah Bay College was established in Sierra Leone in 1827. Now called the University of Sierra Leone, this is the oldest university in tropical Africa. Today, a modern school system exists in every West African country. Still, no country is able to afford the number of schools or trained teachers needed to educate all of its school-age children. And the region's rapid population growth has made the problem worse.

Many West African children do enter kindergarten or elementary school. To be eligible for secondary school or a university, students must pass difficult examinations. Only the very brightest and the hardest workers succeed. Perhaps 20 percent of all children who enter

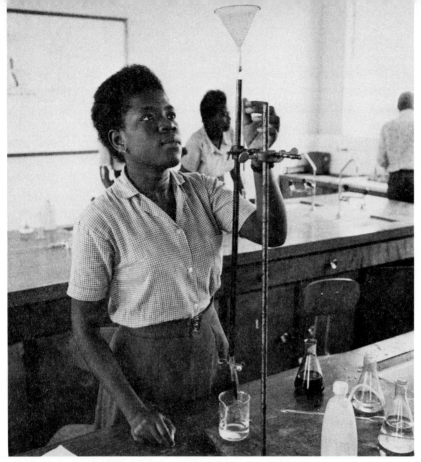

A student carefully executes an experiment in a chemistry class at a girls' college in Freetown, Sierra Leone.

elementary school enroll in high school. Only 2 to 4 percent go from there to a university. Women as well as men attend the schools and universities.

Almost every West African country has at least one university. A few countries, such as Ghana and Nigeria, have several. Many countries also have a law and a medical school.

To train people for a specific craft or trade, many West African businesses follow an **apprentice system**. In such a system a young person is hired as a trainee at less than full wages. He or she receives instruction in a trade such as carpentry, metalwork, painting, auto repair, or textile dyeing. An apprentice will often work for a master for four or five years before establishing his or her own business.

Art, Music, and Literature. African artists have always played a central role in their societies. The arts—particularly music, literature, and sculpture—have always been an important part of everyday life as well.

This tradition continues today even though the forms through which artists express themselves have sometimes changed. For example, Yoruba wood-carvers in what is now Nigeria have for centuries told stories on the doors that they carved. Now they are creating similar narrative sculptures to decorate gas stations and other public places. Sometimes they show scenes from Yoruba history. At other times their carvings depict stories of more recent origin.

Another traditional art whose style reflects the changing times is textile dyeing. West African women have been **resist-dyeing** cloth for hundreds of years. That is, they have been decorating cloth by treating it so that the colors are prevented from adhering to certain areas when it is dipped into a dye vat. This process is also called **batik**. European traders in the fifteenth century highly valued the indigo-dyed material made in Nigeria and Sierra Leone.

In Sierra Leone, women dominate the textile-dyeing industry. Originally local cloth was patterned with dyes mixed from vegetable materials, such as roots and plants. Now, however, various commercial dyes are used, as are imported cottons and satins.

Skilled women dyers, besides earning a good income, are also considered leaders in style. It is part of their business to study fashion. They must know how colors and designs work together and how fabric will look when it is wrapped or stitched into the latest style. Often a successful dyer will employ many of her female relatives and several apprentices in her shop.

Literature is another of Africa's arts that has expanded into new forms since precolonial times. Much of West Africa's literary tradition was oral until only a few centuries ago. As Africans attended Western schools, however, they began to adapt Western literary devices to their own culture.

Amos Tutuola (too-TOH-luh), a Nigerian writer, was one of the first Africans to have his writings reach a worldwide reading public. His best-known work, *The Palm Wine Drinkard*, is the story of a man who visits the underworld to retrieve his dead palm-wine supplier. In the story Tutuola mixes Western and Yoruba images and myths to create a distinctly African tale.

Chinua Achebe (CHIN-oo-ah ah-cheh-BAY), another Nigerian author, has written novels that deal with the clash of African and European cultures and the conflicts that face Africans today. His audience is not only educated Nigerians but others who wish to understand how Africans view the world.

Some African writers have concentrated on children's literature, so that youngsters learning to read will have another way of learning about their culture. A leading writer of children's literature is Efua Sutherland, a Ghanaian. She has also written and produced plays for adults and has started two theater companies. Her *Vulture, Vulture* contains two verse plays that use the "call and response" method usually found in traditional African theater (see Chapter 2). These dramatized stories teach children good behavior.

Musicians, too, are fusing old and new styles. One Nigerian composer, Akin Euba (AH-kin ay-oo-BAH), received most of his musical training in England and the United States. But he enjoyed African music growing up as a child in Nigeria. He has used a common characteristic of African music, the combination of poetry and music, in his work.

When the composition "Dirges" was to be performed in Munich, Germany, in the early 1970s, however, Euba faced a problem. European musicians could not play African instruments, and the African musicians could not read European musical notations. Euba's solution was to combine a tape recording of the African melodies and rhythms with the live poetry recitation, accompanied by Western musical passages.

As you have read, there is great diversity in the West African region. There are also a number of links among the nations—the early development of trade, the impact of powerful kingdoms, the shared colonial experience, and the cultural heritage of the people. By looking more closely at three West African nations, Ghana, Côte d'Ivoire, and Nigeria, we can get a better idea of their similarities and differences.

GHANA

Shortly after midnight on March 6, 1957, amid great excitement, a new flag was raised over Africa. After 80 years of British rule, the Gold Coast was proclaimed independent. It was the first colony in sub-Saharan Africa to gain independence. It was also the first member of Britain's Commonwealth of Nations to be governed by black Africans.

History.   For centuries people living in the land that is now Ghana engaged in trade with outsiders. The Akan-speaking (AH-kan) peoples in the interior forest kingdoms gave their goods to traders who took them to Djenné on the upper Niger River, and Timbuktu. There the goods were sold to traders who transported them by camel across the Sahara to North Africa. The major items of trade were gold and kola nuts, which were exchanged for salt from the Sahara.

After 1471, when the Portuguese first visited the area that they named the Gold Coast, Africans living along the coast established and maintained an active trade with the Europeans—the Portuguese, English, Dutch, Germans, and Scandinavians. The principal items of the Atlantic trade were gold, ivory, and (after the 1600s) slaves. These were exchanged for a variety of goods, including cloth, metals, guns, beads, and brandy.

Great competition for the Gold Coast trade developed among the Europeans, who built forts to protect their interests. A Portuguese fort at Elmina (el-MEE-nuh), built in 1482 and enlarged and rebuilt in the 1600s, still stands. Remains of other European forts can be seen at various points along Ghana's Atlantic shore, including Cape Coast and Anomabu (ah-NOH-mah-boo).

Because of their long history of contact with the outside world, Gold Coast residents in the 1800s were generally more outward looking than other West Africans. A small number of them attended schools established by English and Swiss missionaries. A few students also traveled to England for advanced study. One such individual was John Mensah Sarbah (MEN-sah SAR-bah), the son of a prosperous merchant. Sarbah studied law and returned home to become a prominent lawyer, politician, and writer in the early 1900s. He was also active in promoting the opening of a secondary school in Cape Coast. At the same time, Gold Coast Africans began publishing newspapers, including the *Gold Coast Times* and *the Western Echo*.

Independence.   When Ghana became an independent nation in 1957, it elected Kwame Nkrumah as its first head of government. Nkrumah, born in 1909, attended Gold Coast schools. After working as a school teacher for several years, he decided to seek advanced education abroad. Traveling to the United States in 1935, he attended Lincoln University in Pennsylvania, where he received a bachelor of arts degree. Then he enrolled at the University of Pennsylvania, where he earned two master's degrees, in education and philosophy.

Nkrumah returned to the Gold Coast in 1947, and in 1949, he founded a political party, the Convention People's Party (CPP). The CPP enjoyed immediate popularity, winning large majorities in every election between 1951 and 1960. Nkrumah became prime minister of the colonial government in 1952. Five years later he became prime minister of an independent Ghana, so named after the ancient kingdom.

Nkrumah was a dynamic leader. He was a good speaker and had much personal charm. He gained an enthusiastic following because he won support from people from all walks of life and from every ethnic group. As a consequence, Ghanaians worked hard for the political success of Nkrumah and the CPP. Recently a biographer wrote of him: "He worked tirelessly for African freedom. . . . He was the most effective and the most widely known black African politician for over a decade. . . . To many, both in his own country and abroad, his name has become legendary."

In 1960 the people of Ghana voted to change their system of government from parliamentary to republican, and they chose Nkrumah as president. Soon Nkrumah began to make major policy changes that moved Ghana away from democracy. He declared the CPP the only legal political party, and he increased his personal power. Critics of the government were imprisoned. Official corruption became com-

Kwame Nkrumah (center, front row), with his cabinet, at the time of Ghana's independence in March 1957. The men are wearing richly colored kente cloth to demonstrate their respect for African traditions and values.

monplace, and people began to fear the government. In addition, mismanagement and unwise decisions damaged the economy and saddled the country with large debts to foreign corporations and governments.

In 1966 while President Nkrumah was traveling to China, high-ranking officers from the military and the police overthrew his government. They established a National Liberation Council, headed by General Joseph Ankrah (an-KRAH), to rule the country. In 1969, as it had promised at the time of the coup, the council returned the country to civilian rule. Once again a constitution was written, political parties competed, and elections were held. Kofia Busia (ko-FEE-uh bu-SEE-uh), leader of the Progressive Party, became prime minister.

Since then, Ghana has experienced several coups d'état, and the country has alternated between civilian and military rule. Most Ghanaians resent the military's interference. There was no public rejoicing in January 1972 or in December 1981, when the army overthrew the civilian governments that had been freely and fairly elected. Ghana is presently ruled by the military. Under its leader, Jerry Rawlings, political opposition is suppressed. Today, as late in Nkrumah's rule, a climate of uncertainty prevails in Ghana.

The Land and People.   Ghana's area is 92,099 square miles, about the size of the state of Wyoming. The country includes grasslands and tropical rain forest. In recent years the extent of the rain forest has declined substantially as people have cleared the land for farming or have harvested the rain forest's unique woods for export.

There are some 13 million people in Ghana, and the population is growing at the rate of about 3 percent per year. The country is not densely populated, with only 152 persons per square mile.

Ghana's peoples belong to many different language groups. The largest group is the Akan-speaking people, who make up 44 percent of the population. Among the Akan speakers are the Ashanti. Other language groups in Ghana include the Mole-Dagbani (mohl-dag-BAH-nee) speakers (16 percent), the Ewe (AY-way) speakers (13 percent), and the Ga-Abangbe (gah-ah-BANG-bay) speakers (8 percent). As you have read, Ghana's official language is English.

Religion.   Ghana is unusual in West Africa in that over 40 percent of the population are Christian. Another 40 percent practice traditional religions, and about 12 percent are Muslim. In addition, some people follow practices of several faiths, seeing no conflict between them. For

157

example, when the father of a noted Ghanaian poet died in 1977, the family performed the traditional funeral rituals and practices, then attended a Christian service in the dead man's honor: "We buried him with full ceremony—first the traditional ablutions [washing of the body], and the prayers of the Ewe tribe. Then we have an uncle who is a Presbyterian minister, so to make him happy we had a service in the church, too."

Agriculture.   During most of the twentieth century, cocoa has been Ghana's most valuable export. The foundation for this prosperous industry was laid in the late 1870s, when cocoa trees were first planted in southeastern Ghana. Since that time cocoa has been grown by Ghanaian farmers, and until recently, Ghana was the largest cocoa exporter in the world. The cocoa business brought prosperity to many Ghanaian farmers. In the cocoa-growing areas, especially in Kumasi, the successful cocoa growers were able to build large houses. With profits from this cash crop, they also could afford to send their children to school. They had the money to pay for school fees, books, uniforms, and, at the high-school level, room and board.

Today, Ghana's cocoa industry is in serious decline. There are several reasons for this. First, because of a lack of planning, older, less productive trees have not been replaced on a regular basis. Even when new trees are planted, it takes seven years before they will bear fruit. Second, many areas have been stricken with swollen-shoot disease, which can be halted only by cutting down the affected trees. And finally, low prices for cocoa on the world market and government policies have combined to reduce the incentive to grow cocoa.

Most Ghanaian workers are farmers. In fact, Ghana's farmers account for about 55 to 60 percent of the nation's labor force. They grow food crops, such as cassava, yams, maize, sorghum, millet, and rice.

Fishing.   Ghanaian fishermen make use of the waters of the Atlantic Ocean and various lakes, including Lake Volta, one of the largest artificial lakes in the world. Lake Volta developed as a result of the construction of the Volta Dam in the 1960s. This dam provides electric power for Ghanaian industries, and the surplus electricity is sold to Ghana's neighbors.

The Atlantic Ocean is fished from shore or from fishing boats that travel miles out into the ocean. In either case, the fish are caught in very large nets. Along the main coastal highway between Cape Coast

158

and Accra, groups of 10 to 20 fishermen stand in the hot sun for hours at a time, letting out and slowly pulling in their nets. Once the fish have been removed from the nets, women take them to sell in the market.

Other Industries.   One of Ghana's major industries is wood processing, and there are many sawmills and plywood factories in the country. In addition, a portion of the cocoa crop is processed in Ghana. Other industries include brewing and distilling, soft-drink production, meat processing, canning, sugar refining, flour milling, and the manufacture of cigarettes, cement, textiles, shoes, and sandals. Ghana also has an oil refinery, which produces gasoline and kerosene from imported crude oil.

Small quantities of gold, diamonds (mostly for industrial use), manganese, and bauxite are mined in Ghana. Very recently, offshore oil has been discovered. Small amounts are now being obtained, reducing Ghana's dependence on imported oil.

Construction, especially home construction, is an important small

The lumber industry is an important source of income for many West African countries. Forests must be replanted, however, if the environment is not to be permanently damaged.

business. Other small businesses include furniture making, auto repair, and textile dyeing. Photography is a particularly good business, since most families want to have photographs taken at important occasions. Tailors and seamstresses, busily working at hand- or treadle-driven sewing machines, produce shirts, dresses, and other articles of clothing.

The port of Tema, 18 miles from Accra, opened in 1961. It is linked to Accra by a four-lane concrete highway, and its industrial area is the site of many factories. Ghana's other port, also constructed since independence, is located at Sekondi-Takoradi (say-KON-dee tah-KOR-ah-dee), on the Gulf of Guinea about 125 miles west of Accra.

Open-Air Markets. Open-air markets operate throughout the country. The buying and selling of many items, including food, is usually carried out in such markets. Run mainly by women, they are usually very well organized and carefully regulated. Each product—cloth, fruits and vegetables, pots and pans, and so on—has its own area. There is even an area for buying and selling meat. The butcher shops, however, do not have refrigeration. Hot food is also available at the marketplace.

The markets are very colorful, and when the economy is operating properly, a wide variety of goods is available. Women, the main retailers, often have their young children with them. The markets are always crowded, with large numbers of people jostling one another. Some are looking for a particular item; others are "just looking." Sellers may be shouting at an individual, urging a purchase, calling attention to a particular item. It is common for a buyer and seller to argue over the price of some items; for other items, such as food, prices are usually fixed.

In Accra most people get around by walking, or they take small, privately owned buses, city buses, or taxis, which are usually decorated with sayings such as "Fear God" or "The Lord will provide." The private buses are the cheapest and most efficient means of transportation, and they are a big industry in Accra. Only a small percentage of the population can afford to own a private car.

Traditional Crafts. Ghanaians still produce a number of traditional crafts. Among the popular craft specialties is the production of canoes, boats about 40 feet long and 5 to 6 feet wide. Each canoe is carved from one log. An important tool in this process is the **adz**, a cutting tool with a thin, arched blade.

Another crafts product is handmade *kente* (ken-TAY) cloth, woven by specially trained men and used for traditional clothing. *Kente* is woven in long, narrow strips, which are sewn together to make a large cloth in a brilliant checkered pattern. Long ago kente cloth was woven from silk thread that was unraveled from imported cloth, and it was worn only by kings. Today, anyone who can afford the very high price may wear *kente* cloth.

Another traditional fabric is *adinkra* (ah-DIN-krah) cloth. *Adinkra* is the word for "farewell," and *adinkra* cloth was originally worn only at funerals. It is cotton cloth, hand stamped with patterns in black ink, and used for a variety of garments:

> The printing stamps are skillfully carved from small pieces of the hard skin of a calabash [a gourd]. . . . Using several different stamps, [the printer] dips each one into the thick black ink and prints the designs swiftly, close together, until the whole cloth is covered. . . .
>
> *Adinkra* cloth has much to say to those who know the meaning of the patterns. Reading the message of the *adinkra* stamps, we learn some of the wisdom of the Ashanti people: their patience and fortitude; their faith in the Supreme God; their loyalty to family and king.

Another ancient craft is the production of stools. The craftsman, using adzes, knives, and chisels, "carves the stool from a single piece of wood. The variety of design comes in the decoration of the legs or the column between the flat base and the curved seat. The carver knows that the designs have meanings and that some of them can only be used on certain stools." Decorated stools were once symbols of status in Ghana—the king of the Ashanti was always identified by his golden stool.

Daily Life in the Cities. Approximately 30 percent of the population lives in towns and cities. Accra, on the Gulf of Guinea, is the largest city. It has a population of about 900,000. Other important cities include Sekondi-Takoradi and, in the interior, Kumasi, an old and important trading center and former capital of the Ashanti Kingdom.

Accra is a large, modern city. The streets are lined with a variety of shops, office buildings, restaurants, and banks. At the street corners many small signs advertise nearby businesses, such as "Understanding Motors," "Peugeot Doctors," or "Doctor of Shoes." Booths on the sidewalks sell individual cigarettes, lottery tickets, and other items.

Along the streets a small number of commercial billboards urge the viewer to patronize a particular bank or business. Other, government-sponsored billboards might encourage citizens to support a certain government policy, such as self-sufficiency in food production: "We must grow what we eat and eat what we grow." The government wants Ghanaians to grow enough food to meet the needs of the population. In this way, the country can avoid the expensive alternative—importing food.

Large, multistoried government buildings are located throughout the city. Among the tall buildings are the headquarters of the Volta River Authority, which is responsible for the generation of electric power from a station completed in 1964 at Akosombo. Near the shore is the Castle, a fort built by the Danes during the 1600s and now the official residence of the head of state. Also in Accra is Kotoka International Airport. From here, the government-owned airline operates international air service as well as domestic air service to the smaller airports in other Ghanaian cities.

Housing.   There is in Ghana a variety of housing. Most people in Accra and the other major cities rent their homes. All rental quarters tend to be crowded, sometimes with four or more persons sharing a room. Apartment houses are being built to provide additional housing, but as more and more people migrate to the cities, construction is unable to keep up with demand.

Wealthier Ghanaians, in both cities and rural areas, may live in private homes. These may consist of a living room, dining room, and kitchen and several bedrooms. These houses have running water and electricity. Successful city dwellers may build such a house for relatives who have remained behind in their home community or for their own eventual retirement.

Teachers in secondary boarding schools and professors at the universities live in houses on their school's campus. This rental housing is available at a low rate and is an important benefit for high-school and university teachers.

Foods.   Ghanaians enjoy snacking on the delicious pineapples, oranges, mangoes, and bananas that are grown in their country. Plantains are considered a special treat when they are fried. When thirsty, Ghanaians drink soda and fruit drinks. They can also cut off the top of a green coconut and drink the young coconut milk. They do not eat the meat, which is still soft. For a sweet, they chew on stalks of sugarcane, which is sold in foot-long pieces. A common food is *kenke* (KEN-kay), a heavy dough made from corn flour. Balls of *kenke*, larger than baseballs and wrapped in banana leaves, are sold at stands along the road or in the market. A popular Ghanaian dish is peanut stew, which is very hotly spiced with locally grown red pepper.

Clothing.   Many Ghanaians, particularly in the cities, wear Western-style clothing. Officials usually dress in dark suits, white shirts, and ties. Women may wear either tailored dresses or the traditional blouses and wraparound skirts made from brightly colored locally woven cloth. School children must wear school uniforms.

Education.   On the outskirts of Accra is the University of Ghana, which was founded in 1948. The university offers bachelor of arts degrees as well as professional degrees in law and medicine. The course of study for a bachelor of arts degree is three years. Eligibility for university entrance is based on a student's success on examinations taken at the completion of high school. The number of available places is limited, and, therefore, entrance is very competitive.

There are two other universities in Ghana: the University of Cape Coast and the University of Science and Technology (in Kumasi), which also has a small medical school. Approximately 8,000 students attend Ghana's three universities.

Between 50 and 60 percent of Ghana's adults can read and write. At present close to 80 percent of school-age children attend primary schools.

Throughout the twentieth century Ghana was ahead of other African colonies in the development of its educational system. Educated Ghanaians worked to establish it and succeeded in building a sizable number of secondary schools. In Cape Coast alone there are currently seven secondary schools, all but one of which was founded before the 1950s. At the time of independence, there were a sizable number of educated people, including a small but influential professional class of lawyers, teachers, journalists, and ministers of religion.

The Role of Women.   In the rural areas and small towns, where the majority of the population lives, women carry water buckets, firewood, egg crates, trays of bread, and so on, on their heads. They rarely carry packages in their hands, no matter how valuable, delicate, or heavy they are. For example, it would not be unusual to see a woman walking down the street with a portable sewing machine delicately balanced on her head. Little girls practice carrying small items, such as pots, almost from the time they can walk. Older girls carry their school books in this manner.

Babies are carried on the mother's back. They rest on her hips and are held in place by a cloth wrapped around their bodies and tied on the mother's chest. Thus the woman with the sewing machine on her head may also be carrying a baby on her back.

Recreation.   Adults and children play *oware* (oh-WAH-ray), a board game using beans. An *oware* board, neatly carved from one piece of wood, has ten cups, and the beans are distributed among the cups. The object of the game is to collect the most beans. Only two people can play at one board at a time, and a game may go on for hours.

CÔTE D'IVOIRE

One of the most politically stable and economically successful countries in Africa is the Côte d'Ivoire, the Ivory Coast. This country, Ghana's western neighbor, was once a colony of France. It gained its independence on August 7, 1960.

The Land.   Côte d'Ivoire, with an area of 124,503 square miles, is slightly larger than the state of New Mexico. In 1983 Yamoussoukro was named the new capital. Abidjan, the old capital, remains in many ways the most important city.

The southern part of the country is covered by rain forest, which yields Côte d'Ivoire's main exports—coffee, cocoa, bananas, and hardwood timber. The rest of the country is savanna. There is a 716-mile railroad that connects Abidjan with Ouagadougou, the capital of Burkina Faso.

The People.   There are 12.5 million people in Côte d'Ivoire, and the population is growing swiftly, at the rate of about 4 percent per year. As in the rest of West Africa, the infant mortality rate is high, with 100 deaths per 1,000 live births. That is, 1 out of every 10 babies born in Côte d'Ivoire dies before reaching the age of one year.

There are at least five major ethnic groups in the country. Yet the largest group, the Baule, makes up no more than 23 percent of the population, and no one group predominates. French is the official language.

About 63 percent of the people of Côte d'Ivoire practice traditional religions, about 25 percent are Muslim, and 12 percent are

Christian. Perhaps half or more of the population can read and write. Just under 1 million children attend school each year.

The Government.   The president of Côte d'Ivoire is Felix Houphouet-Boigny (oo-FWAY bwah-NYEE). He was born in 1905 in the central part of the country and was educated in French schools in the colony and in Senegal. He worked as a colonial government employee for almost two decades. He then turned to cash-crop farming, becoming wealthy as a result. Houphouet-Boigny entered politics in 1945 to win improved labor conditions for farmers, and he became the leader of the Democratic Party of Côte d'Ivoire (or PDCI, for the French form of the name, Parti Démocratique de la Côte d'Ivoire). He was also elected to represent Côte d'Ivoire and neighboring Upper Volta (now Burkina Faso) in the French Assembly from 1945 through the late 1950s.

Today the PDCI remains Côte d'Ivoire's main political party, although opposition parties became legal in 1990. Houphouet-Boigny is the architect of the nation's political stability and economic prosperity. Now president for more than 30 years, he has managed to keep the country on a moderate course and to avoid military interference in the government. He uses talk and persuasion rather than force to convince people that his is the best policy for Côte d'Ivoire.

Economic Activities.   Economically Côte d'Ivoire has concentrated on building up and diversifying its agricultural sector first and then encouraging industry. Coffee and cocoa production has been expanded, and pineapples, bananas, and sugar have been added to the export list. Agriculture employs almost 80 percent of the work force.

Houphouet-Boigny differs from other African leaders in one significant way. Unlike many, he has since independence been willing to accept assistance from Côte d'Ivoire's former colonial ruler, France, and has encouraged large amounts of foreign investment. One result is that in 1980, with outside financing, Côte d'Ivoire began to produce oil in small quantities from its off-shore wells. Enough oil comes from these wells to meet most of the country's needs.

The combination of political stability, the emphasis on agriculture, the policy of gradual industrialization, and foreign investment has contributed to making Côte d'Ivoire one of the most prosperous countries in Africa. This prosperity has brought about an improved standard of living for the citizens of the country. It has also helped many thousands of other West Africans, who are able to find work in Côte d'Ivoire.

CASE STUDY:

The City and the Village

Chinua Achebe is one of Africa's most notable writers. Through his work he reveals his ideas of social justice and the importance of African tradition. In 1988 Achebe published a new novel, called *Anthills of the Savannah*. It tells of the rise of an African dictator and the effects of dictatorship on his fictional African country. One character in the novel, Ikem Osodi (ee-KEM oh-SOH-dee), is a well-known newspaper editor in Bassa, the nation's capital. Ikem goes to a hotel to meet a delegation of elders from his village, Abazon. Others from the village who work in the capital have also gone to pay their respects to the delegates. When Ikem arrives, he is immediately recognized and welcomed:

> "Our people say that when a titled man comes into a meeting the talking must stop until he has taken his seat. An important somebody has just come in who needs no introduction. Still yet, we have to do things according to what Europeans call protocol. I call upon our distinguished son and Editor of the *National Gazette* to stand up."
>
> Ikem rose to a . . . tremendous ovation.
>
> "When you hear Ikem Osodi everywhere you think his head will be touching the ceiling. But look at him, how simple he is. I am even taller than himself, a dunce like me. Our people say that an animal whose name is famous does not always fill a hunter's basket."
>
> At this point Ikem interjected that he expected more people to beat him up now that his real size was known, and caused much laughter.
>
> In spite of the . . . laughter the speaker was still able to register his disappointment that this most famous son of Abazon had not found it possible to join in their monthly meetings and other social gatherings so as to direct their ignorant fumblings with his wide knowledge. He went on with this failing at such length and relent-lessness that the bearded old man finally stopped him by rising to his feet. He was tall, gaunt-looking and with a slight stoop of the shoulders.
>
> The shrillness in the other man's voice was totally absent here but the power of his utterance held everyone captive from his very first words. He began by thanking Abazon people in Bassa for receiving him and the other five leaders from home. He thanked the many young men . . . turning out in their hundreds to accompany the delegation to the Palace and showing Bassa that Abazon had people. Then he turned sharply to the complaint of the last speaker:

African grasslands.

"I have heard what you said about this young man, Osodi, whose doings are known everywhere and fill our hearts with pride. Going to meetings and weddings and naming ceremonies of one's people is good. But don't forget that our wise men have said also that a man who answers every summons by the town-crier will not plant corn in his fields. So my advice to you is this. Go on with your meetings and marriages and naming ceremonies because it is good to do so. But leave this young man alone to do what he is doing for Abazon and for the whole of [the country]. The [rooster] that crows in the morning belongs to one household but his voice is the property of the neighborhood. You should be proud that this bright [rooster] that wakes the whole village comes from your compound."

Chinua Achebe. *Anthills of the Savannah.* (New York: Doubleday, Anchor Press, 1987), pp. 111-112.

1. Find the proverb each speaker uses to illustrate what he wants to say. What points are the speakers trying to make?

2. Why is the first speaker angry that Ikem does not attend monthly meetings? How does the leader defend Ikem?

3. What evidence do you have from the reading that the people of Abazon value politeness, modesty, humility, and hard work?

One admirer sums up Houphouet-Boigny's success when he writes that the president of Côte d'Ivoire is not a revolutionary, "yet what he accomplished is nothing less than a revolution, a fundamental change in his country's socioeconomic structure. It is a revolution in which no one has died."

NIGERIA

It is said that two out of every three people in West Africa live in Nigeria, Africa's most populated country. No accurate census has been taken since independence, but it is believed that there are almost 120 million people living in an area of some 356,669 square miles. Lagos, the capital, and the surrounding area have an estimated population of some 4 million, putting enormous pressure on the city's limited housing, transportation, and job opportunities. (A new city, Abuja (ah-BOO-juh) has been named the capital after many years of planning, although most government offices remain in Lagos.)

History. Nigeria has a long and eventful history. More than 1,000 years before Europeans arrived in West Africa, the Nok people who lived there worked iron into tools. They created beautiful sculpture in terra-cotta, some of which has survived. Later, in the 1100s, the Hausa and Bornu empires prospered, serving as important trading centers on the trans-Saharan caravan route. In the 1600s and 1700s the area was drawn into the European world through the growing slave trade and other forms of commerce. A British colony and protectorate after 1914, Nigeria moved toward self-government after World War II. In October 1960 it gained independence.

Conflict. Since independence in 1960, Nigeria has experienced a civil war, harsh military rule, and an effort at democratic government. From the outset, there were disputes among the northern, western, and eastern regions that made up the new nation. At one time or another each sector threatened to secede. Religious tensions between Muslims and Christians and struggles among ethnic groups in each region led to continued conflict.

In early 1966 a small group of army officers overthrew the new constitutional government and attempted unsuccessfully to quiet tensions. Later that year, after another coup d'état General Yakubu Gowon (yah-Koo-boo GOH-won) was named head of a federal military government. At about the same time, the massacre of thousands of Ibo in the north led to their flight to the eastern region. There they threatened to withdraw the eastern region, calling it Biafra (bee-AH-fruh), from the federation of states. A bloody civil war raged for several years, ending in Biafra's defeat in 1970. Following the war, however, tensions eased, and the country turned to developing its economy. It was helped by the spectacular rise in the demand for and the price of oil.

General Gowon was overthrown in 1975, and Nigeria underwent several changes of government. Its attempt at a representative government similar to that of the United States failed, however, and since 1983 it has once again been ruled by the military.

The Economy. Nigeria's oil fields have made it at times one of Africa's wealthiest nations. Since 1980, however, its oil exports, which accounted for over 90 percent of its income, have suffered a serious decline, due to reduced production and falling prices in the world market. Agriculture, too, has suffered reverses. In the early years of independence, Nigeria ranked as a major exporter of cocoa, peanuts, and palm products. Today only cocoa remains a profitable crop. Moreover, the decline of agriculture has also led to severe food shortages. In 1983, for example, Nigeria was forced to import over $2 billion in food.

WEST AFRICA TODAY

Ghana, Côte d'Ivoire, Nigeria, and the other 13 nations of West Africa face uncertain times. Their people, like people everywhere, work hard. And like people everywhere, they would like to improve their standard of living. They would like better health facilities and fewer deaths among their children. They would like running water and electricity in their homes. And they would like greater educational opportunities.

A poem from Ghana emphasizes the importance of human relationships:

> I call Gold.
> Gold is mute.
> I call cloth.
> Cloth is mute.
> It is mankind that matters.

REVIEWING THE CHAPTER

I. Building Your Vocabulary

In your notebook, write the correct term that matches the definition.

apprentice system   cataracts   coup d'état
per capita income   batik   machete

1. the decorating of cloth by treating it so that the colors are prevented from adhering to certain areas when dyed

2. the hiring of a young person as a trainee at less than full wages

3. rapids that interrupt the flow of rivers and make them unnavigable

4. a large, heavy knife

5. the average annual income for each person in a particular area

6. the sudden, violent overthrow of a government by a small group

II. Understanding the Facts

In your notebook, write the numbers from 1 to 5. Write the letter of the correct answer to each question next to its number.

1. Which of the following countries is not located in West Africa?
   a. Sierra Leon   b. Mauritania   c. Uganda

2. Which West African country is the most populated country in all of Africa?
   a. Senegal   b. Nigeria   c. Ghana

3. Which country has the highest per capita income in West Africa?
   a. Ghana   b. Mali   c. Côte d'Ivoire

4. Who is in charge of the markets in most West African countries?
   a. women   b. village councils   c. the military

5. Which West African author has written novels that deal with the conflicts that face Africa today?
   a. Amos Tutuola   b. Chinua Achebe   c. Efua Sutherland

III. Thinking It Through

In your notebook, write the numbers from 1 to 4. Write the letter of the correct answer to each question next to its number.

1. Ghana is unusual in West Africa because
   a. agriculture is one of its major industries.
   b. its government has been unstable since independence.
   c. over 40 percent of its population is Christian.
   d. its population is growing at a very high rate.

2. Côte d'Ivoire differs from other African countries because
   a. it doesn't depend at all upon agriculture.
   b. its population is made up of several ethnic groups.
   c. most of its population is Muslim.
   d. it has encouraged investment by its former colonial ruler.

3. A major problem that faces all the West African countries is
   a. they have nothing of value to export.
   b. more than ten percent of the area's infants die between birth and one year of age.
   c. no country has a per-capita income higher than $200 per year.
   d. they have no transportation systems between countries.

4. A resident of West Africa who was unemployed would be more likely to find work in
   a. Guinea-Bissau.   b. Cape Verde.
   c. Côte d'Ivoire.   d. Gambia

DEVELOPING CRITICAL THINKING SKILLS

1. Explain why the government is the largest employer in many West African countries.
2. Show how the policies pursued by Côte d'Ivoire have made it one of the most politically stable countries in Africa.
3. Discuss the needs of West Africa today.
4. Describe the educational system that exists today in West Africa.

INTERPRETING A MAP

Study the map, on the next page, and answer the questions that follow it. You might also consult the physical map of Africa on page 12.

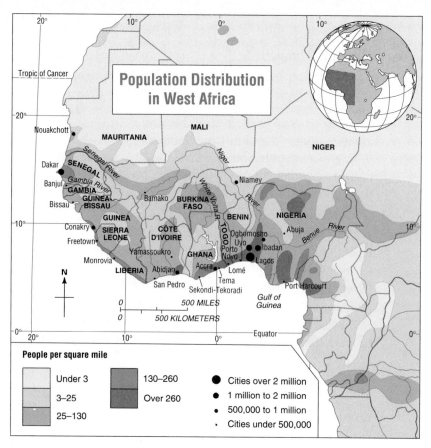

Population Distribution in West Africa

People per square mile

Under 3	130–260	● Cities over 2 million
3–25	Over 260	● 1 million to 2 million
25–130		• 500,000 to 1 million
		· Cities under 500,000

1. Next to what geographical feature are the largest cities in West Africa located?

2. Why do Mauritania, Mali, and niger have the lowest population density in the area?

3. Which country has the largest urban population?

ENRICHMENT AND EXPLORATION

1. Select one of the countries of West Africa. Do research on the country by consulting a variety of library resources. Gather current information on its population, ethnic groups, languages, type of government, and economy. Prepare a written report and make an oral presentation of your findings.

2. By consulting travel agents or the tourism councils of the various nations, draw up an itinerary for a tour of West Africa. Be prepared to explain why you chose the cities listed on your itinerary.

7 Central Africa

On October 18, 1983, leaders of the 10 nations of Central Africa met in Libreville, Gabon. There they signed an agreement to form the Economic Community of Central African States, or CEEAC (the letters come from the French form of the name, Communaute Économique des États de l'Afrique Centrale). Although all the nations of Central Africa had achieved political independence years before, they were still economically dependent on non-Africans. And although Central Africa has a large share of the world's natural resources, most of its 73 million people live in poverty. Now, the founders of CEEAC felt, it was time to work together to gain economic independence. They wanted to help establish a "new international economic order for Africa."

In this chapter you will learn about Central Africa, and you will consider why CEEAC and other efforts at cooperation among the nations in the region have been slow to move forward. First we will take a look at the geography, culture, and history of Central Africa. Then we will focus on Zaire, the region's largest and most heavily populated country.

THE REGION

The countries of Central, or Equatorial, Africa are Burundi, Cameroon, the Central African Republic, Chad, Congo, Equatorial Guinea, Gabon, Rwanda, São Tomé and Príncipe, and Zaire.

The Land.   As you can see from the chart on page 175, the countries of Central Africa vary greatly in population and size. The little group of islands forming São Tomé and Príncipe could

CENTRAL AFRICA AND THE WORLD

1300–Today

1300s	Strong central kingdoms in Zaire Basin and Angola; Kongo kingdom founded.
1400–1500s	Luba kingdom flourishes. Portuguese arrive; slave trade booms.
1492	*Columbus lands at San Salvador.*
1500–1600s	Lunda kingdom replaces Luba.
1550s	Kongo wars with Angola.
1665–1710	Attempts made to revive Kongo kingdom.
1704	Dona Beatrice leads Antonian movement.
1776	*U.S. Declaration of Independence*
1800s	Slave trade abolished in Africa.
1861–1865	*U.S. Civil War*
1884	Leopold of Belgium rules Congo Free State.
1884-1885	Berlin conference partitions Africa.
1908	Leopold cedes Congo Free State to Belgian government.
1914–1918	*World War I*
1921	Simon Kimbangu arrested for attempts to Africanize Christian church.
1960	Congo becomes independent.
1961	Katanga army fights U.N. troops.
1965	Mobutu Sese Seko proclaims self president of Congo.
1966	Military coup in Central African Republic.
1968	Equatorial Guinea gains independence.
1969	*Astronauts land on the moon.*
1971	Mobutu renames his country Zaire.
1991	Mobutu allows opposition parties in Zaire.

fit into an area the size of the U.S. city of Indianapolis. Zaire, on the other hand, would occupy one-fourth of the total continental United States.

The Geography.   Central Africa is dominated geographically by the Zaire River Basin, tropical forests, and savannas. There is desert in

		Some Facts About Central African Countries			
COUNTRY	CAPITAL CITY	POPULATION (millions)	AREA (square miles)	PER CAPITA INCOME (U.S. dollars)	LITERACY RATE (percentage)
Burundi	Bujumbura (boo•joom•BOOR•uh)	5.6	10,747	$ 239	34%
Cameroon	Yaoundé (yah•oon•DAY)	11.0	183,568	1,171	56
Central African Republic	Bangui (ban•GEE)	2.8	242,000	376	40
Chad	N'Djamena (un•jay•MAY•nuh)	5.0	496,000	158	25
Congo	Brazzaville (BRAZ•uh•vil)	2.2	132,000	1,100	63
Equatorial Guinea	Malabo (mul•LAH•boh)	.4	10,820	300	40
Gabon	Libreville (lee•bruh•VEEL)	1.1	102,317	3,300	62
Rwanda	Kigali (kee•GAH•lee)	7.6	10,169	323	47
São Tomé and Príncipe	São Tomé (sou•tuh•MAY)	.12	372	384	50
Zaire	Kinshasa (kin•SHAH•suh)	36.6	905,063	170	46

northern Chad, while most of the countries of the region have mountains, some of them snowcapped.

Mount Cameroon, the highest peak (13,354 feet), is an active volcano. Other volcanic mountains are found in the Great Rift Valley area on Zaire's borders with Burundi and Rwanda.

Zaire has only a tiny stretch of coastline, and four of the other countries—Chad, the Central African Republic, Burundi, and Rwanda—are completely landlocked. Central Africa has a number of large lakes and rivers that serve as important inland waterways. The major river is the Zaire. The Zaire is the second longest river in Africa, after the Nile, and one of the longest rivers in the world. Through its many tributaries, such as the Ubangi River (oo-BANG-gee) in the Central African Republic, it drains all of Zaire and parts of Congo, the Central African Republic, Cameroon, Burundi, Tanzania, Zambia, and Angola.

THE PEOPLE

A majority of the people in Central Africa are members of the Bantu-speaking group, believed to have come originally from an area near the border of modern Nigeria and Cameroon. They are divided into many subgroups, with different cultures and languages. Many of them share similar customs, however, and in some cases they can understand each others' languages.

As you have read, most of the political divisions that exist among African people today are the result of colonial occupation. As early as the 1300s, there were strong central kingdoms in the Zaire Basin and farther south, in modern Angola. Then Europeans and other outsiders arrived. They took over the Africans' land, gave their own names to the areas, and altered drastically many aspects of African life. Ignoring the traditional local religions, the Europeans claimed to be civilizing the Africans by converting them to Christianity.

Much earlier, in the eighth century, Arabs from the north had introduced the Islamic faith into what is today Chad and parts of Cameroon. Islam remains strong in the region today.

As you have read, the slave trade played a major role in disrupting the lives of thousands of Africans. It began with the Portuguese arrival in Africa in the 1400s and 1500s and spread rapidly to meet the growing demand for labor in the new colonies in the Americas. Arabs, Europeans, Americans, and some Africans participated in the slave trade, which was finally abolished in the 1800s.

176

Colonization and the slave trade left their mark on the population of Central Africa. For example, the people who live on the islands of São Tomé and Príncipe today are mostly of mixed European and African ancestry. They include descendants of African slaves brought from areas of modern-day Benin, Gabon, Congo, and Angola; descendants of forced laborers from the Portuguese colonies of Angola and Mozambique; and some descendants of Europeans, mostly Portuguese.

Of the foreigners who came to Central Africa, some had good intentions. In 1913, for example, Albert Schweitzer (SHWYT-sur), a medical missionary, musician, and philosopher from Alsace-Lorraine (then part of Germany), established a hospital at Lambaréné (lam-buh-RAY-nay) in Gabon. During his 52 years working there, he drew worldwide attention and was awarded the Nobel Prize for Peace in 1952. Africans, however, were less enthusiastic about his work. Like many others, Dr. Schweitzer was kind and caring but not really understanding of what the Africans already knew or could learn.

Today, many years after independence from colonial rule, the people of Central Africa are still tied in many ways to their former rulers. They are separated into countries that were created by the Europeans during the late 1800s. And because so many African lan-

Foreigners left their mark on Central Africa in many ways. Often it was European military officers who met with African leaders to impress upon them the power of the colonial ruler.

guages are spoken in the region, each country has adopted the language of its former colonial ruler as the official language, which is used in schools, business, government, and other public affairs.

Obviously, the use of four different official languages—English, French, Spanish, and Portuguese—poses a problem for communication among the ten countries of Central Africa. Many Africans are multilingual, however, speaking several different African languages as well as one or more European languages.

Education. In the 1800s Europeans introduced Western-style education—especially reading and writing—into Central Africa. The Africans who led their countries to independence were among those who had had access to Western education. Today, education for every person, directed toward African needs, is a priority of the Central African governments. Cameroon, Congo, and Gabon have made the most progress in this area. For example, Gabon, with a literacy rate of 62 percent, devoted 26 percent of its 1990 operating budget to education. Its universities are crowded to capacity. A literacy campaign for adults is also in operation.

A Cameroonian teenager does her homework on a portable typewriter. Her brothers and sisters watch with curiosity and respect.

Cameroon has an extensive educational system at all levels, and over 70 percent of all children attend school. The University of Yaoundé, established in the capital of Cameroon in 1961, was the first African university to offer courses in both French and English. Today it has three branch campuses.

Gabon has achieved **universal primary education,** that is, primary education for almost all its children. And it is giving high priority to rural schools. Emphasis now is on technical, secondary, and higher education. The University of Libreville was established in Gabon in 1971. Gabon's educational system has been criticized for being French dominated. But like Congo and Cameroon, it is trying to lessen the influence of its former rulers. These countries are attempting to add African history and culture to the school curriculum.

Literature and Art.   As you have read, African history and literature were passed down orally from one generation to the next. Historians, who were employed in the courts of kings, often specialized in the "official" versions of events. Parents and other elders kept alive less formal history by retelling stories to their children. While these traditions are still alive, they are being expanded by Africans who are writing in European languages, mostly French and English. Their works are read not only by Africans but also by foreign audiences.

Central Africa has produced many writers of international fame. The novels of the Cameroonians Mongo Beti (BEH-tee) and Ferdinand Oyono (oh-YOH-no) were published in both French and English. Both writers have described the colonial experience with great humor and insight. Francis Bebey (beh-BAY), another Cameroonian, has published poems, stories, novels, and a book on African music. He has also produced several recordings of his own musical compositions. Congo's Tchicaya U Tam'si (CHEE-cah-yah oo TAM-see) is considered one of the leading poets of French-speaking Africa. Cameroon's major publishing company serves as an outlet for young writers, especially from French-speaking countries. Like many other African writers, these artists often pursue other professions while they write. Ferdinand Oyono, for example, a career diplomat, was for many years the head of Cameroon's mission to the United Nations in New York City.

Several Central African countries—particularly Cameroon, Congo, Gabon, and Zaire—are the source of some of the finest examples of traditional African art found in museums and private collections all over the world. Crafts people in Zaire and Gabon, especially, excel in making sculptures of wood and metal. In Zaire women weave palm-

The Kongo people create statues of wood and iron which sometimes depict ideas of law and justice. This figure, decorated with nails, is of a dog because it is an animal who can hunt and find criminals even in the dark.

fiber velour, a velvetlike fabric, and beautiful examples of this cloth are seen all over Africa.

Equatorial Guinea does a great deal to promote African culture through lectures, performances, exhibits, and its own cultural centers. A museum of art at Bata (BAH-tuh) contains the works of Guinea's internationally acclaimed sculptor and painter, Leandro Mbomio (mm-BOTT-mee-oh).

Economic Activities.   Central African nations inherited from the colonial period economies designed more to serve European needs than to serve African needs. Foreign governments and private investors made great profits from the region's natural resources—copper, diamonds, gold, ivory, timber, and palm products. But little was shared with the Africans. Under colonial direction agriculture was geared less toward growing food for the African people and more toward production of crops for export to Europe—coffee, cotton, and cocoa, to name only a few. Roads and railways were built to transport products to overseas shipping ports rather than for internal trade or trade with neighboring African countries. The lack of a good transportation network within and between the countries of Africa remains a problem.

Today, African countries still rely on outsiders for the money and technology they need for growth. These include their former colonial rulers and other non-African countries, multinational corporations, and international agencies such as the World Bank and the International Monetary Fund (IMF).

GOVERNMENTS AND POLITICS

With their shaky economies and their inability to achieve national unity, the nations of Central Africa are troubled by unstable governments. National armies play a major role. Except for São Tomé and Príncipe and Cameroon, all of the Central African countries have had at least one military coup d'état.

All ten countries have a republican type of government. These governments vary greatly in the amount of power they give to the president or to the people. As elsewhere in Africa, many regimes did away with their opposition by adopting a one-party or no-party system. Few, however, have been able to resolve all the problems that faced the multi-party governments that preceded them. By the early 1990s, several countries had taken steps to return to multiparty rule.

Before examining Central Africa's largest nation, Zaire, let us consider the problems that some of the other Central African countries have had in developing governments that represent the interests of the majority of the people.

Gabon.   By just looking at its thriving economy, Gabon could be considered one of Africa's success stories. It has the continent's highest **Gross Domestic Product** (GDP) **per capita,** that is, the total value of goods and services produced in a country, divided by the population. In 1990 it was one of the four largest suppliers of oil in sub-Saharan Africa. It has used its oil revenues and its income from other exports to develop its transportation systems, such as a railroad network. As you have read, it has also made progress in education.

But these facts and figures are deceptive. Most of Gabon's wealth is in the hands of a very few. The richest 2 percent of the population earn about the same share of the national income as the poorest 50 percent. In other words, if 2 people earned $5,000 collectively, or $2, 500 apiece, then 50 other people earned $5,000 among them, which comes to only $100 apiece. Life expectancy is 53 years. And the country's great natural resources—among them oil, manganese, uranium, and wood— are largely controlled by foreign investors. More French people live and work here now than in colonial times. Gabon relies far too much on outsiders both for money for investment and for trained labor. Most of the labor force is engaged in agriculture, but the majority of crops are exported. Thus Gabon is forced to import about 65 percent of its food.

Cameroon.   Cameroon, another country with oil reserves as well as crops for export, has made steadier progress toward a balanced economy. Like all African countries, Cameroon depends on help from the IMF and other foreign agencies. But the average Cameroonian still has few sources from which to borrow money. Banks usually require a borrower to own property. Since most Africans do not own land, many Cameroonians often take advantage of a *tontine* (tawn-TEEN), a type of traditional credit union. In a *tontine*, a group of people pools their money. The money is then lent to the tontine members, who use it for such purposes as paying for a wedding, building a hotel, or buying a taxi. The tontine establishes rules for loans and repayment, and tontine meetings are held on a regular basis. Unlike customers of a bank, who are not likely to know the bank directors personally, the tontine members know one another. Therefore the social pressure from fellow members serves to prompt borrowers to repay their loans. Not to repay a loan means more than just losing a source of credit. It means the loss of friends and earning a bad reputation.

Almost 72 percent of the population of Central Africa is engaged in farming and cattle raising. In Cameroon, herders drive their cattle from the Niger River region to the capital at Yaounde, where they will be sold in a great open-air livestock market.

In 1986 Cameroon was the site of a tragic natural accident. An explosion in a volcanic lake unleashed poisonous gases, killing more than 1,700 people. This was another in the series of environmental disasters to strike Africa in recent years.

Chad.   Chad is named for a lake once described by an African writer as "the great lake of blue water, lightly salted and covered with papyrus [a water plant]." It is a country of two distinct groups of people. Those in the desert and savanna regions of the north are mostly Muslim cattle herders. Those in the equatorial forests of the south practice a mixture of Christianity and traditional religions and are farmers.

In 1965 a civil war broke out in Chad between the north and the south. Until 1990, the war dominated the nation's affairs and resulted in numerous changes of government. The war was aggravated by support from outside. Libya supported the north, while France, Zaire, and the United States gave aid to the south.

Burundi and Rwanda.   Burundi and Rwanda were once strong kingdoms, and each is populated today by people from two major ethnic groups—the Huto (HOO-too) and the Tutsi (TOOT-see). Rivalry between the two groups over land ownership began in the days of the kings, who were called *mwami* (MWAH-mee). Since then, intermarriage has blurred the differences between the Hutu and the Tutsi. Yet their traditional rivalry has been one cause of unstable governments in both countries.

Equatorial Guinea.   Equatorial Guinea fared better than many other African territories under colonial rule. When it gained independence from Spain in 1968, it ranked among the highest in Africa in literacy and per capita income. It also provided good health-care service. After independence Equatorial Guinea came under a dictatorship set up by its first president, Francisco Macias Nguema (mah-see-as un-GWAY-mah). During the 11 years of his rule, conditions in the country rapidly became worse. Since Macias's overthrow in 1979, Equatorial Guinea has been trying to repair the damage that was done during his regime and to build a government that better represents its people.

The Central African Republic.   The Central African Republic, too, is slowly recovering from the waste and abuse of a power-hungry ruler. In a military coup in 1966, Jean-Bedel Bokassa (boh-KAH-suh) installed himself as president. He abolished the constitution adopted by the country at its independence in 1960 and took over most of the powers of the government. In December 1976, Bokassa abolished the republic and established a monarchy. In an elaborate ceremony a year later, he had himself crowned Emperor Bokassa I.

Since Bokassa's overthrow in 1979, the country has returned to a republican form of government and is trying to build up its economy. One of the least developed countries, the Central African Republic has many natural resources, including diamonds, as well as agricultural and animal products for export. It supplies most of its own food needs and could be a regional exporter of food—for example, to neighboring countries like Gabon, which import most of their food.

Congo. A former French colony, Congo is one of Central Africa's more economically successful nations. This is largely due to its oil revenues. In addition, with some 63 percent of its area covered with forests and woods, lumber and wood products are among its chief exports. Life expectancy is 60 years, one of the highest rates in the region, and almost half of the population lives in towns and cities.

Congo had limited contact with the United States until recently. Its governments looked to the Soviet Union for political and economic direction. Today it continues to have a nonaligned foreign policy, but its relations with the United States have improved, and a number of U. S. development programs in health and agriculture are under way.

ZAIRE

On October 27, 1971, Joseph-Désiré Mobutu (moh-BOO-too), self-proclaimed president of the country then called the Democratic Republic of the Congo, announced that his country would now be called the Republic of Zaire. Cities and towns with European names were given African names. The National Assembly passed a law requiring all Zairians to give up their Christian first names and adopt African names. Mobutu himself changed his name to Mobutu Sese Seko.

These actions were part of a policy of Africanization known as *authenticité* (aw-tan-tis-ee-TAY), or "authenticity," declared by Mobutu. The aim was to strengthen the nation by encouraging pride in its African heritage and by reducing European influence. The call for *authenticité* by Mobutu in 1971 was by no means anything new in Zaire's history. While at first the people of this area welcomed the Europeans, they soon resisted foreign domination. As you will learn,

Doña Beatrice (DOH-nyah BEE-uh-tris) in the 1700s, Simon Kimbangu (KEE-mm-ban-goo) in 1921, and Patrice Lumumba (loo-MOOM-buh) in 1960 all lost their lives for the cause of Africanization.

Early Kingdoms. The Kongo Kingdom was founded in the 1300s by a Bakongo *mani,* or landholder. Through wars with neighboring groups, he acquired a major share of the lands in the region. By the time the Portuguese navigator Diogo Cão arrived at the mouth of the Congo River in 1482, the Kongo Kingdom, which included parts of present-day Congo, Zaire, and Angola, was the leader of all the coastal states of Central Africa.

In comparison with other African rulers, the Kongo kings were unusually open to European culture. They adopted Roman Catholicism as the kingdom's religion and sent their young men to be educated in Portugal. As gifts, they gave slaves to the Portuguese, as well as ivory trinkets and cloth made from raffia.

Eventually this attempt at European-type "civilization" failed. This was not only because of African resistance to change, but also because the Portuguese, greedy for land and slaves, exploited the Africans. After 1550 neighboring African groups took advantage of the growing weakness of the Kongo Kingdom and almost destroyed the whole area. The kingdom was saved by Portuguese troops, but it went into a decline. Afterward, Angola, a colony founded in the south by the Portuguese, began a series of wars with Kongo. By the end of the 1600s, Kongo was no longer a major political power.

From 1665 to 1710, there were a number of attempts to revive the Kongo Kingdom. In 1704 a young Kongo woman, Kimpa Vita (KIM-puh VEE-tuh), given the name Beatrice at her Catholic baptism, led an African Christian movement aimed at restoring Kongo to its former prosperity and power. Dona Beatrice based her mission on dreams and visions she had had. Claiming that Saint Anthony had entered her body, she preached against the "white" practices of the Roman Catholic Church. She told her followers to stop singing the Ave Maria and to destroy the European-made crosses and images of Christ. Christ was an African, she said, and his apostles were black.

For a while, Dona Beatrice had a large following. Nobles honored her and claimed she had magical powers. To set themselves apart from the whites, her followers, calling themselves Antonians, dressed in cloth made of fig bark. Other Africans, however, accused Beatrice of making false claims, and in 1706 she was burned to death at the stake. The Antonians continued the movement for several years after her death, proclaiming Kongo as the true Holy Land.

Over 200 years later, in 1921, Simon Kimbangu attempted to introduce African hymns and prayers into, and to otherwise Africanize, Christian worship. Kimbangu was arrested by the Belgian government and lived out his life in prison. Today, however, a Christian church bearing his name—the Church of Jesus Christ on Earth through the Prophet Simon Kimbangu—has millions of members in Zaire, Congo, and other neighboring countries.

Besides Kongo, several other great kingdoms flourished in the Zaire River Basin. The most important were the Luba (LOO-buh) Kingdom (in the 1400s and 1500s), the Lunda (LUN-duh) Kingdom (in the 1500s and 1600s), and the Kuba (KOO-buh) Kingdom (in the 1800s).

Cultures throughout the region were, and still are, similar. The use and ownership of land was considered a sacred trust from the ancestors. Land titles were passed down from one generation to the next. Most of the groups are **matrilineal**—that is, ancestry is traced through one's mother. Thus property is passed down through the female side of the family, and social standing is determined by the mother's line rather than the father's. The brothers (rather than the husband) of a mother have legal control over her children.

Agriculture, hunting, and fishing were always important occupations. Many of the food crops that are staples in the diet today—corn, cassava, peanuts, and sweet potatoes—were introduced from the Americas after 1500. Bananas, yams, and taro, a starchy root plant, came from Malayasia. Older African crops—millet, sorghum, numerous kinds of peas, and beans—were widely cultivated for food. Various types of palms provided both food and materials for clothing and houses.

The Congo Free State.   For many years few Europeans knew much about Central Africa. It was first brought to worldwide attention when the New York Herald sent a reporter, Henry Morton Stanley, to Africa to search for the Scottish explorer David Livingstone (see Chapter 5). After Livingstone's death, in 1873, Stanley continued to explore the Congo River. On his return to Europe in 1877, he tried to interest Great Britain's Queen Victoria in the region, but with no success. The Belgian King Leopold II was receptive to Stanley's proposals, however, and chose Stanley to head another expedition.

In 1884 Stanley returned to Belgium and presented Leopold with treaties from 450 chiefs he claimed had given up their rights to lands in the Congo Basin. The next year, as you have read, the European powers met in Berlin to settle distribution of the African territories. King Leopold was officially recognized as the personal owner of the Congo area, which he named the Congo Free State.

The people of the Congo suffered under Leopold's rule. According to the agreement that gave him control of the Congo, Leopold was supposed to put an end to the slave trade in the region. (Although a worldwide decree had abolished the slave trade 50 years earlier, it still continued in many places.) Leopold did stop some Arab slave traders, and he pressured local chiefs to free their slaves. Then, however, he contracted the freed slaves to employers in order for these former slaves to have what he called the "civilizing benefits of regular work."

Leopold's agents treated the Africans cruelly. Workers were forced to build railroads and collect rubber from trees on his private plantations. They were physically tortured for failing to meet production goals. Many people died as a result of harsh treatment.

Reports of Leopold's exploitation of Africans brought many protests. The British Parliament began an investigation of the colony in 1897. Finally, in 1908, Leopold turned the colony over to the Belgian government, which renamed it the Belgian Congo.

The Belgian Congo. A conservative administration representing the interests of the Roman Catholic Church managed the affairs of the Belgian Congo. Africans had no real representation in the government until late 1959, just before independence. Immediate concerns of the colonial administration were, in order of importance: to make a profit from the colony, to "civilize" and Christianize the Africans, and to protect the Africans from further abuses. The Belgian regime has been called one of the most paternalistic of all the colonial administrations in Africa.

In terms of the first object, making a profit, the Belgians had at their disposal in the Congo some of the richest natural resources in the world. Most important were the vast diamond and copper deposits in the east-central (Kasai [kuh-SY]) and southern (Shaba [SHAH-buh], formerly Katanga [kuh-TANG-guh]) regions. Belgian companies gained mining rights and grants of land from the colonial government. There was little competition and little government regulation. The companies made large profits, but little benefit came to the Africans, whose wages were low and living conditions poor.

After World War I an increased demand for labor in industry and agriculture brought some improvements in the conditions of these Africans. They were offered better working conditions and higher wages. Men were no longer forced to leave their families. Now they were encouraged to bring their wives with them to the mining regions. The Belgian government felt the need to diversify the economy, and some attention shifted from mining to agriculture. Attempts to introduce modern agricultural technology had good results. The Africans were not trained in the new methods, however, and most of the farming settlements collapsed after independence.

Education was provided largely through mission schools run by the Belgian Catholic Church and a few Protestant denominations from other Western countries, including the United States. At independence the primary education program in the Congo was one of the best in Africa, reaching over seven out of every ten children between the ages of 6 and 11. Yet only 2 percent of these children went on to secondary schools. The two universities were not established until the 1950s, just before independence. As a result, when the colony of the Belgian Congo became the independent Republic of Congo in 1960, it had only a handful of university-educated citizens. These few were not enough to govern effectively a country of its size and importance.

Independence. In the late 1940s, after World War II, Africans in the Congo began to pressure Belgium for reforms. At first French-speaking Africans known as *évolué* (ay-vol-yoo-AY)—French for "developed" or "enlightened"—demanded a chance to hold civil service positions and to earn equal pay for equal work. By the mid-1950s the *évolué* were demanding participation in the government.

Within a very short time, over 40 political groups had formed. These were alliances of the country's many different ethnic groups. The

Troops of the Katangese army cluster about their armored truck during the fighting against the United Nations force in December 1961.

Alliance of Bakongo (ABAKO) was the only one representing a single group, the Bakongo. The only party that tried to form a broad-based party with no particular ethnic focus was the National Congolese Movement (or MNC, for the French *Mouvement national congolais*), which was established in October 1958.

The president of the MNC was Patrice Lumumba. Lumumba had only a primary-school education, but he was fluent in French, Swahili, and Lingala. He was also president of one of the évolué organizations and had tremendous appeal to mass audiences. In 1958 Lumumba attended the Pan-African Conference held in Accra, Ghana. Here he met Kwame Nkrumah, the man who had led Ghana to independence the year before. The two kept in close contact after the meeting.

Because of his growing popularity among Africans in the Belgian Congo, the Belgians arrested Lumumba for stirring up the people. Other Africans were imprisoned as well, and in 1959 riots broke out against Belgian rule. Belgium was quickly forced to respond to the Africans' demands. At a meeting in Brussels in early 1960, the independence date for the colony was set for June 30, 1960.

General elections for the new country were held in May 1960, a month before independence. Over 100 political parties participated, but none of them received a clear majority. **A coalition government,** that is, a government composed of members of several parties, was formed. Lumumba became prime minister of the Republic of the Congo. Joseph Kasavubu (kah-suh-VOO-boo), leader of ABAKO, became president.

The Lumumba-Kasavubu government lasted only two months. In July 1960 Congolese soldiers revolted against their Belgian officers, who, despite Congolese independence, still commanded the army. The African soldiers had expected that independence would bring them immediate promotion to the senior positions they had long been requesting. The revolt spread throughout the country. Belgian **para-troopers**—soldiers equipped with parachutes—arrived, and most Europeans were **evacuated** from—sent out of—the country. Lumumba acted quickly to Africanize the forces. In addition to promoting all the soldiers one rank, he replaced the Belgian commander in chief with an African. He also appointed Joseph-Désiré Mobutu as the army's chief of staff. The name of the army was changed to the Congo National.

The events that followed increased pressure on the government. Copper-rich Katanga, one of the Congo's wealthiest areas, threatened to **secede,** or withdraw, from the new nation. Rebellion broke out in Luba territory. United Nations (UN) and other foreign troops (including those requested from the Soviet Union by Lumumba) arrived to restore order. Blaming each other for the situation, prime minister Lumumba dismissed President Kasavubu, and President Kasavubu dismissed Prime Minister Lumumba. Then the army chief of staff, Joseph-Désiré Mobutu, dismissed them both. Thus began the long career of Zaire's current president, Mobutu Sese Seko. Lumumba was arrested by Mobutu and died mysteriously shortly afterward. Because his death has never been fully explained, it has been the subject of many inquiries, books, and plays.

Today, there are two opposing views of Patrice Lumumba. Some people remember him for his friendship with the Soviet Union, his angry outbursts, and his impatience with Western indifference to African interests. They judge him as having been dangerous or even mentally disturbed. For others, however, many of whom have named their children for him, Lumumba is a symbol of freedom. To them he expresses the values and hopes of black people everywhere. As Lumumba wrote in his last letter from prison to his wife, Pauline: "History will one day have its say, but it will not be the history that is taught in Brussels, Paris, Washington, or in the United Nations, but the history which will be taught in the countries freed from imperialism and its puppets. . . . Long live the Congo! Long live Africa!"

Mobutu Comes to Power.   Following Lumumba's downfall, the new nation of Zaire continued to experience great upheaval. A wave of civil wars caused by ethnic rivalries resulted in frequent changes in the government. Finally, on November 24, 1965, Mobutu declared himself president for five years. He enacted a new constitution that created a strong central government and strengthened his personal power. In 1970 Mobutu was elected to serve a seven-year term, and he has been reelected ever since.

For more than ten years after Mobutu came to power, Zaire was relatively peaceful. Then, in 1977, rebels from Katanga (now Shaba) who had been living in neighboring Angola invaded Zaire. Their objective was to take over the Shaba region. The following year they succeeded in occupying an important mining town in that region. Yet in both conflicts the rebels were defeated by Zairian and French troops, with some help from the United States. Following these invasions the Zairian army was strengthened, and other attempted raids have been promptly put down.

The Government and People.   Zaire, with a population of over 36

President Mobutu Sese Seko of Zaire greets Pope John Paul II as he arrives in Kinshasa, the capital, to start an African tour in 1980.

million, is divided for administrative purposes into a number of regions: Lower Zaire, Upper Zaire, Bandundu, Equator, West Kisai, East Kisai, Kivu, and Shaba. Kinshasa, the capital, is **autonomous**—that is, it is a separate district with its own local government. Publicly referred to as Guide and Founder President, Mobutu is both president and commissioner of state for defense. He is also president of the only legal political party, the Popular Movement of the Revolution (or MPR, for Mouvement populaire de la révolution). People who disagree with the government are treated harshly, and some have gone into exile.

November 24, the date Mobutu took power, is observed as Zaire's national holiday. Until recently, June 30, the date of independence, was almost ignored, although Mobutu has built monuments to Lumumba and praised him in public speeches.

French is the official language of Zaire, but Lingala (ling-GAH-luh), Swahili, Kongo, and Luba are also used in broadcasts and newspapers. Kongo and Luba are spoken by a large number of descendants of the Kongo and Luba kingdoms. Neither Lingala nor Swahili is associated with any original Zaire group, but both have become the first language of children growing up in the multiethnic cities and towns.

191

The Economy. Because of its great natural resources, Zaire has had no trouble attracting foreign investors. It has also easily gotten loans for development projects from international agencies, such as the IMF and the World Bank. Zaire has much unused land and forests and the largest hardwood reserves in Africa. It also has enough hydroelectric potential to provide electricity for the entire country and many of its neighbors, and it has extensive mineral resources. Except for a few government-sponsored agricultural projects and the hydroelectric dam at Inga I in Lower Zaire, most attention to development has been focused on mining, Zaire's most important economic activity. In the late 1980s Zaire was the world's largest producer of industrial diamonds and cobalt, and seventh in the production of copper.

A good transportation system is vital to the development of a country as large as Zaire. At independence Zaire had one of the best transportation systems in Africa. There are 8,400 miles of navigable waterways as well as 3,000 miles of railroad, which were built by the Belgians. These systems still work fairly well. The Belgian road system, however, built mainly to serve the rail and river lines, is in need of repair. In addition, Zaire badly needs new roads to connect the cities with the regional capitals as well as with the isolated rural areas. The country has a national airline, Air Zaire, which provides domestic and international service. Some private planes and foreign international airlines also operate in Zaire.

In the first years after independence, the mines and other industrial projects continued to operate under Belgian ownership and direction. Other foreigners were also welcomed to help expand industrial development, including transportation. In 1973, however, President Mobutu announced that all foreign businesses in agriculture, commerce, and transport must be turned over to Zairian owners. Because the new owners were inexperienced and unqualified, the businesses began to fail. Mobutu then **nationalized** them, that is, placed them under government ownership and control. But the Zairians who were put in charge were also inexperienced and unqualified, and nationalization failed. Finally, in 1976, Mobutu issued a decree that returned 60 percent of the businesses to their original owners. The rest were sold to Zairians to run in partnership with the government.

Zaire, like most countries in Africa, needs **foreign capital**, money from outside sources, to develop its economy. Consequently, much of the country's industry and agriculture is focused on producing goods for export, so that foreign money will be exchanged for goods sold abroad. For example, palm oil, used for soap and lubricants, and palm kernels

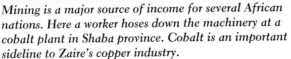

Mining is a major source of income for several African nations. Here a worker hoses down the machinery at a cobalt plant in Shaba province. Cobalt is an important sideline to Zaire's copper industry.

have become important commercial exports. In the agricultural sector the neglect of food crops for the people in favor of export crops like coffee, cocoa, and palm products has resulted in a rise in hunger and malnutrition. Small rural farmers, who raise many of the local food crops, are poorly paid for their produce. They also receive little help from a government that favors larger, commercial plantations.

Despite its great potential, Zaire's economy has dropped to a low level. Some reasons for this, such as falling prices of copper and other exports, are beyond the country's control. Other reasons, such as mismanagement and corruption at all levels of government, are internal. As a result, the country's foreign debt of over $8 billion has made the IMF and other agencies less ready to make new loans.

Religion. An estimated 80 percent or more of Zaire's population is Christian. Of this total, roughly 45 percent are Roman Catholic, 27 percent are Protestant, and the rest belong to the Kimbanguist Church and other independent groups. About 1 percent of Zairians are Muslims. The remainder of the population practice traditional religions.

193

Many of the Christians keep some beliefs and rituals from the African religions. The use of African music and instruments is common in both Catholic and Protestant churches.

As you have learned, the Kimbanguist Church was founded in 1921 by Simon Kimbangu. Kimbangu, who had been converted to Christianity, tried to introduce into the Protestant service prayers and hymns that were more suitable to African cultures than those imported from Europe. After Kimbangu's imprisonment his followers continued to worship secretly. They composed the music, prayers, and rituals that are heard in the Kimbanguist cathedral in Kinshasa today. During their nearly 40 years underground, the Kimbanguists developed their own schools and community programs to provide for their food and health care needs. The spirit of cooperation and self-reliance continues among the Kimbanguists, who call their church center in Lower Zaire Nkamba Jerusalem. In their organizations, women and men are recognized as having equal status.

Education and Health.   During Belgian rule both education and health care were largely run by foreign missionaries. Since independence both of these programs have had successes and failures. Today, even with Africanization, some foreigners—missionaries, Peace Corps volunteers, and others—are still part of the system, working with the government.

All schools in Zaire, including those run by the state and those run by church organizations, operate under the state, with the government paying teachers' and administrators' salaries. In 1988 about 84 percent of boys and 68 percent of girls between the ages of 6 and 11 were enrolled in the primary schools. In the 12-to-17 age group, there are considerably fewer students, with about twice as many males as females. In 1985 about 40,000 students were attending Zaire's three universities and a number of technical schools.

Zaire's goal is to provide all of its citizens with a basic education. The object is not only literacy but a knowledge of up-to-date science and technology. The depressed economic situation has seriously hindered the achievement of this goal, however. There have never been enough secondary schools, and the rural areas in particular have been neglected by all education programs. Recent cuts in the number of schools have greatly affected the rural areas. Therefore village youths are moving to the cities in the hopes of getting the education necessary for their survival. The cities are crowded with disappointed young people who can find neither the education nor the jobs they want.

The people of Zaire face a number of health problems. Many conditions are brought on or made worse by poor sanitation and malnutrition. Major diseases include malaria, pneumonia, tuberculosis, measles, leprosy, sleeping sickness (caused by the bite of the tsetse fly), and syphilis.

In recent years Zaire, like much of Africa, has been hard hit by the AIDS epidemic. Zaire, however, has been in the forefront of AIDS prevention. As early as 1983, researchers were welcomed into the country so that an accurate assessment of the situation could be made. They estimated that about 7 percent of the 36 million Zairians have been infected with the deadly virus that attacks the body's immune system. Of these, many are women and children.

In 1987 the Zairian government introduced a coordinated AIDS prevention campaign. First, a massive education project was carried out through radio and television broadcasts, poster campaigns, dramatic presentations, and printed brochures. Second, the government sponsored a widespread condom distribution program. Third, a special clinic for women was established in Kinshasa, in which free checkups, condoms, and information were made readily available. Through measures such as these, Zaire is beginning to make progress in its war against AIDS.

Art.   Zairians have been known for centuries for their creativity in the arts. Foreigners were first familiar with the statues, ivory carvings, masks, metal objects, raffia cloths, and jewelry brought back to Europe from the Kongo Kingdom and from later explorations into the country. Indeed, art from all parts of Zaire is in major museums and private collections all over the world, and collectors still pay high prices for Zairian art. In Zaire itself there has been an attempt to collect and preserve the art of the country's various peoples, but the programs of a few small museums in Zaire's cities have been hurt by the country's economic problems.

At Mushenge (moo-SHEN-gay) in the Kuba area of western Kasai, there is a training school for wood-carvers. Started by Catholics, this school is incorporating some of the ideas and patterns that were associated with the Kuba Kingdom. In keeping with Kuba tradition, the wood-carvers are all males. The women are weavers, making the raffia fabrics that are special to the area.

CASE STUDY:

Teaching a Lesson

A group of students at the University of Lubumbashi, in Zaire, were researching their roots and traditions. They noted that the legends and stories of their childhood often instructed them on morals and values. One young man from Burundi recalled a tale about Samandari, a popular character in Burundi literature. Amusing, sympathetic, and clever, Samandari created this situation for the king in order to teach him a lesson.

Samandari went to the court one day to see the king.

"Samandari wishes you a good day," he said. "He would like to ask you for a few vegetables, because he is dying of hunger."

The king gave him a young bull. But Samandari refused it.

"No," he said, "that's not what I want."

The king then offered him a he-goat, but Samandari again refused, saying, "I beg you, do me a favor. That is not what I want."

"Then, what do you want?" asked the king.

"Spinach!" said Samandari.

"Go to my field and cut a basket full of spinach," said the king.

"Furnish me also a small pot," said Samandari, "and a corner where I can cook the greens."

The king gave him the pot and showed him a place where he could do his cooking. While the king sat watching, Samandari filled the pot to overflowing and put it on the cooking stones. After he lit the fire, he said to the king,

"King of the Burundi, stay here while I go over there to gather a bit of wood. I will be back."

So the king watched over the fire while Samandari went away. Now, everyone knows, of course, that spinach shrinks when it is cooked. When Samandari came back he went over to the pot and said, "I'll have a look at the greens now to see if they are ready to eat."

He lifted the cover and when he saw that the greens had sunk low down in the pot, he cried out, "Look, you've eaten my vegetables!"

The king protested, "No, I haven't eaten any of them." But Samandari started shouting very loudly, telling everyone that the king had eaten his spinach.

Central African baskets

"Stop, I beg you, Samandari!" cried the king. "Don't let my wife and children hear you say I have eaten your spinach!"

But Samandari shouted even louder, "No, I will not keep still! Give me back my spinach!"

The king offered ten cows in exchange for his silence.

"I don't want your cows," said Samandari, "only my spinach. I am dying of hunger." He cried out so loud everyone could hear him. The king offered him five herds of cows. Then Samandari answered.

"King, call all your men, all your men, all your women. Before accepting these cows I have something to say to you."

After the king had called all the people together, Samandari spoke.

"O King of the Burundi, I wanted to show how wrong it is to accuse someone out of spite. You know very well that no one could believe you ate my spinach but that I slandered you. I wanted to confuse you, because you, the judges, condemn people unjustly and cause them to die without giving them a fair trial. From now on you must settle each dispute in order, with justice. Never again will you condemn the innocent."

1. What lessons do you think children might have found in this story? Did you learn stories as a child that taught lessons? Describe some of the stories and their lessons.

2. What are some qualities people in the story prized in their king?

3. How does the Burundi idea of justice compare with Western ideas of justice? What stories do we have that illustrate similar ideas?

Music.   The Lulua (loo-LUH-ah) people of western Kasai have a proverb that says "Do not be afraid to listen to strangers. Wisdom comes from everywhere." In their music, Zairians heed that advice. Zaire's popular music has borrowed rhythms, forms, and instruments from other countries. One hears calypso from the West Indies, rumba and bolero from Brazil, and, most recently, reggae (REG-ay) from Jamaica. There has been much exchange with black musicians throughout the world, including black Americans. The bands marching through the streets at the 1960 independence celebrations sang "Independence Cha Cha," accompanied by saxophones and other European instruments.

Music plays an important role in the life of Zairians. Many traditional songs have changed with the times as they have been adapted to different situations. For example, a Luba song, "Kamulangu," began as a song in praise of a chief named Kamalangu (kah-mah-LAN-goo). Later it became a children's play song, then a Christmas song about a great king. Today, it is used to praise Mobutu.

Zairian music is famous all over Africa. Tabu Ley (TAH-boo lay) is Zaire's most famous musician today. He and his band, African International, have performed in the United States and are also popular in Europe and Japan.

Zairian popular songs are sung in a variety of languages, including French and the African languages Kongo and Luba. The most widely used language, however, is Lingala. Lingala is not associated with any particular Zairian ethnic group, and its use indicates that the ethnic divisions among the people are weakening. Once the official language of the army, Lingala is now associated with music, and some people say it is the language most sung in Africa.

Most Zairian songs are concerned with aspects of daily life: love, death, lack of money, and even world problems, including domination by Western culture. Some songs describe problems created for Zairian men by the women's liberation movement. The growing gap between wealthy urban dwellers and rural Zairians is the subject of one popular song. It compares a Kinshasa girl who can speak French and rides in a Mercedes Benz automobile with a village girl who sleeps on a straw bed and cleans her feet with pebbles.

Religious music is also being composed in Zaire. Christian missionaries have slowly grown to appreciate African culture and to see that it can have a role in worship. It was the encouragement of Catholics working among the Luba people at Kananga, in western Kasai, that produced *Missa Luba*, a mass based on African traditions. This work is now popular in the United States and Europe. One Catholic priest,

Bernard van den Boom, worked for over 20 years with children's singing groups, helping them to popularize African culture. The last one of his youth groups was called Chem Chem Yetu (chem chem yay -TOO), Swahili for "Our Source." Their recordings of music using traditional African instruments have introduced outsiders to Zairian folk songs as well as to some African church music.

CENTRAL AFRICA TODAY

As you have read, the Central African nations are joined together in the Economic Community of Central African States, or CEEAC, an organization devoted to promoting regional development. They also belong to the Organization of African Unity (OAU) and to the United Nations.

Most Central Africans nations have been part of the movement in the OAU and the UN to condemn **apartheid** (uh-PART-hayt), South Africa's policy of strict separation of the races. (You will read more about apartheid in Chapter 9.) To show its commitment to this goal, Cameroon cut off trade relations with South Africa totally. Gabon and Zaire, on the other hand, continued to trade with South Africa on a limited basis, although they expressed disapproval of apartheid.

Relations between Congo and Zaire have often been tense. The two nations share a long border, and when relations between them are good, ferry systems carry people and products across the Zaire River. Often, however, the ferries are shut down. A major cause of disagreement was the result of the world power struggle between the Soviet Union and the United States. Zaire generally aligned itself with the United States, while Congo aligned with the Soviet Union. Today, Congo has good relations with the United States and other countries of the West. And a joint Congo-Zaire commission has been meeting regularly to discuss mutual problems.

There are a growing number of such links between the countries of Central Africa. This suggests that the people in this area can work together to solve their regional problems and contribute their skills and resources to helping solve other problems facing Africa.

REVIEWING THE CHAPTER

I. Building Your Vocabulary

In your notebook, write the correct term that matches the definition.

matrilineal   coalition   nationalize
tontine   secede   apartheid

1. the tracing of ancestry through one's mother
2. a type of credit union in which people who know each other pool their money and lend it to members.
3. to withdraw from affiliation with a country
4. the South African policy of strict separation of the races
5. to place a business under government ownership and control
6. a government made up of members of several political parties

II. Understanding the Facts

In your notebook, write the numbers from 1 to 5. Write the letter of the correct answer to each question next to its number.

1. Which leader of Zaire died under mysterious circumstances?
   a. Joseph-Désiré Mobutu   **b.** Joseph Kasavubu   **c.** Patrice Lumumba
2. Which country in Central Africa has achieved universal primary education?
   a. Gabon **b.** Central African Republic **c.** Burundi
3. Which of the following Central African countries is not land-locked?
   a. Zaire **b.** Chad **c.** Rwanda
4. What activity is most of the population of Central Africa engaged in?
   a. mining **b.** farming and herding **c.** forestry
5. Who was the personal owner of the Congo Free State?
   a. Queen Victoria **b.** King Leopold II **c.** Henry Morton Stanley

III. Thinking It Through

In your notebook, write the numbers from 1 to 5. Write the letter of the correct answer to each question next to its number.

1. Under colonial direction, agriculture in Central Africa was
   a. totally ignored.
   b. geared toward the needs of local people.
   c. organized for the production of crops for export.
   d. devoted exclusively to the production of cocoa.

2. As is the case throughout Africa, the borders of the nations in Central Africa were drawn
   a. with ethnic groups in mind.
   b. with the importance of mineral resources in mind.
   c. to meet the convenience of the colonial rulers.
   d. to foster improved transportation.

3. The fact that all but two of the Central African nations have experienced coups d'état suggest that
   a. the governments are extremely unstable.
   b. the colonial influence is still present.
   c. the nations will never be able to cooperate.
   d. democracy has great potential in the area.

4. For a country the size of Zaire to reach its economic potential, it must
   a. put more emphasis on producing cash crops.
   b. increase its foreign debt.
   c. nationalize its industries.
   d. exploit and maintain its good transportation system.

5. Cooperation among the ten countries that make up Central Africa will be made more difficult by the fact that the countries
   a. are of different sizes.
   b. employ four different official languages.
   c. have no democratic heritage.
   d. have very low literacy rates.

DEVELOPING CRITICAL THINKING SKILLS

1. Discuss what occurred with the industries in Zaire after the country achieved its independence.

2. Explain why Zaire and other African nations need foreign capital to

develop their economies, and point out the problem that arises in gaining the capital.

3. Describe what Zaire is doing in the area of education, and evaluate its success or lack of success.

4. Show what Zaire has done to fight the battle against AIDS.

INTERPRETING A COMPARISON CHART

A comparison chart allows you to set down important data about related items. In your notebook, copy the comparison chart outline below. Use material from the chapter and from standard reference works to complete the chart for the countries of Central Africa. Discuss what it suggests about each country and about the area as a whole.

Country	Colo- nizing Power	Type of Government	Principal Languages	Main Industries	Major Problems

ENRICHMENT AND EXPLORATION

1. Learn more about some of the current activities of CEEAC, the Economic Community of Central African States. Write a short report on the organization's progress or lack of progress. Consult *The Reader's Guide to Periodical Literature* for current information.

2. Do some library research to gather information on Leopold II's private colony of the Congo Free State. Find out how the colony came to be his private property, and describe how his agents served his interests. Present your findings to the class.

3. Conduct research on the life of Albert Schweitzer, the medical missionary, musician, and philosopher who worked for over 50 years among the people of Gabon. Explain what he did each day. Find out how the African peoples viewed him and his work. Deliver your findings in an oral report to the class.

8 East Africa

Perhaps the region of Africa best known to Westerners is East Africa, an area that stretches from Ethiopia on the Red Sea to Tanzania on the Indian Ocean. Many Westerners are familiar with the famous game preserves of Kenya, the Serengeti Plain of Tanzania, and the abundant wildlife seen nowhere else in Africa. They also know East Africa as the source of the Nile River, the longest in the world, and as the cradle of humanity. The Olduvai Gorge, where evidence of the earliest human-like people was found, lies in the Great Rift Valley. This vast divide cuts through the region from north to south.

In addition, writers such as the American Ernest Hemingway and the Dane Karen Blixen (Isak Dinesen) have introduced East Africa to many Western readers. Hemingway's novels describe safaris and white hunters, while Blixen, in her memoir *Out of Africa*, described the beauty of the land and her life as a planter in Kenya. Most recently, Westerners have become aware of East Africa through photographs and news accounts of the devastating droughts and the massive famines in Ethiopia and Somalia.

In this chapter we shall first discuss the common aspects of the region's history, geography, and people. Then we shall take a closer look at the nations of Kenya and Tanzania.

THE REGION

Ten countries are included in the East African region: Djibouti, Ethiopia, Kenya, Somalia, Tanzania, Uganda, Comoros, Madagascar, Mauritius, and Seychelles. The last four are island nations, located off the coast of East Africa. Réunion, an island east of Madagascar, is a jjjjh

EAST AFRICA AND THE WORLD

300–*Today*

A.D. 300s	Axum dominated by Persia; emperor accepts Christianity.
A.D. 600–700	Axum declines.
1500s	Portuguese arrive in Indian Ocean.
1540	Omani Arabs control Red Sea Swahili rebellion
1600s	Omani Arabs occupy Tanzanian region.
1700	Portuguese expelled south of Tanzania.
1776	*U.S. Declaration of Independence*
1800s	Demand for slaves increases.
1884–1885	Berlin Conference partitions Africa.
1895	Great Britain organizes Kenya as East Africa Protectorate.
late 1800s	Germany annexes Tanganyika.
1914–1918	*World War I*
	Britain takes German lands in Africa.
1920s	Jomo Kenyatta emerges as leader in Kenya.
1939–1945	*World War II*
1952–1956	Mau Mau revolt in Kenya.
1953–1961	Kenyatta imprisoned.
1960	African majority government formed in Kenya.
1962	Tanganyika becomes republic; Julius Nyerere elected president.
1963	Kenya adopts constitution; Kenyatta becomes Prime Minister.
1964	Zanzibar and Tanganyika unite as Tanzania.
1977	All East Africa now independent.
1978	Kenyatta succeeded by Daniel Arap Moi.
1990	Nyerere retires from all political positions.

| | | | | PER CAPITA | LITERACY |
COUNTRY	CAPITAL CITY	POPULATION (millions)	AREA (square miles)	INCOME (U.S. dollars)	RATE (percentage)
Comoros	Moroni (maw·ROHN·ee)	.46	719	$ 340	15%
Djibouti	Djibouti (juh·BOOT·ee)	.34	8,996	400	20
Ethiopia	Addis Ababa (ad·uh·SAB·uh·buh)	51.7	472,432	121	55
Kenya	Nairobi (ny·ROH·bee)	24.6	224,460	322	59
Madagascar	Antananarivo (an·tuh·nan·uh·REE·voh)	11.8	230,035	255	68
Mauritius	Port Louis	1.1	787	1,400	83
Seychelles	Victoria (vik·TOR·ee·uh)	.07	175	2,600	60
Somalia	Mogadishu (mog·uh·DISH·oo)	8.4	246,199	170	12
Tanzania	Dar es Salaam (dar es suh·LAM)	26.0	364,900	160	79
Uganda	Kampala (kam·PAL·uh)	17.9	91,343	280	57

Some Facts About East African Countries

department of France. East Africa is an area of great diversity, and its peoples and traditions show the influence of centuries of contact with Arab and Asian cultures to the north and east.

Ethiopia, in the north, boasts a 3,000-year-old civilization. It has maintained its independence longer than any African country. Except for a five-year period of Italian occupation during World War II, Ethiopia never experienced European colonialism. It is also the largest country in East Africa, about the size of New Mexico, Oklahoma, and Texas combined. Djibouti, situated at the southern end of Ethiopia's coastline, is, in contrast, the area's most recently independent country (1977), and its smallest, being slightly larger than Massachusetts.

All of the East African countries have faced many of the same problems since independence. Among these are the struggle for stability, the rapid growth of cities, the pressure to create transportation, education, and health-care systems, and the need to develop the economy. A further problem, especially acute in East Africa, is the destruction of the land. Some of this destruction, as in Ethiopia, is the result of prolonged drought. In other areas, it is partly the result of overgrazing and partly the fault of urbanization. In addition, in such countries as Kenya and Tanzania, the people must share the land with the wildlife, which their governments are determined to preserve.

The Land.   The land varies from snow-capped mountains to desert, from wet to dry savannas, from rain forests to flood plains, from highlands to deep gorges. Vast coastal plains lie in the east, and great plateaus rise in the western, central, and eastern areas. The climate is as varied as the landforms, with irregular rainfall over much of the area.

Rivers and Lakes.   Ethiopia and Uganda are, respectively, the sources of the Blue Nile and the White Nile, which converge in Sudan. Among East Africa's other rivers are the Tana, in Kenya, and the Kagera, a natural divide between Uganda and Tanzania. Many of the rivers in the region are wadis, filling with water only during some seasons. Thus they are not reliable for irrigation or for transport.

East Africa has some of the world's largest lakes. Lake Victoria, the source of the White Nile, is bordered by Kenya, Tanzania, and Uganda. It is the world's second largest. Only Lake Superior, in the United States and Canada, is larger. Tanzania and Zaire share Lake Tanganyika. The deepest lake in the world, Lake Malawi (also called Lake Nyasa), is on Malawi's border with Tanzania and Mozambique. In addition, Lake Turkana is in Kenya, Lake Kyoga is in Uganda, and Lake Albert is between Uganda and Zaire.

Agricultural Resources.   The heaviest population concentrations are in the foothills of the snow-capped mountains and on the shores of the lakes and rivers. Given the physical setting and the climate of East

Africa, most people work at farming, herding, fishing, or, often, a mix of these.

Much of the northeast of this area is suited for herding. Unlike the southern area, where the tsetse fly makes cattle raising difficult, most of the northern savannas in East Africa provide disease-free grazing land. From Somalia to northern Kenya, pastoral people herd cattle, goats, camels, and sheep. Because cattle provide their main livelihood, East African herders highly value their animals.

Farmers raise maize, millet, bananas, and cassava for food. Coffee, tea, cotton, rice, sugar cane, and **sisal** a plant used to make rope, are the principal export crops. They are produced mainly in Tanzania, Kenya, and Ethiopia. Livestock provides other export products, such as hides and meat.

Mineral Resources. East Africa has a long history of iron working. Africans engage in this craft to make tools and other objects for themselves and to provide items for trade. More recently, Western

Sisal continues to be an important cash crop in some East African countries. Here Tanzanian workers brush the fiber to make it suitable for manufacture into rope. Recently sisal production has fallen, as cheaper plastic rope has become available.

countries have been interested in the region's diamonds, copper, cobalt, potash, and other minerals. With the exception of Djibouti, Kenya, and the Seychelles, East Africa has numerous rich mineral deposits, many of which have yet to be fully exploited. In most cases this is because the minerals lie deep in the interior of the countries, and a transportation network for their export is not in place. Most countries, moreover, do not have the technology necessary to mine or process these minerals. Therefore they must rely heavily on the technology provided by Western mining companies.

Tanzania has one of the world's most important deposits of diamonds—the Williamson diamond mines in its north-central region. In addition, it has gold, coal, iron, and tungsten. These remain, however, relatively undeveloped. Ethiopia also has deposits of gold, copper, and potash, and Somalia has untapped sources of petroleum. Other countries in the region are also exploring their coasts and parts of their interior for oil.

Economic Activities.   As you have read, the economies of the nations in East Africa are primarily based on agriculture. Exports, too, are largely agricultural, while imports generally are manufactured goods. But planners in East African nations are trying to rely less on agricultural products and are beginning to develop manufacturing industries. The development of natural resources, however, requires capital. And the necessary funds are not readily available in these developing nations.

Raw materials are needed to build and operate factories. If they are not available, they must be imported. Recently, some countries have been importing crude petroleum and exporting refined petroleum products. One developing industry, particularly in Kenya, is assembly lines for automobiles and buses. In Kenya 90 percent of safari visitors travel by minibus. These vehicles are assembled in Kenyan factories from imported parts, mostly from Japan but also from other foreign automobile manufacturers. In 1987 the 5,000th minibus rolled off an assembly line in Kenya.

THE PEOPLE AND CULTURE

The nations of East Africa have struggled to create national unity from groups with diverse ethnic origins, traditions, languages, and religions. In Kenya alone, where the population is 98 percent black African, more than 40 ethnic groups are represented. Asians, Arabs, and Europeans make up the other 2 percent. In Tanzania there are more than 100 different ethnic groups.

Languages.   One way in which historians divide Africa for study is by language groups (see Chapter 2). They use these groups to trace the way Africans in ancient times moved about and populated various parts of the continent.

In eastern Africa at least four of the language groups are present. People in Ethiopia, Somalia, and Djibouti speak related languages of the Afro-Asiatic group.

Farther to the south are peoples whose languages belong to the Niger-Congo family. These peoples, who speak Bantu languages, such as Swahili, are thought to have been farmers who migrated, over many centuries, from the west coast of Africa to the east and central regions. Scattered among the Bantu-speakers are peoples whose roots are in herding and fishing cultures and who speak languages of the Nilotic family. For example, the Masai, who are still mainly cattle herders, speak a Nilotic language.

In the island nation of Madagascar, the languages spoken are not members of one of the four African language families. Instead, they belong to the Malayo-Polynesian family. The people of Madagascar are a mixture of Southeast Asian and African settlers. While they are mostly African in origin, their languages are mainly Southeast Asian.

Religious Beliefs.   "Where there are many people, there is God" is a Swahili proverb heard in Tanzania. In East Africa, Christianity, Islam, and African religions exist side by side. Many Africans practice their traditional religion as well as another.

In Kenya, Uganda, and the Seychelles the majority of the people are Christian, while more than 90 percent of Djibouti's population is Muslim. Ethiopia has a Christian tradition going back to the fourth century, when that religion was brought to the region by missionaries from Egypt and Syria. There is also a small number of black Ethiopian Jews, the Falasha, who date from yet earlier times. Today, nearly 50 percent of its people are Ethiopian Orthodox Christians. Many other Ethiopians, perhaps 30 percent, are Muslim.

Education.   As elsewhere on the continent, traditional education has always been the responsibility of the family and the village. There children learned the history of their people, their roles in their family and group, and practical skills.

East African nations have struggled to expand their educational systems. Here, in 1966, Tanzanian President Julius Nyerere presents a degree to one of the first students to graduate from Dar es Salaam University.

In the 1800s European missionaries introduced Western-style education, mostly to train Africans to work in the governments set up by the colonial powers. Primary and secondary schools were established to teach reading and writing. Most often these schools stressed European culture, often ignoring local traditions and history.

Many East Africans who were to become leaders in their countries' struggles for independence received a Western-style education. Jomo Kenyatta, the first president of Kenya, was educated by Church of Scotland missionaries. Julius Kambarage Nyerere (kam-BAH-rah-guh nyuh-RARE-ray), former president of Tanzania, attended Roman Catholic schools and, later, a teacher's college.

Since independence literacy has soared in some countries. In Tanzania, for example, it is now at 79 percent, with most children attending primary school.

Today, the nations of East Africa are struggling to expand their formal systems of education. In doing so, they face many of the same problems experienced by developing nations throughout the world. For example, the rapidly growing population puts enormous pressure on schools. With almost 50 percent of the population under 15 years of age, there is a constant shortage of teachers, materials, and buildings.

Literature. The myths, legends, folk tales, riddles, and praise poems of East African peoples have been preserved by storytellers. The function of these literary specialists was, and remains, to pass on the history and traditions from one generation to the next.

Most written literary works belong to the twentieth century. The exception is the written Swahili literature in East Africa. As you will learn, this is an old tradition, dating from at least 1700. It may have been encouraged by the influence of Islamic culture in the region. Strong traditions in written African-language literature also developed where Great Britain, rather than France or Portugal, was the colonizer. British colonial policy enabled Africans to retain some of their institutions and traditions. Sometimes the British even allowed the use of indigenous languages, such as Swahili, for instruction in the schools.

One of Kenya's leading novelists, Ngugi wa Thiong'o (un-GOO-gi wah thee-on-GOH), typifies modern African literature. He had been an early enthusiast for nationalism. In his first novels, such as *Weep Not, Child,* Ngugi's characters hoped that independence would provide Kenyans with the opportunity to solve problems brought on by their colonial experience. In more recent works he criticizes the Kenyans in power for not working to achieve this goal. He speaks of disillusionment with the postindependence period. He has also said that he will now write only in African languages, since only the privileged know English.

East African writers Bethwell Ogot (oh-GOT) and Ben Kipkorir (KIP-kor-rir) express sadness at the loss of African identity and cultural values. The poet Okot p'Bitek uses popular comedy to express serious social and political ideas and concerns.

The Visual Arts. Rock paintings, one of the oldest forms of visual art, have been found in a number of East African locations. In the highlands of Tanzania, there are more than 1,000 rock paintings created by Stone Age hunters. These paintings are naturalistic portrayals of people and animals. Rock paintings of cattle are found in Ethiopia, and paintings and cave inscriptions are found in northern Somalia. The age of these paintings indicates that early East Africans had developed a paint that could last for centuries.

Today in Kenya, woodcarvings of figures, as well as sculptures in soapstone, are traditional forms of art. People along the Kenyan coast are famous for their elaborate stools, chests, and doors, which are carved and inlaid with ivory and metals.

Crafts people are also highly skilled in the decorative arts. In Somalia they are noted for their gold and silver jewelry and their finely woven cloth and baskets. Ethiopia has an ancient tradition of art, especially connected with its churches and monasteries. Crowns, daggers, swords, as well as goblets and tableware, were crafted of gold

211

and silver and adorned with rubies and emeralds. Ethiopia's monasteries are treasure houses of **illuminated manuscripts** (books hand-painted on parchment and beautifully decorated). These are among some of the earliest such works ever produced.

Health Care.   In many parts of East Africa, people in rural areas must travel long distances to obtain modern health care. In much of the region, however, traditional medicine continues to be practiced. Often people will consult a traditional healer as well as a doctor.

Like many people elsewhere, East Africans believe that illness often may be caused by natural factors, such as bad weather, bad food, or impure water. They also believe that illness can be caused by mystical, or supernatural, forces. When someone becomes sick, the family may call on a specialist, often a **diviner,** to help cure him or her. In the ritual part of the treatment, the diviner evokes the spirits of the patient's ancestors. He or she asks for forgiveness for the patient's misdeeds or for his or her failure to make a proper sacrifice. The specialist asks to have the patient's health restored and requests prosperity for the patient and his or her kinspeople.

Healers are highly trained in traditional medicines and rituals. They may prescribe root, bark, leaf, or mineral medication. He or she might also place **taboos** on certain foods or actions; that is, the healer forbids the patient to eat or do certain things. Today, in many instances, a patient will take herbal as well as doctor-prescribed medicine.

Health Problems.   An old Kikuyu saying goes, "May you live to a ripe old age to be carried on a *gathuma*" (gah-THOO-mah). (A *gathuma* is a mat that formerly was used to carry fragile old people from their homes out into the sun.) Today, care for the aging is a major problem for people who respect and honor the elderly. Old people are concerned that they not be a burden to the younger members of their family.

There are many other health problems in the region, among them drought, famine, malnutrition, AIDS, and illnesses caused by insects or impure water. Information is now available on nutrition, treatment, and disease control. But the shortage of money makes it hard for governments to implement health-care programs.

Research in traditional medicine is being encouraged in East Africa. The World Health Organization (WHO) has officially recognized the importance of the effect of a people's culture on medicine and health practices.

African children continue to learn skills from their elders.
Here Masai boys are being taught to use the bow and
arrow, a weapon herders rely on when guarding cattle.

The Family. Many East African peoples continue to respect and cling
to the old traditions of family and village life. Some, such as the Masai,
have tended to resist cultural change. The Masai are still nomadic
people. They tend their herds of cattle on the savannas of Kenya and
Tanzania, living in temporary shelters of grass, reeds, and mats. When
they move their herds to new pasture lands, they leave their dwellings,
building new ones where they settle next. The Masai continue to practice polygyny, and boys, when they come of age, continue to be initiated into the warrior group.

In much of East Africa, however, urbanization is contributing to
the breakup of traditional family patterns. In one recent study of a Kikuyu village, researchers found that older people now insisted on doing
more than their share of domestic and agricultural chores. They hope
thereby to free the younger members of the group to concentrate on
education for the jobs they might want to find in the cities.

THE HISTORY OF EAST AFRICA

East Africa has a long coastline on the Indian Ocean. It is not surprising, therefore, that trade and commerce have been important
throughout its history.

213

Early Civilizations. As you read on page 76, from the first to the sixth century, Axum, in northern Ethiopia, was the capital of a series of empires. While most people of Axum were farmers and herders, the kingdom's wealth and fame came from its trading activities. In the 300s the area was dominated by Persia (modern-day Iran), then the major sea power in the Indian Ocean trade. Then, however, Axum's emperor accepted Christianity and declared it the state religion. In response, the Roman emperor Constantine the Great forged an alliance with the kingdom. Together the two rulers were able to control the shipment of goods from the Indian Ocean to the ports of Egypt, which were controlled by Rome.

Axum flourished for several centuries as a prosperous trading center. It lost its power in the seventh and eighth centuries, as Muslims and traders from the Arabian Peninsula moved into its coastal lands. Evidence of Axum's civilization still exists in records written in Geez, its classical language, and in huge, carved obelisks that were erected during this early period.

The Christian king of Axum and his subjects retreated south into central Ethiopia as Muslims began to take over the trade routes on the Indian Ocean and in the coastal towns. These routes were already well established. For centuries Indians and Arabians had sailed down the East African coast on the southward **monsoon** (the wind that blows across the Indian Ocean and southern Asia) from November through March and back again on the northward monsoon from April through August.

The slave and ivory trade soon expanded to include gold from Central Africa; rice from the islands of Comoro and Madagascar; animal skins, ores, and rock crystal from the East African interior; and varieties of birds and beasts not known in Asia. In return, people in towns from Somalia to Mozambique and on the islands off the eastern coast obtained cloth from India, glass beads, Chinese pottery, and Chinese and other Asian coins and currency.

This trading network flourished for several hundred years and gave rise to significant cultural changes. Foremost among them was the rise of Swahili culture in coastal East Africa. It probably first emerged long before 1500 in Lamu, an island off the Kenyan coast, and quickly spread north and south.

Swahili culture, of which the language is just one part, included a growing body of poetry and prose. This literature was written down around 1700 in a modified Arabic script. Written Swahili probably existed long before then, however.

214

Arrival of the Portuguese.   The rich Swahili culture was flourishing when the Portuguese began sailing into the Indian Ocean at the beginning of the 1500s. Rather than cooperate with the East Africans and their trading partners, the Portuguese sought to centralize all control of trade in their own hands. Official Portuguese policy led to merciless attacks on Muslim towns and sailing vessels. By 1515 the better-armed Portuguese had succeeded in making large areas of the western Indian Ocean subject to them.

The Portuguese were most interested in obtaining slaves, gold, and ivory. Indeed, their demand for these items was so great that they caused fighting among African peoples of the interior to intensify as groups competed to sell their goods to the Europeans. These wars were made more deadly as the Portuguese sold large supplies of firearms to their African allies who aided them in their search for resources.

The Africans and their Indian and Arabian trading partners were not subdued for long. In 1540 another powerful people, the Omani Arabs, gained control of the Red Sea. The Arabs began to raid the East African coast. At the same time, the Swahili townspeople began to rebel against the Portuguese. By 1700 they, together with the Arabs, had succeeded in expelling the Portuguese from every foothold north of the present Tanzania-Mozambique border.

Portuguese power was also challenged by the French, who were developing coffee plantations on the islands off the East African coast. Mauritius was one of the first islands on which the French established themselves. They used slaves from Mozambique, Kilwa to the north, and Madagascar to cultivate their extensive farms.

East Africa in the 1800s.   Ethiopia entered the nineteenth century with four important provinces vying for power. By the middle of the century, Tigre (tee-GRAY), Amhara, Gojam (GOH-jam), and Shewa (SHAY-wuh) were being united by a series of strong rulers. The real binding force of modern Ethiopia was Menelik II. He rose from being king of Shewa to rule Ethiopia at the end of the century. He succeeded in uniting the provinces, expanding Ethiopia's frontiers, and instituting a number of economic and social reforms. He was also able to keep Italy from claiming Ethiopia as a colony.

At the same time, as you read in Chapter 5, the Germans, British, and other European powers were showing considerable interest in eastern Africa. On the coast to the south of Ethiopia, many changes were taking place. The beginning of the 1800s saw an increase in the demand for slaves. For example, on the island of Zanzibar, off the coast of Tanzania, a new crop, cloves, had been introduced, and plantation owners needed more and more slaves to cultivate it. Eventually, however, other countries officially abolished the slave trade, even if they did not enforce the laws restricting this commerce.

Elsewhere the demand for ivory was growing, as Europe and America realized it could be used for piano keys, jewelry and ornaments, and billard balls. In pursuit of ivory, animal skins, and minerals, European traders began to penetrate the interior of the continent in greater numbers. They followed the trade routes that the African themselves had been using for centuries, often making alliances with the more experienced African traders.

Thus by the late 1800s European nations were eager to take part in the sharing of Africa's wealth. When they met at the Berlin Conference in 1884-85, they agreed among themselves to partition Africa (see Chapter 5). By 1914, Great Britain and Germany controlled most of East Africa. After World War I, Great Britain took over the lands previously held by Germany.

The Rise of Nationalism.   After World War I conditions in the region created an ideal setting for the development of ideas about independence. Why did feelings of nationalism arise in East Africa? During the colonial period, you will recall, colonies were formed with little or no regard for communities, ethnic groups, or natural territories. Peoples were divided with little regard for their history.

In addition, the British-controlled colonies of East Africa, particularly Kenya, became home to a large number of whites. Settlers from Great Britain and South Africa were attracted by the cool highland climate, the rich soil, and the fact that these areas were relatively free of disease. The settlers bought vast tracts of the best farm and grazing land, while Africans were excluded from their traditional homelands.

It was in this atmosphere that a group of leaders began the drive for independence. As the struggle intensified, the confrontation between the white minority settlers and the Africans was often violent. Most of the settlers were determined to stay on the land. They planned to take control of the governments as the colonial powers began to withdraw after World War II. The Africans were just as determined that they, the majority population, would control their nations.

As you will read, the conflict in Tanzania was less severe than elsewhere in the region. Tanzania became a United Nations trust territory in 1946, making it more difficult for white settlers to gain control. Nevertheless, whether by conflict or by the gradual taking of power by African leaders, the nations of East Africa all gained their independence by 1977.

KENYA

Located on the Indian Ocean, Kenya is crossed by the equator and divided north to south by the Great Rift Valley. It is approximately 224,960 square miles in land area, slightly larger than Texas and twice the size of Nevada. Its neighboring countries are Ethiopia, Sudan, Tanzania, Uganda, and Somalia.

The Land.   In both landforms and climate Kenya is a country of striking contrast. Its northern three-fifths are arid semidesert. The southern two-fifths are rolling savanna with adequate rainfall. Along the coast the tropical temperatures and beautiful beaches have given Kenya the chance to develop a flourishing tourist industry. The highlands, in the center of Kenya, have some of Africa's most fertile soil in addition to a cool, temperate climate. Mount Kenya's snow-capped peak rises above the equator in the center of the country, on the edge of the rift.

The People.   The people of Kenya are as varied as their land. In the semidesert region of the north, the nomadic Turkana, Samburu (sam-BOO-roo), and Somali people herd cattle, goats, and camels. In the Great Rift Valley live agricultural peoples such as the Kikuyu, Kipsigi (kip-SIG-ee) and the Nandi (NAN-dee). The Great Rift Valley is also the home of the Masai.

The Luo people live mainly around the shores of Lake Victoria in the west. The Kisii (kis-see) and the Abaluyia also live in the west, where they farm the fertile highlands around Lake Victoria. In the east, between the highlands and the coast, live the Kamba (KAM-buh) who herd cattle on the plains and farm in the hills. Early explorers and traders considered the Kamba superb fighters and often employed them as guides and soldiers.

The largest ethnic group is the Kikuyu, who make up 21 percent of the population. The Kikuyu dominate the business community and politics. Jomo Kenyatta, Kenya's first president, was a member of this group.

About 88 percent of Kenyans live in rural areas, and most are farmers. Of the wage-earning population, about 21 percent work in

217

industry and commerce, and more than double that, some 48 percent, work in government and public services.

Swahili and English are the languages of government and business. Today, Swahili is an important subject in school, and candidates who stand for parliament must know Swahili as well as English.

The Cities.   People living in the cities of Kenya enjoy one of the highest standards of living in sub-Saharan Africa. Nairobi, the capital, is situated on a high, fertile plateau. It is the largest city in East Africa. (*Nairobi* is a Masai word that means "place of cool waters.") It is the commercial, industrial, and communications center for all of East and Central Africa, as well as the site of many international conferences and agencies. Among the other important cities are Mombasa and Kisumu (KIH-so-moo).

The History.   In 1895, ten years after the Berlin Conference, Great Britain organized the region into the East Africa Protectorate. To transport the minerals they intended to extract from the interior, they planned a railway from Mombasa to Kisumu in the west. For this project the British imported 32,000 laborers from India, about 25 percent of whom remained when the railroad was completed. Many

Since the early 1900s the cool Kenyan highlands have attracted settlers who came to farm and raise herds. Here, on the edge of the Rift Valley, ranchers prepare their sheep for shearing.

who stayed became cooks, artisans, and merchants. They were to form the future core of Kenya's commercial community, particularly in Nairobi.

The railroad followed the route of old caravan trails. It went through the dry bush country near Mombasa and climbed, gradually, toward the Great Rift Valley, 300 miles from the coast. At a place called Nongo Bargo (NON-goh BAR-goh), railroad repair shops were established. Here Kikuyu women had long gathered to exchange food needed by the traders for beads, cloth, and small items.

It was at Nongo Bargo that white settlers, attracted by the highland climate, founded the city of Nairobi. The British then opened the area to other settlers, who used the black Kenyans living on the land as workers on their farms. These new settlers had a large voice in the government even before Kenya was officially declared a British colony in 1920.

Independence. In this atmosphere nationalism took root. Jomo Kenyatta, who would lead Kenya to independence, was born in a place north of Nairobi. He became involved in politics at an early age. He realized, he once said, that "when the missionaries came, the Africans had the land and the Christians had the Bible. They taught us to pray with our eyes closed. When we opened them they had the land and we had the Bible."

In the 1920s rising prices, low wages, and the unemployment that followed World War I led to political unrest among the young people. Another problem was increasing **land alienation.** This term refers to the thousands of acres of unused lands that lay in the highlands where whites had settled. Africans were being evicted from this land and sent to overcrowded reserves, much as in the United States in the 1800s Native Americans were removed to reservations. In time, four-fifths of the best land in Kenya belonged to about 4,000 whites. Yet 1 million Kikuyu were expected to live on the remaining one-fifth that had been set aside as reserves.

In protest, Africans began to form political parties, and Jomo Kenyatta emerged as a leader. Kenyatta traveled to London to petition for African representation on the Kenya Legislative Council, the colony's governing body. In the 1930s he again journeyed to England to present other African grievances. Finally, in 1944, the first African was named to the Kenya Legislative Council.

By the late 1940s, however, the tension erupted into what has been called by the colonial government the Mau Mau (MOU mou) revolt.

CASE STUDY:

Independence for Kenya

The speech below was given by Jomo Kenyatta, Kenya's first president, at its independence ceremonies in 1964.

Today, on the first birthday of our independence, the Republic of Kenya is born. This is another great moment for us all.

Today we have freedom and unity as the pillars of the state. That is what *republic* means. The Republic is the people of Kenya. All through the colonial days, for the purpose of divide and rule, we were constantly reminded that we were Kikuyu or Wakamba, or Giriama or Kipsigis or Masai or English or Hindu or Somali. But now, the Republic has embodied those features of equality and respect which cut through any differences of race or tribe. . . .

I say to you this: in freedom and with unity, there is nothing that we cannot accomplish. An approach to our future, in this spirit, is something else that the Republic means.

We have much cause for rejoicing at this moment. We can reaffirm here our dedication to the tasks that lie ahead. But let us spare some thought as well for those, our brothers in Africa, who are still in bondage and despair. And let us resolve that, within this coming year, racialism and bigotry must be finally conquered, not through the blood and the evil that come of setting one community against another, race against race, but through the forces of enlightenment, service and dignity that can be harnessed by all decent men. . . .

Our objective here in Africa is justice, after long years of desolation, exploitation, and neglect. Africa is fast awakening, not for conquest or disruption or revenge, but to contribute to the world a new philosophy. All men are equal. All men are equally entitled to respect. The talents and resources of the world are enough to banish squalor, and to bridge the gap between the richer nations and those where poverty has stifled man's creativeness.

Jomo Kenyatta. "The Inauguration Ceremony," in *From Black Africa*, selected by David Wells, Marjorie Stevenson, and Nancy King (New York: Harcourt Brace Jovanovich, 1970), pp. 69-71.

1. What did "divide and rule" mean in Kenya? Why does Kenyatta think it is important to stress unity?

2. How does Kenyatta define *republic*?

Some saw this as an organized terrorist plot, and it was marked by violence and atrocities on both sides. Today, however, it is generally considered to have been a desperate attempt by the Kikuyu to regain the land that had been taken from them by highland whites.

The rebellion lasted from 1952 to 1956. Kenyatta was imprisoned from 1953 through 1961 for his part in the struggle to bring about land reform. In 1957 the first African elections were held in Kenya, and by 1960 the Legislative Council had an African majority for the first time. In the same year, the Kenya African National Union (KANU), a political party, was formed, and Kenyatta was elected its leader.

At independence in 1963, Kenyatta became the nation's prime minister. He later became president and remained in office until his death in 1978. He had led his nation along a moderate path, encouraging land reform, foreign investment, and links with the Western world. He was respected by both whites and blacks, who referred to him as *Mzee* (mm-ZAY), the Elder.

Government and Politics. In 1963 Kenya adopted a constitution outlining the duties and responsibilities of the different branches of government. It guaranteed the vote to men and women over 18 years of age and promised to protect fundamental rights and individual freedom.

During the 1960s Kenya's government went through several changes. The federal system, with a prime minister, became a republic, with a president. The original two-house legislative body became a unicameral legislature. After the assassination in 1969 of Tom Mboya, a leading government official, opposition political parties were banned and KANU became the only legal party. Now every candidate for president must be a member of KANU and is nominated by the party. Following Kenyatta's death, Vice President Daniel arap Moi (uh-RAP moy) was elected president.

In East Africa many nations have been plagued by famine, poverty, and civil war. Kenya, in spite of political change, has been "an island of stability," as one writer put it. Although as a one-party state the government and the president have most of the power, lively and heated debates take place in the legislature. And Europeans and Asians are encouraged to take part in politics. Recently, however, unrest and political tension have been rising, as the government has become less tolerant of criticism. The president has concentrated more power in the executive, and university students and lecturers have been particularly outspoken about these policies. Because they have frequently disrupted classes and demonstrated, the government has often closed down the universities to quiet opposition.

The Economy. The word *harambee* (hah-ram-BAY) represents the spirit of Kenya much as the eagle represents the spirit of the United States. In Swahili *harambee* means "let us pull together." A concept announced by President Kenyatta and his successor, Daniel arap Moi, it stands for the idea that Kenyans should not expect their government to do everything for them. For example, if a community needs a new school, it decides what it needs and raises money by having a *harambee*, or fund-raising party. At the party, a guest of honor donates a sum of money or something for sale. Other guests then match or add to the gift showing their respect for the guest of honor. All the money from the party is then used to pay for the school building and equipment. *Harambee* parties are popular in Kenya as a way of raising money for all sorts of projects.

To extend the spirit of *harambee*, President Moi has also begun the idea of *Nyayo,* which means "footsteps." *Nyayo* reminds people of all that Kenyatta stood for. It urges citizens to follow in his footsteps, continuing to work together for the improvement of the country.

Agriculture is the mainstay of the economy. Coffee, tea, cotton, and pyrethrum (dried chrysanthemums used for insecticides) are its principal exports. It imports crude petroleum, machinery and transportation equipment, iron and steel, pharmaceuticals, fertilizers, and manufactured goods. Recently, Kenya discovered oil off its coast in the Indian Ocean. There is hope that the oil field is large enough so that

A variety of popular Kenyan baskets are displayed at a street market in Nairobi. Kenyan baskets have also become an export item and can be bought in shops all over the United States and Europe.

the country can soon become self-sufficient in petroleum, thus freeing itself from expensive import costs.

Tourism and the Arts.   To save its wildlife, Kenya has set aside about 6 million acres for national parks and animal preserves in different geographic areas. This land serves as a sanctuary for nearly all the species of animals native to Africa—buffalo, lions, jackals, zebras, giraffes, elephants, and many more, as well as a great variety of birds.

Some 400,000 tourists visit Kenya's parks annually. With an efficient tour system and an excellent network of roads, visitors can go on safari, not to hunt the animals, as in the past, but to watch them in their natural surroundings.

Tourism is a major industry in Kenya, adding about $80 million to the nation's income each year. It provides occupations for many Kenyans. Some manage hotels, restaurants, and tour services. Others work in game parks, at beaches, or in the entertainment industry. Even artists have become involved in the tourist market. Kamba carvers, for example, are now responsible for a million-dollar art industry.

The carving industry began following World War I. At that time a young Kamba, Mutisya wa Munge (moo-tis-yah wah mun-GAY) was stationed with other East African troops in Dar es Salaam, Tanganyika. There he observed the Makonde carvers making a living from their work. He apprenticed himself to a carver there to learn the artist's skills. When he returned to Kenya, Mutisya added to his farming income with the money he earned from the sale of his carvings. And he taught the craft to others in his village. Some of his pupils later moved to Mombasa, a center for tourism, where they found a wide market for the figures of animals and people that they carved.

Population Growth.   Kenya's rapid population growth is putting enormous pressure on the nation's resources. It has one of the world's highest birthrates, 3.8 percent a year. This fact is important because of its impact on economic development. If Kenya is to achieve an improved Gross Domestic Product, perhaps 40 percent or higher, for the population projected for the year 2004, its economy would have to grow by 6.2 percent each year for the next 17 years. This seems unlikely to happen, since Kenya's economic growth rate has not gone above 6 percent since 1978.

For a government committed to improving the lives of its citizens—as Kenya's is—this is a serious projection. Kenya's government must figure out how to expand economic development to meet the needs of its rapidly increasing population. On the other hand, the government must grapple with the question of whether it wishes to promote a policy of population control. It might encourage people to have fewer children, as China has done. In this way, the benefits of economic development would improve the everyday lives of Kenyans.

TANZANIA

Tanzania, which includes the islands of Zanzibar and Pemba off its coast, is one of the largest countries in East Africa. It borders on the Indian Ocean, between Kenya and Mozambique. On its west are Burundi, Rwanda, and Zaire. Zambia and Malawi lie to the southwest.

The Land.   Located between Lakes Victoria, Tanganyika, and Malawi, Tanzania has 23,000 square miles of inland water. Its four main climate zones are the hot coastal plains, an arid zone on the central plateau, the high, humid lake regions, and temperate highland areas in the north and south. It also boasts the highest point in Africa: near its border with Kenya, Mount Kilimanjaro rises 19,340 feet above the sea. Dar es Salaam, on the coast, is the capital. However, Dodoma (DUH-doh-muh), which in the center of the country, has been named to be the new capital. This move is meant to show that Tanzania is no longer looking outward but at its own country for prosperity. Tanga, (TAN-guh), Arusha (uh-ROO-shuh), Mwanza (MWAN zuh), and Iringa (ih-RIN-guh) are other important cities.

The People.   Tanzania's flag is black, green, yellow, and blue. The black represents its people. The green is a symbol of the land. Yellow represents Tanzania's mineral resources, and blue stands for the sea.

The estimated population of 25 million is unevenly distributed throughout the country. In the arid regions population density is about 51 people per square mile. In the well-watered highlands, however, there are an average of 134 per square mile.

Because no one group predominates, Tanzania has not experienced great ethnic rivalries or conflict. Of its nearly 130 different groups, only the Sukuma people number more than 1 million. Among the other groups are the Nyamwezi, the Makonde, the Luo, and the Masai.

The population is fairly evenly divided among Christians, Muslims, and followers of traditional African religions. On the islands of Zanzibar

Draftsmen work on plans for the new Tanzanian capital at Dodoma. The government decided to move the capital from the coast to the center of the country to show their interest in developing the country from the inside.

and Pemba, the majority are Muslims, most of whom are a mixture of peoples who emigrated from the mainland and the Middle East. One group, the Shirazi (shi-RAZ-ee), trace their heritage to early Persian settlers.

The History.　Scientists have found remains of the earliest ancestors of human beings in Olduvai Gorge. Here also the descendants of the early humans crafted some of the first stone axes and other tools (see Chapter 3). By the year 500 Bantu-speaking people from what are now Zaire and Zambia migrated into the area, bringing with them their knowledge of iron working. Trading villages along the coast existed as early as Roman times, and, later, Arabs took a more important role in trade. The Portuguese took over Zanzibar in 1503, only to be overtaken in the next century by Omani Arabs, who occupied Zanzibar, Pemba, and the thriving port city of Kilwa on the mainland.

Meanwhile highly developed kingdoms such as the Busingao (BOO-sing-gow) the Haya-Singa, the Nyamwezi, and the Chagga arose in the interior. Trade spread deep into the interior. The main slave-trade route was from Bagamoyo through Dodoma and Tabora to Kigoma. Along this route men, women, and children were captured and taken to Bagamoyo. From there the survivors were sent to Zanzibar, for clove cultivation, and to the Arabian peninsula.

At the end of the 1800s, Germany annexed 60,000 miles of what had been regarded as the Omani sultan's mainland territory. It was then called Tanganyika. As you have read, control of German territory passed to Great Britain after World War I. And following World War II, Tanganyika became a United Nations trust territory administered by Great Britain.

Independence.   *Uhuru* (oo-HOO-roo) means "independence" in Swahili. Julius Kambarage Nyerere, known in Swahili as *Mwalimu* (mwah-LEE-moo) (Teacher), and *Baba Wa Taifa* (bah-buh wah tah-EE-fuh) (Father of a Nation), was born in 1922 in Butiama, in the Musoma district, home of the Zanaki people. From his student days, around 1943, until his retirement from the presidency in 1985, Nyerere was among the most influential leaders of the emerging African states. Through his leadership, his Tanganyika African National Union (TANU) Party pressured Great Britain first for self-government and then for independence.

When Tanganyika became a republic in 1962, Nyerere was elected president by 97 percent of the vote. Shortly thereafter, Zanzibar got independence from Britain but with a sultan as leader instead of a parliamentary form of government. The people then rose up and deposed the sultan, forming a new government. Because the islands are small and not heavily populated, the new leaders accepted President Nyerere's invitation to unite with Tanganyika. In 1964, the two nations joined, forming Tanzania.

Nyerere was succeeded as president in 1985 by Ali Hassan Mwinyi (MWIN-yee). However, he remained head of the political party and continued to exert influence until he retired in 1990. Nyerere was a leading figure in African regional organizations. He was chairman of the "front-line" states, concerned with the freedom of South Africa and the development of Southern Africa. He also helped form the Organization of African Unity.

The Government.   Nyerere, in outlining his policies for the development of Tanzania, named his guiding beliefs *ujamaa* (oo-jah-MAH). This Swahili word translates into English as "family-hood" and refers to the promotion of cooperative self-government and cooperative economic development. *Ujamaa* has its roots in traditional African cooperation between members of families and communities. In his *Arusha Declaration* of 1967, Nyerere wrote, "The development of a country is brought about by people, not by money. Money, and the wealth it represents, is the result and not the basis of development. The four

226

[needs] of development are different. They are (l) People, (2) Land, (3) Good Policies, (4) Good Leadership."

Tanzania is a republic with executive, legislative, and judicial branches. Its executive head is the president. A prime minister is chosen from among the 244 members of the National Assembly, the single legislative body.

The Economy. In the past most people in Tanzania lived in simple, scattered homes around which women tilled small plots of collectively owned land. When a plot became unfertile, the local chief assigned a new one. This system produced enough to eat but not enough money with which to buy consumer goods, pay taxes, or finance improvements such as schools or roads.

Under *ujamaa* scattered houses were collected into villages that could be supplied with water, schools, clinics, and roads. Many people were at first unwilling to move into these villages, preferring their old ways. The government, however, was determined to provide clean water and other services. Nyerere said, "It's not a question of whether [the people] are happy . . . that's a philosophical question. I'm not trying to make them happy. But there's a difference between clean water and dirty water. My problem is a healthy child."

Tanzania follows a socialist economic policy, in which the government maintains control over most business activities. It sets prices for goods and buys surpluses to distribute through state corporations. Much of the manufacturing is also controlled by the state.

Dar es Salaam is one of Africa's principal and busiest ports. It is the port of entry and exit for goods carried to and from the landlocked nations surrounding Tanzania—Zambia, Malawi, Burundi, and Rwanda. To help develop trade, the Tanzanian government is expanding and modernizing the city. A major step was the construction of the 1,100-mile Tazara, or Tanzam, Railroad. The railroad was built by Tanzania in the 1970s with financial aid and technical support from China. It connects Dar es Salaam on the Indian Ocean with Zambia's interior, a major copper-mining center. Zambia is now able to ship to the coast of a friendly neighbor rather than through South Africa, whose apartheid policies Zambia and Tanzania oppose.

Most of Tanzania's farm land is in the northern and southern highlands, along the coast, and in the lake regions in the west. Because of a lack of water and the presence of the tsetse fly, almost two-thirds of the land is unusable for extensive agriculture. Still, agriculture remains the main economic activity. Major export crops are sisal, pyrethrum, coffee, cotton, tea, cashew nuts, peanuts, and tobacco. A fishing industry has the potential for boosting the economy. Mineral resources such as gold, coal, iron, and tungsten have yet to be fully exploited. But, as you have read, diamond mining is already a major industry.

In the 1970s and 1980s the economy suffered as a result of drought, a war with Uganda, and falling prices for its exports. More and more food had to be imported. And at the same time, income from food exports declined rapidly. Because of a shortage of raw materials, industry declined. Although foreign investments and aid from the IMF have helped, Tanzania's economy continues to face serious problems.

Tourism. An important part of Tanzania's economy is tourism. Most of the tourism is focused on the magnificent game preserves. Nearly one-quarter of the nation is made up of national parks, game preserves, and forest reserves. There are 12 national parks, the most famous of which is the Serengeti, located in the northern part of the nation. The largest game preserve in the world, it contains more than 1. 5 million animals .

One of the spectacular features of the Serengeti is the yearly migration of plains animals. In the dry seasons most herds move from the central part of the Serengeti Plains to the water in the north and west. Zebras and wildebeest thunder across the plain in long, seemingly endless droves. Once they have reached the water, the great herds turn and migrate back again to the central plains.

Education. Under *ujamaa* President Nyerere wanted Tanzanians to begin working cooperatively rather than competitively. To achieve this change in values, he suggested that the educational system be over-hauled. Thus Nyerere led the government in restructuring the educational system.

Now education through high school is in Swahili, not in English, as it was in colonial times. English had been the language of the elite. Now all people would speak Swahili.

Schoolchildren in villages cultivate gardens so that they can contribute to the payment of their education. They eat the food that they grow and sell the surpluses to raise money for school activities. Before students may go on to a university or training school, they must spend two years in the National Service. This is an organization whose members teach adult literacy classes, provide tutoring services, and even build roads.

The point of this educational system is to make students aware of

To save their wildlife, East African countries have set aside vast areas of land as animal preserves. Each year thousands of tourists from around the world visit the parks to see animals in their natural environment.

their country's problems. At the same time that they are preparing for their adult lives, they are contributing to the nation.

EAST AFRICA AND THE FUTURE

East Africa, as you have read, contains many different countries, peoples, and ways of life. It is an area that is featured in our newspapers and on television from time to time. We learn that parts of it have been devastated by droughts and famines and that international wildlife groups are concerned with the dwindling number of wild animals in the game parks.

But East Africa is, more importantly, a region where governments have made great strides in educating their people. Most governments, as well, have developed health programs that have improved their citizens' life expectancy and have made health care services available to more and more of their people. East African leaders have also developed programs to give farmers—the people on whom their agricultural economies depend—more and better land on which to grow food and crops to sell.

In developing solutions to the problems that they have faced in the past 20 years, East Africans have come up with many different and creative solutions. They have also seen many problems grow more difficult to solve. In facing the challenges of the 1990s—rapidly growing population, shrinking resources, and urbanization—they will expand on their experiences as they strive to meet them.

REVIEWING THE CHAPTER

I. Building Your Vocabulary

In your notebook, write the correct term that matches the definition.

diviner   taboo   monsoon
animal preserves   sisal   land alienation

1. the wind that blows northward and southward across Africa, the Indian Ocean, and southern Asia

2. one who helps to cure the sick by calling upon the spirits of the patient's ancestors

3. areas of land set aside for the viewing of wild animals in their natural surroundings

4. referring to European ownership of lands once used by the African population

5. a prohibition against things or actions

6. a plant used to make rope

II. Understanding the Facts

In your notebook, write the numbers from 1 to 5. Write the letter of the correct answer to each question next to its number.

1. In which East African nation is the source of the White Nile located?
   a. Kenya b. Uganda c. Tanzania

2. Which African lake is the second largest in the world?
   a. Malawi b. Tanganyika c. Victoria

3. In which East African country is the Serengeti located?
   a. Tanzania b. Kenya c. Somalia

4. Which East African country has the longest history of independence?
   a. Djibouti b. Somalia c. Ethiopia

5. Which people in East Africa are still nomadic?
   a. the Masai b. the Kikuyu c. the Abaluyia

III. Thinking It Through

In your notebook, write the numbers from 1 to 5. Write the letter of the correct answer to each question next to its number.

1. Trade and commerce have always been important in East Africa because
   a. the area's climate is suitable.
   b. the interior areas are rich in minerals.
   c. the area has a long coastline on the Indian Ocean.
   d. the area is generally unsuitable for agriculture.

2. The preservation of wild animals is important in both Kenya and Tanzania because
   a. the animals are sources of food for the population.
   b. the animals make a thriving tourist industry possible.
   c. African religions mandate the preservation of wild animals.
   d. the animals help make the land suitable for agriculture.

3. White settlers were particularly attracted to Kenya because of
   a. favorable financial incentives that the British gave to settlers.
   b. the country's location near the equator.
   c. the country's excellent rail system.
   d. the cool highland climate, rich soil, and relative absence of disease.

4. The fact that Tanzania has moved its capital from the seacoast to the interior suggests that
   a. the country is looking inward for future growth.
   b. the country is abandoning all trading activities.
   c. the country is removing itself from all foreign contacts.
   d. the largest portion of the population lives in the interior.

5. Which of the following is a concrete sign of the Tanzanian concept of *ujamaa*?
   a. A railroad was built to connect Dares Salaam with the interior of Zambia.
   b. A program was launched to encourage the opening of private businesses by citizens.
   c. Scattered houses were collected into villages that could be supplied with water, schools, clinics, and roads.
   d. Tremendous efforts were made to attract foreign capital.

DEVELOPING CRITICAL THINKING SKILLS

1. Show how the concept of *harambee* is used by the government of Kenya to encourage citizens to work together.

2. Discuss the common problems that have faced all East African countries since they gained their independence.

3. Explain why white settlers have always been attracted to East Africa in general and to Kenya in particular.

4. Describe the importance of wild animals to both Kenya and Tanzania.

INTERPRETING A MAP

The map on the facing page shows the physical quality of life in the nations of Africa. Study the map and use it to answer the following questions.

1. Which East African countries have the best physical quality of life? Which have the worst?

2. Check the literacy rate for Tanzania on page 205. In which area or areas would improvements have to be made for the physical quality of life to go up?

3. How does the physical quality of life in the four island nations compare with the rest of East Africa? With the entire continent of Africa?

ENRICHMENT AND EXPLORATION

1. Divide the class into small groups. Each group should research an East African nation reporting on the land, the people, the cities, the history, the government and politics, and the most pressing problems currently facing the nation. Each group should report orally in class.

2. As a class project, collect photographs and make drawings that could be used for a brochure to promote a photo safari to either Kenya or Tanzania. Write a caption for each photograph or drawing. Choose the best photographs and drawings and use them to make a model of the brochure. Write copy for the brochure that will appeal to people who may want to join such a safari.

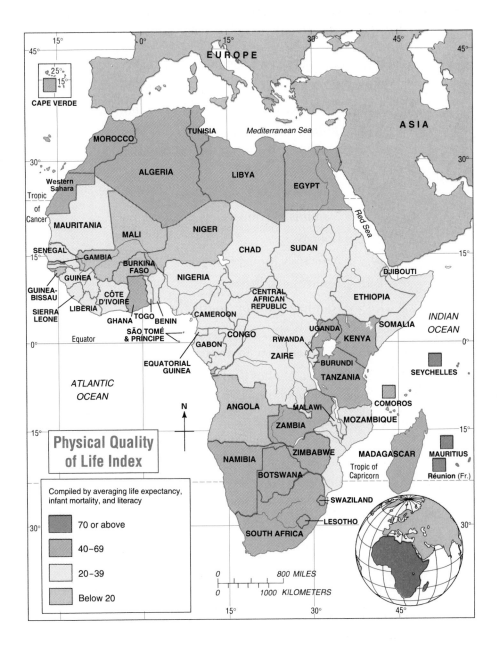

15°   0°   15°   30°   45°

45°   EUROPE   45°

CAPE VERDE

                                                            ASIA

            MOROCCO   TUNISIA   *Mediterranean Sea*

30°   30°
            ALGERIA   LIBYA
Western   EGYPT
Sahara
Tropic
of
Cancer MAURITANIA
        MALI   NIGER
                              CHAD   SUDAN
SENEGAL   15°
15°   GAMBIA   BURKINA
      GUINEA   FASO   NIGERIA   DJIBOUTI
GUINEA-   CÔTE   CENTRAL
BISSAU   D'IVOIRE   AFRICAN   ETHIOPIA
SIERRA LIBERIA   REPUBLIC
LEONE   GHANA TOGO BENIN CAMEROON
          SÃO TOMÉ   UGANDA   SOMALIA   *INDIAN*
Equator & PRÍNCIPE GABON CONGO RWANDA KENYA   *OCEAN*
0°   0°
        EQUATORIAL   ZAIRE   BURUNDI   SEYCHELLES
        GUINEA   TANZANIA

ATLANTIC
OCEAN   COMOROS
            N
            ↑   ANGOLA   MALAWI
                    ZAMBIA   MOZAMBIQUE
15°   15°
Physical Quality
                        ZIMBABWE   MADAGASCAR   MAURITIUS
of Life Index   NAMIBIA
                    BOTSWANA   Tropic of   Réunion (Fr.)
                              Capricorn

Compiled by averaging life expectancy,
infant mortality, and literacy   SWAZILAND

                                      LESOTHO
30°   30°
        70 or above   SOUTH AFRICA

        40–69

        20–39   0   800 MILES

        Below 20   0   1000 KILOMETERS

                        15°   30°   45°

                                                                      233

SOUTHERN AFRICA AND THE WORLD
A.D. 500–*Today*

A.D. 500s	Bantu-speaking people move into Southern Africa.
1600s	Dutch settle Cape of Good Hope.
1700s–1800s	Portuguese in Angola and Mozambique.
early 1800s	Zulu uprising Gold and diamonds discovered.
1836	The Great Trek
1879	British defeat Zulu.
1892	Namibia becomes German colony.
1899–1902	Boer War
1912	African National Congress (ANC) formed.
1914–1918	*World War I*
1919	Namibia ruled by South Africa.
1939–1945	*World War II*
1948	National Party in power in South Africa.
1952	ANC launches campaign of defiance.
1960s	Frelimo emerges in Mozambique.
1964	Malawi and Zambia become independent. Nelson Mandela jailed in South Africa.
1965	Ian Smith declares Rhodesia independent.
1968	Lesotho, Botswana, and Swaziland become independent.
1970–1979	War against white Rhodesian government.
1974	Independence of all Portuguese colonies.
1980	Rhodesia becomes independent Zimbabwe.
1985, 1986	State of emergency in South Africa
1989	Frederick de Klerk leads South Africa; legalizes ANC, frees Mandela.
1990	Namibia becomes fully independent.
1991	Apartheid laws repealed.

9 *Southern Africa*

Of all the regions of Africa, Southern Africa, with its large mineral resources, fertile soils, and relatively well developed manufacturing industries, has the greatest economic potential. It is also one of Africa's most politically troubled regions. The major source of both the region's economic potential and its political troubles is the Republic of South Africa.

South Africa is the most heavily populated, richest, and most militarily powerful state in Southern Africa. But efforts by its minority government, to preserve the rule of 5 million whites over the nation's more than 28 million blacks have led to violence at home and contributed to conflicts throughout the region.

In this chapter you will learn about Southern Africa. You will find out how it is similar to other regions in Africa and how it differs. You will also learn how white rule developed in South Africa and how generations of black South Africans have struggled against that rule to gain their freedom. And you will learn how the white South African government, in its attempt to maintain its power, has created chaos in all of Southern Africa.

THE REGION

With a total area of 2.3 million square miles, Southern Africa covers roughly 20 percent of the African continent. It includes ten countries—Angola, Botswana, Lesotho, Malawi, Mozambique, Namibia, South Africa, Swaziland, Zambia, and Zimbabwe. As you can see from the chart on page 236, the countries of Southern Africa vary tremendously in size. The two largest—Angola and South Africa—cover over 450,000 square miles apiece. In contrast, the two smallest countries—Lesotho and Swaziland—are only about 12,000 square miles and 7,000 square miles, respectively. South Africa has the area's largest population. About 40 percent of the area's people live there.

		POPULATION (millions)	AREA (square miles)	PER CAPITA INCOME (U.S. dollars)	LITERACY RATE (percentage)
Some Facts About Southern African Countries					
COUNTRY	CAPITAL CITY				
Angola	Luanda (loh·AN·dah)	8.5	481,350	$ 500	41%
Botswana	Gaborone (gab·uh·ROH·nee)	1.2	232,000	1,050	60
Lesotho	Maseru (MAZ·uh·roo)	1.8	12,000	410	59
Malawi	Lilongwe (lih·LONG·way)	9.2	46,747	160	41
Mozambique	Maputo (muh·POO·toh)	14.6	303,073	319	38
Namibia	Windhoek (VINT·hook)	1.5	318,269	1,020	100[a] 50[b]
South Africa	Pretoria (preh·TOHR·ee·uh) and Cape Town	39.5	437,876	2,290	100[a] 50[b]
Swaziland	Mbabane (em·buh·BON)	.8	6,704	790	68
Zambia	Lusaka (loo·SAK·uh)	8.1	290,586	304	76
Zimbabwe	Harare (huh·RAH·ray)	10.4	150,699	275	74

[a] whites
[b] others

The Land. Six states in the region—Botswana, Lesotho, Malawi, Swaziland, Zambia, and Zimbabwe—are entirely landlocked. For access to the sea they must depend on railroads and ports in neighboring countries, especially Mozambique and South Africa. Because of this, events in one country significantly affect the other countries. For example, because of wars in Angola and Mozambique, it has been difficult for neighboring countries to transport goods to and from those countries' ports. As a result, the landlocked neighbors are forced to ship goods at greater cost over longer distances to ports in South Africa.

The landscape of Southern Africa ranges from the arid Namib and Kalahari deserts in Namibia and Botswana to the more lush coastal areas in the east. But most of the region is covered by tropical savanna or semiarid plateaus. There are several mountain ranges in the region. The largest is the Drakensberg, which runs parallel to the coast in eastern South Africa.

The region has some of the most beautiful natural scenery in the world. Victoria Falls, in the northwestern corner of Zimbabwe, is the world's 10th longest waterfall—and one of the most spectacular. The Okavango (oh-kuh-VANG-goh) Swamps of northern Botswana, inhabited only by very few San people, is one of Africa's most untouched wildlife areas. Other natural features of great beauty include the Zambezi River, Lake Kariba, and the coastline of the Indian Ocean.

The People. More than 80 million people live in the region of Southern Africa. Most of them are in the eastern and northern areas and in the Republic of South Africa, which has over one-third of the region's population. The majority of Southern Africans are descendants of Bantu-speaking peoples who migrated into the region from Central Africa. But there are also a sizable number of Southern Africans whose ancestors came from Europe and Asia.

The diverse racial and ethnic makeup of Southern Africans is the result of several major waves of migration. Bantu-speaking peoples first began to move into the region from Central Africa around the year 500. By 1500 this migration had proceeded as far southward as the Transvaal (trans-VAL) in what is now the nation of South Africa. A number of the groups that established themselves over the course of this migration developed highly organized political and economic systems. In what is now Zimbabwe, for example, the ancestors of the Shona-speaking (SHOW-nuh) peoples (a Bantu subgroup) established a far-reaching empire built on trade, especially in ivory and gold.

Southern African societies were severely disrupted in the early

237

While black Africans work and shop in Johannesburg, South Africa, they cannot live in the city's apartment buildings and houses, which are reserved for whites.

1800s by a revolutionary upheaval called the **mfecane** (mm-feh-CAH-nay), or "crushing of peoples." The *mfecane* began among rival Nguni-speaking (un-GOO-nee) clans located along the southeastern coast in what is now Zululand, in South Africa. One clan, the Zulu, led by a chief named Shaka (SHAK-uh), built a superior military organization and began to conquer neighboring groups. As a result of the bitter wars that followed, the people of the region were scattered, and the political organization was changed. Two nations—Lesotho and Swaziland—were founded during this period by chiefs seeking to defend their peoples against Shaka. Several of Shaka's rivals fled northward with small bands. Imitating the Zulu, they conquered other less organized groups. One of these leaders, Mzilikazi (mm-zih-lee-KAH-zee), founded the Ndebele Kingdom in what is now southeastern Zimbabwe.

Early European Settlers. The first European immigrants to Southern Africa were the Dutch, who established settlements at the Cape of Good

238

Hope in the 1600s. In the 1700s and 1800s French, German, and English immigrants joined the Dutch on the cape, while the Portuguese government established settlements in Angola and Mozambique. Europeans began to arrive in greater numbers in the late 1800s. This followed the discovery of gold and diamonds in South Africa and the establishment of colonies by the British and the Germans. Many Indians and Malays arrived in the region at that time, brought to work in the sugar fields of Natal (nuh-TAL) province of eastern South Africa. Today Natal province has roughly 1 million citizens of Indian descent.

The European population of Southern Africa underwent another major change in the mid-1900s. In 1960 there were more than 1 million Portuguese settlers in Angola and Mozambique and more than 300,000 English settlers in Southern and Northern Rhodesia (present-day Zimbabwe and Zambia). Fifteen years later Angola and Mozambique gained their independence. Hundreds of thousands of Portuguese settlers left these two countries for Portugal and South Africa. In 1980 British-ruled Southern Rhodesia became independent Zimbabwe. Within a few years over two-thirds of the white Rhodesians had chosen to emigrate rather than live in black-ruled Zimbabwe.

Ethnic Divisions.   Southern Africa is more racially diverse than other regions in Africa. While black Africans are in the majority, there are also significant numbers of whites, Asians, and people of mixed race. Ethnic groups are often distinguished by their language. Among whites there are three main groups: the Afrikaners, who speak an Africanized version of Dutch; the English; and the Portuguese. Black Africans can also be classified by language group. In Zimbabwe, for example, the two major groups are the Shona-speakers, who represent roughly 75 percent of the population, and the Ndebele-speakers, who represent roughly 19 percent.

Differences in language are often accompanied by differences in culture, religion, economic interests, self-identity, and political loyalty. These differences—and how they can change over time—are critical to understanding African societies. For example, Afrikaners traditionally have had close ties to the land. They are deeply religious and fiercely hostile to the British. In contrast, English-speaking South African whites tended to be more worldly and business-oriented. From the late 1800s until the mid-1900s, South African politics were dominated by the struggle for power between parties representing these two different groups. By the late 1980s, however, as more and more Afrikaners left their farms for the cities, differences between the Afrikaners and the English-speaking people had narrowed.

One of the major goals of most African governments is to reduce ethnic conflict. They attempt to do this by promoting nationalism—loyalty to the nation. Yet in countries like Botswana, Lesotho, and Swaziland, there are fewer sources of conflict. This is because in these nations a single ethnic group represents over 90 percent of the population. In countries like Angola and Zimbabwe, however, there are two or three major groups who have historically competed for resources.

Ethnic differences tend to become less important and economic differences more important as a country becomes industrialized and urbanized. Thrown together in cities and workplaces far removed from the areas where they grew up, people change their ideas about the world and themselves. In South Africa's black townships, for example, ethnic identities are becoming less important. Instead, South African blacks today are influenced by ideas that stress the experiences that all the victims of white rule share. The leading institutions are now churches, trade unions, civic associations, and national opposition movements.

Independence. As you have read, long before the arrival of the Europeans, the peoples of Southern Africa had established a number of kingdoms with highly sophisticated political and economic systems. By 1900, however, Southern Africa, like most of the rest of the continent, had been colonized by the Europeans. Southern Africa was divided into Basutoland (buh-SOO-too-land), Bechuanaland (bech-oo-AH-nuh-land), Nyasaland, Northern Rhodesia, Southern Rhodesia, Swaziland, and the Union of South Africa, all ruled by the British. Angola and Mozambique were ruled by the Portuguese. South West Africa (Namibia) was ruled by Germany until World War I and after the war by the Union of South Africa.

The colonial history of Southern Africa is extremely varied. There were for example, significant variations in the ways the seven British territories were governed.

In Nyasaland and Northern Rhodesia the patterns of colonial rule and decolonization closely resembled patterns found elsewhere in Britain's African colonies. After World War II British authorities had assumed that these colonies would eventually gain independence—either as separate states or in federation with neighboring Southern Rhodesia. In the meantime, however, protests by nationalist political parties caused the British to speed up decolonization. Thus, in 1964 these two colonies achieved independence as Malawi and Zambia, respectively. Following the pattern established elsewhere on the continent, power was handed over to an African majority.

240

In contrast, throughout most of the colonial period British officials had assumed that the three so-called high commission territories— Basutoland, Bechuanaland, and Swaziland—would eventually become part of South Africa. By the late 1950s, however, because of changing public attitudes, the British realized they could not hand over control of these territories to white-ruled South Africa. Thus they rapidly set about preparing them for independence, and by 1968 the independent nations of Lesotho, Botswana, and Swaziland were born.

The five states that gained independence in the 1960s had identical constitutions. Each established a parliamentary form of government. Yet despite their shared experience, they quickly developed very different political systems. In 1991 Botwsana was still a parliamentary democracy. Three other nations had amended their constitutions to become one-party states. Zambia, after a period of one-party rule, returned to free elections in 1991.

Government since Independence.   Toward the end of the colonial era in Nyasaland, Dr. Hastings Kamuzu Banda (BAN-duh), who had practiced medicine for many years in England and had not played a major role in politics, was asked by nationalist leaders to return to his native land and head the territory's leading party. When Nyasaland became the independent country of Malawi in 1964, Banda was elected its first president. He quickly established near dictatorial control over Malawian society, allowing no political opposition. Today, despite his advanced age (over 80, by most estimates), Banda is still in power. Almost nothing is done in Malawi without his approval. President Banda is one of the most conservative leaders in Africa. Under his leadership, Malawi stands apart from the rest of Africa by maintaining close relations with white-ruled South Africa.

Zambia's first president, Kenneth Kaunda (kah-OON-duh), had played a leading role in nationalist politics. Kaunda exercised great political power, but his regime was far less strict than Banda's. His official ideology was a form of African socialism that he called humanism. Kaunda opposed white rule in South Africa, but he encouraged change by peaceful methods. In 1991 he allowed free elections for the first time in many years. By a huge majority the voters replaced Kaunda with a new president, Frederick Chiluba (chee-LOO-bah).

Botswana is one of the few remaining multiparty democracies in Africa. As of 1988 Botswana had four political parties. Since independence, however, the country has been governed only by the Botswana Democratic Party. Its first president was Seretse Khama (suh-RET-say KAH-muh) one of independent Africa's most respected leaders. In 1980, when President Khama died, he was succeeded by his vice president, Quett Masire (ket mah-SEE-ray).

In Swaziland the constitution written at independence was replaced by one that provides for government according to the tradi-tional practices of the Swazi people. Swaziland is the only country in sub-Saharan Africa to be ruled by a traditional king. When he died in 1983, King Sobhuza II (so-BOO-zuh) was the longest reigning monarch in the world, having been on the throne for 61 years. Following custom, the Swazi council selected one of Sobhuza's sons to be the new king. Like his father, King Mswati (mm-SWAH-tee) was only a young teenag-er when he was chosen to rule.

Despite the fact that over 90 percent of its population comes from the same ethnic group, Lesotho has had a troubled political history. Shortly after independence President Lebua Jonathan turned Lesotho into a one-party state. He ruled from 1966 until 1986, when he was overthrown by a military coup d'état. Officially Lesotho is now a con-stitutional monarchy led since 1990 by King Lestie III. But the king has little authority. Instead, political power rests in the hands of General Justinius Lekhanya (leh-KAN-yuh), chairman of the country's military council. Lesotho's political life is dictated to a large extent by its loca-tion, totally surrounded by South Africa.

Although the experiences of the five Southern African nations that received their independence in the 1960s have been varied, they did not differ in any important ways from the experiences of African countries in other regions of the continent. In contrast, the modern political history of Southern Africa's other five nations—Angola, Mozambique, Namibia, South Africa, and Zimbabwe—has been unique in Africa. In the pages ahead, we will look at each of these countries in greater detail. But first it is useful to understand some of the political features they share:

1. All five countries had large white-settler populations.
2. In all five countries political parties led by black leaders were forced to fight wars of liberation in order to gain independence. (As of 1992, South Africa, which has been independent since 1910, was still ruled by a white minority government.)

Southern Africa and the World. Americans have a special interest in Angola, Mozambique, Namibia, South Africa, and Zimbabwe. Many black Americans identify strongly with the suffering of the blacks in Southern Africa. Moreover, many American leaders believe that the

United States, because of its own struggle with racial oppression, should work actively to end racial injustice in Southern Africa. The United States also has an important economic stake in the area, which could become a major trading partner. Finally, the role that the United States plays in Southern Africa will influence the way people through-out the world view it.

United States policymakers have paid a great deal of attention to Southern Africa since 1975. In 1976, for example, Secretary of State Henry Kissinger began a major effort to help bring independence to Southern Rhodesia and Namibia. And in 1986 the United States Congress passed a Comprehensive Anti-Apartheid Act to help bring racial justice to South Africa. The United States has also sought to influence events in Angola and Mozambique.

Other countries have also taken a great interest in Southern Africa. Some, like Great Britain, West Germany, and Portugal, have done so because of their colonial ties with the region. Others, such as the Soviet Union and Cuba, had ties to national liberation movements in the region.

Mining.   Southern Africa has an amazing wealth of mineral deposits. Much of the world's supply of gold and diamonds, as well as important quantities of copper, platinum, uranium, and manganese, is mined there. The most important mineral-producing areas are the copper belt of Zambia, the gold reefs of the Transvaal, and the Great Dyke area of Zimbabwe. Oil has been discovered in Angola, and there are natural gas fields off the coasts of Namibia and Mozambique. Except in Malawi and Mozambique, income from mineral exports and money sent home by foreign mine workers account for more than half of all foreign-exchange earnings. In Zambia copper exports alone account for over 90 percent of foreign-exchange earnings.

The development of the mining industry in South Africa has had a major impact on life throughout the region. Beginning in the late 1800s, mine owners created a system of labor migration. This system brought men from the rural areas of South Africa and surrounding countries to work in the mines of the Transvaal. The use of migrant labor in the mines of South Africa continues today. As a result, millions of black African men are forced to live much of their adult lives separated from their homes and families. As of mid-1986, in addition to the native South Africans who had left their homes to work in the mines, there were nearly 300,000 blacks from neighboring countries, including 140,000 from Lesotho, working in South African mines.

Diamonds are one of South Africa's major exports. Here workers excavate and sweep the terraces at Alexander Bay.

Agriculture. Southern Africa contains much of the most fertile farming land on the continent. South Africa is the largest grain-producing country in Africa. It is also a significant exporter of citrus fruit, sugar, and tobacco. Zimbabwe grows large amounts of grain and is a major exporter of tobacco. Angola was once the largest coffee-producing country on the continent and a significant cotton exporter. Malawi grows tea and tobacco. Despite its small size, Swaziland grows a relatively wide range of crops, including citrus fruit and sugarcane. Mozambique is the world's leading producer of cashew nuts.

Southern Africa, therefore, could become one of the major agricultural producers in the world. Yet it has failed to fulfill this promise. One reason for this failure is drought, which year after year afflicts countries such as Botswana, Namibia, South Africa, and Zimbabwe. But although drought has had serious effect in Southern Africa, the main problem has been politics.

Colonialism and white rule have had a major impact on farming in the region. White settlers brought with them skills and technologies that improved productivity. But their presence—and the growth of the mining industry—also distorted agricultural development. The Europeans stressed the raising of cash crops for export. In addition, white farmers, fearing competition and needing workers, urged colonial governments to prevent black Africans from farming. They were joined in this request by mine owners, who needed labor for their mines. In South Africa laws were passed preventing Africans from owning property in over 85 percent of the country.

When the colonial period ended, politics began to interfere with agriculture in new ways. At independence in 1964, Zambia was agriculturally self-sufficient. By the 1980s, however, it had become a food importer. This shift was largely due to the fact that the government failed to provide farmers with adequate economic incentives.

In Angola and Mozambique agricultural production has dropped since independence in 1975. The reasons are primarily political. First, the mass exodus of the Portuguese left both countries without skilled managers of the nations' farms and estates. Second, these countries adopted the socialist economic policy of **collectivization**, or group ownership of land. Many Angolan and Mozambican peasants refused to cooperate, preferring to work their own land. Finally, **guerrillas**, or small bands of soldiers engaged in irregular warfare, opposed their governments and began to attack farms and disrupt transportation between the rural areas and the cities.

By 1991 both Angola and Mozambique had adopted new policies that offered more economic freedom and greater incentives for farmers. Fighting in Mozambique continued, however. Until it ends, this country will not be able to increase its agricultural production significantly.

One country that has maintained agricultural productivity since independence is Zimbabwe. Zimbabwe's black leaders learned from the experience of their neighbors. When they came to power in 1980, they convinced many white farmers to remain in the country. They also gave incentives and support to African farmers. As a result, agricultural production increased significantly in the first two years after independence.

Trade with South Africa. Three countries—Botswana, Lesotho, and Swaziland—are linked to South Africa through a **customs union agreement.** This means that there are no **tariffs**, or taxes on goods traded between these countries. In spite of this agreement, however, the economies of these three countries have not fared equally. Lesotho, with few mineral resources and no industry except handicrafts, is one of the poorest states in Africa. Its only major source of income is money sent home by migrant workers in South Africa. Botswana, in contrast, is one of the richest states in Africa. It has substantial deposits of nickel, diamonds, and soda ash and is one of Africa's best-managed economies. Like Lesotho, however, it has failed to develop any significant manufacturing industry. Of the three states, Swaziland has the most balanced economy. Its major products include coal, citrus fruit, sugar, and wood pulp. In addition, it has developed several small manufacturing industries.

You have read about the region of Southern Africa—its geography, its people, its politics, and its economy. In the following sections of this chapter you will look in greater detail at five Southern African countries—Angola, Mozambique, Zimbabwe, Namibia, and South Africa.

ANGOLA AND MOZAMBIQUE

Throughout the colonial period Portuguese officials regarded Angola and Mozambique as parts of Portugal. Thus they encouraged settlement by the Portuguese and made no effort to prepare the African peoples to govern themselves. In most settler colonies Europeans were employed as skilled artisans and managers, while Africans worked in the unskilled jobs. In Angola and Mozambique, however, Portuguese settlers occupied jobs at all levels. For example, they worked as waiters, taxi drivers, and clerks. This greatly restricted the opportunities for Africans and added to their hatred of colonialism.

Nationalist parties were slower to form in the Portuguese colonies than elsewhere in Africa. In Angola two major parties emerged in the 1950s. They became known as the MPLA (from the Portuguese for Popular Movement for the Liberation of Angola) and FNLA (for National Front for the Liberation of Angola). In 1961, as it became clear that Portugal did not intend to grant its colonies independence, these two parties launched a guerrilla war in northern Angola. They were joined by a third party, UNITA (for National Union for the Total Independence of Angola), in 1964, under the leadership of Jonas Savimbi (SAH-vim-bee). But although the groups carried on a guerrilla war against Portugal throughout the 1960s and early 1970s, they were never able to defeat the Portuguese army.

In Mozambique several political parties emerged in the early 1960s and then united to form Frelimo (for Front for the Liberation of Mozambique). In 1964 Frelimo launched a guerrilla war against the Portuguese. Frelimo eventually succeeded in liberating the two northern

Members of an Angolan family gather to cook food at a camp near Lusaka, Zambia. They are refugees from the fighting between government forces and rebels in their own country.

provinces from the Portuguese and established schools, clinics, and political structures. But the party was never able to establish itself in other, more populated and more highly developed areas of the country.

Although Portugal was not defeated in Angola and Mozambique, the military effort imposed a heavy human and economic burden on Portuguese society. In April 1974, in Portugal, army officers overthrew the nation's president. Upon taking power, the new military government announced that it would grant independence to all of Portugal's colonies, including Angola and Mozambique. Independence thus came suddenly.

Independence. In Mozambique, where Frelimo was the only widely recognized national party, a smooth transfer of power occurred. Negotiations between the Portuguese government and Frelimo resulted in the establishment of an independent African government in 1975. Samora Machel (muh-SHEL), head of Frelimo, became the first president. Machel governed Mozambique until 1986, when he was killed in a plane crash. He was succeeded by Joachim Chissano (CHIH-sah-noh).

In Angola, the Portuguese were unable to negotiate a peaceful transfer of power. When they departed, a civil war broke out between the three rival nationalist parties. On one side was the MPLA, aided by Cuban troops and military assistance from Soviet-bloc countries. On the other side were the FNLA and UNITA, aided by South African troops and supported by **covert**, or secret, military assistance from the United States. By the end of 1975, the MPLA had gained control of the capital, Luanda, and its leader, António Agostinho Neto (ah-gos-TEE-noh NAY-too) became the first president of Angola.

Civil War.   After the MPLA gained control in Angola, the FNLA withdrew from the field. Encouraged and aided by South Africa, however, UNITA continued to fight. Cuban troops remained to assist the MPLA. After more than a decade of warfare, and after thousands of civilians had been killed or wounded, the civil war in Angola finally came to an end in 1990.

War also raged in Mozambique. For five years following independence, members of Frelimo helped black nationalists in neighboring Rhodesia to fight the white government there. In the late 1970s the angered Rhodesian government aided in the organization of a Mozambican guerrilla group, called Renamo (for Mozambique National Resistance), to overthrow the Frelimo government. In 1980, after the collapse of Rhodesia's white regime, the South African government also began to assist the Mozambican guerrillas. The war spread across the country as the guerrillas attacked railways, roads, schools, and clinics. The war in Mozambique continued into the 1990s with neither side close to achieving victory.

Before he died, Mozambique's President Machel said, "There are two things you cannot choose—brothers and neighbors. We cannot move our country." This statement expresses in a few words the major problem confronting Mozambique and Angola (as well as the rest of Southern Africa) today. Caught in a struggle to maintain its power, the white-ruled government of South Africa was doing all it could to keep its neighboring black countries weak and divided. From their own territory, and from friendly Malawi and the Coromos Islands, South Africa was sending troops into Angola and Mozambique to make sure that the wars in those nations did not end.

Foreign Relations.   Both the MPLA and Frelimo considered themselves to be **Marxist-Leninist** parties. That is, they followed the socialist principles developed in the late 1800s by the economist Karl Marx and in the early 1900s by the Russian revolutionary Lenin. After independence Angola and Mozambique adopted the economic policies of and signed treaties of cooperation with the Soviet Union. The economies of these two nations did not fare well under socialism, however.

In the late 1970s and early 1980s the governments of both countries began to reconsider their situations. Mozambique changed a number of its economic policies. For example, it granted farmers greater freedom to sell their goods, increased its efforts to attract Western investment, and joined the International Monetary Fund and the World Bank. It also improved its diplomatic relations with the United States and other Western countries and attempted to reduce its dependence on the Soviet Union.

In Angola, the MPLA government had been careful to maintain good relationships with the American multinational companies that operated its oil industry. But as economic conditions worsened in the 1980s, Angola also adopted new policies. It authorized private farming, did away with price controls, and encouraged foreign trade. Like Mozambique, it applied for membership in the IMF. It also sought to improve its relations with the United States. At the same time, however, it remained dependent on Soviet and Cuban military assistance.

ZIMBABWE

As you have read, members of two major language groups—the Shona and the Ndebele—live in Zimbabwe. Shona-speakers have lived in the area since at least the eleventh century. Prior to the 1800s they were divided into several subgroups, linked in a loose political confederation. The Shona developed an advanced trading empire. But they lagged behind the Nguni of South Africa in military technology. In the 1830s a Nguni subgroup gained control over the Shona and established a kingdom in southeastern Zimbabwe.

Colonial History. The colonial history of Zimbabwe began in the late 1880s when Cecil Rhodes, a wealthy British mine developer, set up the British South African Company (BSAC) to explore and develop the area north of the Limpopo River. In part by treaty, but mostly by military conquest, the BSAC established control over the territory, which it named Rhodesia, after Rhodes. In 1898 Britain recognized Southern and Northern Rhodesia as separate territories. By the 1920s about 25,000 white settlers were established there.

Upon independence in Zimbabwe many Africans got the right to vote for the first time. Here an election official instructs the people how to mark ballots.

In 1922 the British government held a **referendum** (a special election in which the people vote on a proposed government law or policy) among the white settlers of Southern Rhodesia to decide the colony's future. The settlers voted for self-government rather than becoming a province of South Africa. Thus in 1923 Southern Rhodesia became a self-governing British colony. (Northern Rhodesia was to become Zambia.) The British government maintained the right to veto laws passed by the settlers, but this right was seldom exercised.

White Rule in Rhodesia. In the early 1960s the white government in the colony, now called Rhodesia, began to pressure Great Britain for full independence. The British government, however, demanded that Rhodesia first take steps to guarantee that blacks, who represented over 95 percent of the population, receive greater political rights. The whites refused. Instead, in 1965 Ian Smith, Rhodesia's prime minister, declared Rhodesia independent. Britain—and most of the rest of the world—rejected the declaration and refused to recognize the breakaway colony. In 1968 the United Nations imposed political and economic **sanctions**, or penalties, on Southern Rhodesia in order to force it to change its position.

The Establishment of Zimbabwe. Blacks in Southern Rhodesia had begun to establish their own political organizations in the 1950s. In

1957 several groups combined to form a unified national party, the Southern Rhodesian African National Congress (SRANC) under the leadership of Joshua Nkomo (un-KOH-moh). In 1959 the colony's white rulers banned the SRANC. New parties were formed, but they too were banned and their leaders imprisoned. Black leaders then began to establish parties in exile. In the early 1970s they launched a guerrilla war against the white Rhodesian government.

The fighting continued until 1979, when a conference was held in Great Britain to arrange for peace. Both sides finally agreed to the formation of a new government. A new constitution was drawn up, and in April 1980 the colony became the independent state of Zimbabwe. Robert Mugabe (moo-GAH-bee), a black and the leader of the Zimbabwe African National Union (ZANU), the largest nationalist party, was elected prime minister.

Zimbabwe Today.   Mugabe adopted a policy of reconciliation toward whites in Zimbabwe. He named two whites as members of his cabinet. He left the economy he inherited largely intact. He also established close ties with Great Britain, the United States, and other Western countries. Because of Mugabe's policies, many whites chose to remain in the country.

Zimbabwe's major political problem has been ethnic conflict between ZANU and the rival Zimbabwe African People's Union (ZAPU), led by Joshua Nkomo. The two parties were allies in the liberation struggle. But shortly after independence a disagreement arose over what role Nkomo and ZAPU should be given in the new government. Conflict between ZANU, which was supported by the country's Shona-speaking majority, and ZAPU, which was supported by the Ndebele-speaking minority, was rooted in Zimbabwe's precolonial history. Prime Minister Mugabe remained committed to ending ethnic rivalries. The conflict appeared to have been resolved with the merger in 1988 of the two parties into a new party, the ZANU-PF.

NAMIBIA

Namibia was the last territory in Africa to receive its independence. South West Africa, as Namibia was formerly called, became a German colony in 1892. Following Germany's defeat in World War I, the League of Nations placed the territory under South Africa's control. After World War II the UN called on South Africa to begin preparations for the territory's independence. The South African government refused and instead began to broaden its control of—and extend its restrictive racial policies into—Namibia.

The repressive racial policies of South Africa gave rise to increasingly militant nationalist movements in Namibia. In 1966 the South West African People's Organization (SWAPO), the largest nationalist party in the territory, launched a guerrilla war against the South African-backed Namibian government. In 1971 the UN declared South African occupation of Namibia illegal. After that time the UN and major Western powers, especially the United States, tried to persuade South Africa to grant Namibia independence. In 1978 the South African government agreed in principle to independence for the territory. However, a final agreement was not reached until 1988. Namibia became fully independent early in 1990, ending the warfare that had begun in 1966.

SOUTH AFRICA

With more than 7 million whites in a country of nearly 40 million people, South Africa cannot be compared with any other African nation. It is a land of extreme contrasts. It is the richest country in Africa, yet many of its citizens live in terrible poverty. Its official leaders consider themselves part of the Western free world, yet they deny over 80 percent of their population the most basic human and political rights. South Africa is a country with great untapped promise—and equally great potential for tragedy.

South Africa's current problems are rooted in its unique history. For most of Africa, colonialism covered only a very short period, and whites never were more than a very small percentage of the population. In South Africa whites have played an important role for 300 years.

Early Inhabitants.   There is some evidence that South Africa was inhabited as many as 10,000 years ago by hunters and gatherers who were the ancestors of the people called the Khoi and the San. When Europeans first began to establish settlements at the Cape of Good Hope in the mid-1600s, the Khoi and San numbered between 100,000 and 200,000. By the end of the 1700s, most of these peoples had been conquered by the Europeans, and many of them had been made slaves.

The majority of today's South African blacks are Bantu-speaking peoples who crossed the Limpopo River, South Africa's northern boundary, sometime around the year 1300. By the middle of the 1700s, the Bantu-speakers had settled much of what are now the provinces of Transvaal, Natal, and the Orange Free State.

The Bantu of South Africa were divided into two major groups. In the east were those who spoke Nguni dialects; in the west were people who spoke Sotho-Tswana (SOO-too-TSWAH-nuh) dialects. Both groups supported themselves by subsistence farming and cattle raising. They differed, however, in that the Nguni lived in widely separated settlements, while the Sotho-Tswana tended to live close together. The groups that today are called the Xhosa, the Zulu, and the Swazi are all descended from the Nguni.

European Settlement and Colonization. Dutch and later French Huguenot (Protestant) settlers arrived in South Africa in the late 1600s and early 1700s and established farming settlements in the countryside surrounding Cape Town. They soon developed their own language, known as Afrikaans, and a fiercely independent identity. They themselves became known as Afrikaners or **Boers**, the Afrikaans word for "farmer." As they moved northward in search of more farmland, the Afrikaners began to come into conflict with the Nguni and the Sotho. Between 1779 and 1819, for example, Afrikaners fought five wars with Xhosa, largely over cattle.

In the 1800s and early 1900s, thousands of Boers trekked—traveled by ox-drawn wagons—as they fled from British domination in South Africa to settle elsewhere.

At the end of the 1700s, the British government gained control of the Cape Colony. They began to encourage English settlement and made English the official language. They also introduced laws banning slavery, which angered the Afrikaners, many of whom used African slaves on their farms.

To escape from British authority, many Afrikaners decided to leave the Cape Colony. Loading their belongings onto ox-drawn covered wagons, they headed north, where they established the independent republics of Transvaal and the Orange Free State. This migration, which began in 1836, is known as the Great Trek. The expansion of white settlement increased conflict between the Afrikaners and Africans.

The discovery of incredibly rich gold and diamond deposits in the Transvaal and the Orange Free State in the late 1800s deeply affected Southern Africa. Thousands of fortune hunters from Great Britain and other countries rushed to the Afrikaner republics. Conflicts between the Afrikaners and the British over control of the territory resulted in the Boer War, fought between 1899 and 1902. Great Britain won the war, and the Afrikaner republics became British colonies.

Treatment of South African Blacks. During this period the British began a campaign to bring the black African peoples of the area under white rule. They defeated the Zulu, the most powerful of the Nguni groups, in 1879. By the end of the century, essentially all of the once-powerful African groups had lost their independence. Only the Swazi and the Basuto escaped conquest, and they signed agreements permitting the British to establish protectorates in their territories.

Once they had the Africans under their control, the colonial rulers destroyed their thriving agricultural settlements. They also imposed heavy taxes, forcing the Africans to seek work on white farms and in white mines to earn money to pay the taxes.

In 1910 the British granted independence to the colonies of Southern Africa—the Cape of Good Hope, Natal, the Orange Free State, and the Transvaal—which united to form the Union of South Africa. A government was formed that included representatives of both the English- and Afrikaans-speaking communities. Black Africans, who had been pressed into military service by both sides in the Boer War, were largely ignored. Furthermore, the limited political rights that had been granted to a small group of blacks in the Cape of Good Hope and Natal in the 1800s began to be chipped away. In 1912 black Africans formed the African National Congress (ANC) to lobby for political rights. But their pleas were ignored by both the English and the Afrikaners.

254

The South African government oppressed black Africans economically as well as politically. In the early 1900s laws were passed that made it illegal for Africans to own land or hold certain jobs. Under the provisions of the Native Lands Acts of 1913 and 1936 over 85 percent of the country's territory was declared part of a "white area." Africans were prohibited from permanently settling in this region. As a result, millions of African laborers were forced to become migrant workers, leaving their families in the "black areas" for much of the year while they worked in the mines and on the farms located in the white areas.

The Afrikaner Rise to Power.   The first governments of South Africa tried to promote close cooperation between the nation's Afrikaners and its people of British descent. The Afrikaners, however, who were poorer and less educated, resented British influence. And during World War II many Afrikaners refused to fight alongside the British against Germany.

Following the war, in 1948, the National Party (NP), which was made up entirely of Afrikaners, came to power. The NP worked to increase the economic power of the Afrikaners. It also sought to eliminate remaining political ties with Great Britain. By the mid-1960s Afrikaner control of South African politics and society was firmly established.

Apartheid.   Upon coming to power, the NP began the policy of apartheid—the Afrikaans word for "separateness." This policy created a system of strict racial separation in all areas of society—cultural, economic, and political. Some of the apartheid laws that were enacted as part of this policy include:

The Population Registration Act, which required that all South Africans be classified on the basis of race (as determined by appearance, general acceptance, and repute) into one of four categories: white, African, Asian, or colored.

The Group Areas Act, which divided South Africa into areas according to race. Each racial group may live only in its own area.

The Black (Urban Areas) Consolidation Act, the Black Labor Act, and the Black Labor Regulations, which required blacks to live in segregated townships. These laws also established controls on the entrance of blacks into white areas and their employment there.

The Promotion of Bantu Self-Government Act, which created separate national states, known as homelands, or *bantustans*, for 10 designated African ethnic groups.

The Bantu Homelands Citizenship Act, which made every black South African a citizen of one of the homelands, even those who had never lived in the homeland to which he or she was assigned or any homeland before.

The Reservation of Separate Amenities Act, which required that separate facilities such as restaurants, trains, and toilets be set up for each racial group.

The Bantu Education Act, which established a separate educational system for blacks that is vastly inferior to that provided for whites.

The Growth of Opposition.   Black Africans had long opposed the racial policies of the South African government. This opposition grew stronger after the rise of the National Party and the implementation of apartheid. As you have read, the African National Congress was founded in 1912 to work for African rights. But the ANC met with little success. Now, pressured by young leaders such as Nelson Mandela (man-DEL-uh) and Oliver Tambo (TAM-boh) the ANC adopted a program of mass protest against the government. Its leaders organized boycotts, strikes, and large-scale acts of noncooperation. In 1952 the ANC launched a nationwide defiance campaign, urging blacks to defy apartheid laws by nonviolent actions. More than 8,000 people were jailed as a result, but the government refused to make any changes in its apartheid laws.

In 1955 the ANC joined with three organizations—the South African Indian Congress, the South African Congress of Democrats, and the Colored People's Congress—to issue the Freedom Charter. This document called for a multiracial democracy in which all groups would have equal rights:

> We, the people of South Africa, declare for all our country and the world to know:
> - That South Africa belongs to all who live in it, black and white, and that no government can justly claim authority unless it is based on the will of all the people.
> - That our people have been robbed of their birthright to land, liberty, and peace, by a form of government founded on injustice and inequality.
> - That our country will never be prosperous or free until all our people live in brotherhood, enjoying equal rights and opportunities.
> - That only a democratic state, based on the will of all the people,

can secure to all their birthrights without distinction of color, race, sex, or belief.

And, therefore, we the people of South Africa, black and white together—equals, countrymen, and brothers—adopt this Freedom Charter. And we pledge ourselves to strive together, sparing neither strength nor courage, until the democratic changes set out here have been won.

Sharpeville.   In 1959 a split developed in the ANC, and some of its members formed the Pan African Congress (PAC). The following year the PAC launched a national campaign against laws requiring all Africans over the age of 16 to carry **passes**, or special identity papers, at all times. PAC leaders instructed Africans to appear on the first day of the campaign—March 21, 1960—at police stations without their passes. In most places the police broke up the crowds without incident. But in the township of Sharpeville, the police opened fire and killed 69 people.

The incident at Sharpeville sparked a nationwide wave of protest. The government declared a state of emergency and arrested over 1,500 African leaders. And the ANC and the PAC were banned.

With their existence declared illegal, the ANC and PAC went underground, secretly organizing resistance to the South Africa government. They also established a guerrilla organization to begin an armed struggle against the government. In 1964, at his trial for acts committed against the government, ANC president Nelson Mandela explained his organization's actions:

All lawful modes of expressing opposition to [white rule] had been closed by legislation, and we were placed in a position in which we had either to accept a permanent state of inferiority, or to defy the government. We chose to defy the law. We first broke the law in a way which avoided any recourse to violence, when this form was legislated against, and when the government resorted to a show of force to crush its policies, only then did we decide to answer violence with violence.

Mandela, along with many other ANC and PAC leaders, was sentenced to life in prison. And, for a while, resistance to white rule ebbed.

Black Consciousness.   In the late 1960s a new political movement, called black consciousness, developed in the African community. The spokesman for this movement was Steven Biko (BEE-koh), a young black

Mourners in a black township carry the coffins of people shot dead by police during the unrest in South Africa. Thousands attend mass funerals such as this one to protest apartheid laws.

medical student. Biko told listeners that "the black man has become a shell, a shadow of man, completely defeated, drowning in his own misery . . . an ox bearing the yoke of oppression with sheepish timidity." He called on blacks to develop a more positive self-image. He instructed them to seize control of their lives, to refuse to participate in white-dominated institutions, and instead to develop institutions of their own. Biko's appeals rekindled the sparks of resistance in the black community.

On June 16, 1976, some 20,000 schoolchildren in Soweto (suh-WEE-too) began a march to protest a government ruling requiring black schools to teach certain courses in Afrikaans. The police opened fire on the marchers, killing 4 students. This incident touched off 16 months of unrest, during which at least 700 people died. It also focused world attention on South Africa.

The South African government responded to growing internal and international pressure in two ways. First, it cracked down on black

CASE STUDY:
A Black Childhood in South Africa

Joyce Sikakane was raised in Soweto and became the first South African black woman reporter at the *Rand Daily Mail*. In 1977 she was arrested and tried with 22 others, including Winnie Mandela, under the Terrorism Act. The charges against the group were eventually dropped. Sikakane, however, spent 17 months in jail, mostly in solitary confinement. Once out of prison, nothing she said or wrote could be published. Sikakane left to live and work in Great Britain. Here she describes one aspect of her childhood in South Africa:

> The Newcastle area where my mother grew up was predominantly composed of people of mixed race. It was also declared a "white spot" by the apartheid regime, and the people were removed into other locations. Its population was split into African and Colored. For many of the inhabitants the official race classification depended on how straight or kinky the hair was, or how dark or fair the skin was. . . . My mother's family was split into Colored and Africans. Those fairer members of the family, who were classified Colored, now live in Johannesburg, in Kliptown. . . .
>
> My parents moved to the Orlando location, which is now part of Soweto. . . . The Sikakane family moved into a standard four-roomed house, one of the few equipped with a shower-room. The lavatory was outside. . . .
>
> My parents named me Joyce, and my grandfather added the Zulu name Nomafa, which means "inheritance." When flattering myself, I am inclined to believe that he named me thus, so that I should continue with the political struggle he was involved in with the African National Congress, fighting against white domination. He had named my elder sister Themb'umusa, which meant "have faith in mercy." By the time I was born, it had become obvious that the African people could have no faith in any mercy, the political struggle had to be pursued with full vigor.

Joyce Sikakane. A *Window on Soweto* (London: International Defence & Aid Fund, 1977), pp. 22-23.

1. How are people classified in South Africa?

2. What peculiarity in the classification system does Joyce Sikakane tell about?

3. What reasons does Sikakane give for the names her grandfather gave to her and her sister?

opposition. Hundreds of black leaders were detained. In September 1977 Steven Biko died in jail after a severe beating by police interrogators. But even as it continued its policies of repression, the South African government was forced to recognize for the first time that some changes would have to be made.

Mounting Pressure.   In 1978 South Africa chose a new prime minister, Pieter Willem Botha (BOO-tuh). Upon taking office, Botha warned South Africa's whites that they would have to "adapt or die." He called on them to support a series of reforms. But Botha and his supporters were not prepared to grant blacks their major demand: full political rights.

The African response to these half-measures was increased resistance to the Botha government's policies. The anti-apartheid activists were now joined by members of the long-exiled ANC, who were able to infiltrate from neighboring countries. During this period the leader of another group of blacks, Mangosuthu Buthelezi (boo-tuh-LAY-zee), Chief of the Zulu nation, joined the struggle when he refused to cooperate with the government's attempts to confine the Zulus in a separate homeland.

Meanwhile the rest of the world became increasingly sympathetic to the struggle against apartheid. Nelson Mandela became famous as a symbol of black resistance. Many foreign companies and countries, including the United States, banned doing business with South Africa. These bans, or **sanctions**, had a serious impact on the economy.

At first the Botha government responded by imposing even tighter internal control. A state of emergency was declared in 1985 and again in 1986. The police were given special powers to make arrests without warrants and to imprison people indefinitely. Secret death squads were sent out to assassinate black leaders. In spite of these measures, the unrest intensified. A growing number of South Africa's white leaders began to realize that the only way to stop the violence was to abolish the hated apartheid laws and give blacks a voice in the government.

A New Era.   In the summer of 1989, ill health forced Botha to step down in favor of Frederick de Klerk. In September de Klerk was elected president and soon began to dismantle the formal structure of apartheid. Within a few months after taking office, he legalized the ANC and released Nelson Mandela from prison. In June 1990 he lifted the state of emergency in most parts of the country. By August the ANC agreed to end nearly 30 years of armed struggle. In return, the government worked out arrangements for the return of some 22,000 exiles. Soon afterwards, the parliament repealed the Separate Amenities Act, thus making public facilities open to everyone. In the following year all apartheid laws were repealed, including the law restricting land ownership, the law limiting freedom of movement, and the law classifying South Africans on the basis of race. Plans were made for all ethnic groups to join forces in drafting a new, more democratic constitution. In response, western countries began to lift their economic sanctions.

In spite of these developments, many problems remain. One problem is divisions within the various ethnic groups. Members of Mandela's ANC have frequently clashed with another black activist group, the United Democratic Front (UDF), as well as with supporters of Chief Buthelezi's Inkatha (in-KAHT-hah) party. Since 1984 feuding among black groups has claimed more than 8,000 lives, a situation that some blacks feel has been promoted by right-wing extremists opposed to change. Serious divisions also split the white minority. Members of a new, rapidly growing Conservative Party opposed de Klerk's reforms and advocated a return to the old repressive legislation.

Even more threatening to peace and stability is the stark contrast that still exists between the "haves" and "have-nots." The country's 7 million whites own more than 80 percent of the land and enjoy prosperous

Frederick de Klerk, left, and Nelson Mandela.

lifestyles, while most of the 27 million blacks live below the poverty line. To gain real equality for them and their children is a daunting task, considering the extent of the changes required, the country's limited economic resources, and a population explosion that is expected to add 20 million citizens by the year 2010.

The Economy.   South Africa is the most highly industrialized nation on the African continent. Since World War II manufacturing has surpassed mining as the chief economic activity. Today, manufactured goods contribute three times as much to the economy as do mining and agriculture combined. Major products include processed food, wine, clothing and textiles, chemicals, iron and steel, and motor vehicles. Mining was the foundation of South Africa's wealth, and today South Africa is still a major mining country. It supplies most of the world's gold and is a leading producer of diamonds, platinum, chrome, vanadium, manganese, and fluorite.

Agriculture is also important to South Africa's economy. In addition to raising a variety of crops, South Africa ranks as one of the world's chief sheep-raising countries and is a major exporter of wool.

Education.   South African schools are divided into four separate, segregated systems. Children from each of the official racial groups attend separate schools. English-speaking and Afrikaner-speaking whites also go to separate schools.

South Africa's segregated schools provide very unequal education. The government spends 10 times as much money educating a white child as it does a black child. Teachers in black schools are not as well trained as those in white schools, there are more pupils per teacher in black schools, and fewer courses are available to black students. Of the black high schools, only 17 percent offer math to final-year students. Dumisani Kumalo, a black activist, describes his early school experiences:

> When I went to school, white education was compulsory and virtually free. . . . Yet I, like other black students, had to pay school fees to the government. [But] the government didn't build schools for black students, so my parents had to help build mine. They had to buy the furniture; they had to buy the books, the chalk, and help pay the teacher's salary.
>
> The school I went to was just four mud walls and a corrugated iron roof. During the summer the school was like an oven because

there were only little holes for windows. When it rained—or hailed—
we couldn't hear each other speak because of the corrugated iron
roof. We had to wear uniforms. But we had no chairs so we had to sit
on the dusty ground. . . .

We had one teacher for a class of 120. All the grades were mixed
up together. The teacher—who had one small piece of blackboard—
divided us into two shifts, one from 7 to 1 o'clock and the next from
1 to 5. . . . The teacher in my school was paid $20 a month to teach
120 kids per day (under rotten conditions). Teaching was something
done out of love. . . .

South Africa has a number of colleges and universities, but higher
education is more available to the white minority. White full-time university students outnumber African students by a ratio of two to one,
and fewer Africans than whites graduate from universities each year.
The situation has improved considerably, however. In 1990 there were
significantly more full-time African university students than there had
been ten years before.

Health-Care.   Like education, health-care services in South Africa are
separate and unequal. There is 1 doctor for every 330 whites, compared
to 1 for every 19,000 black Africans. Among Africans 90 infants out of
every 1,000 die before the age of one, compared to 13 per 1,000 for
whites. Life expectancy for white men is 67 years; for African men it is
55 years. For white women it is 74 years; for African women, 60 years.

Sports.   South Africa's national sport is rugby. Cricket and soccer are
also very popular. Like everything else in the country, sports in South
Africa have been affected by apartheid. Despite some relaxation in the
law since the 1970s, most sporting events involving whites and nonwhites are prohibited.

The Arts and Apartheid.   The arts have become a major force in the
struggle against apartheid. White writers played an early role in bringing
the injustices of that system to the world's attention. Among the best-
known works about South Africa are Alan Paton's (PAYT-un) *Cry, the
Beloved Country*, Andre Brink's *A Rumor of Rain*, J. M. Coetsee's (Coh-
ET-say) *The Life and Times of Michael K.*, the plays of Athol Fugard
(FOO-gard), and the many novels and short stories of Nadine Gordimer
(GORD-ih-mer). In 1991 Gordimer was awarded the Nobel Prize for
Literature.

Black and mixed-race authors have received less world attention until recently. Dennis Brutus, who teaches in the United States, has gained fame both for his poetry and for his leadership in the sports boycott of South Africa. One of his books, *Letters to Martha*, is actually a book of poetry. When Brutus was jailed in South Africa he was forbidden to write poetry. In order to continue his writing, he put his poems into letters to his sister, Martha.

Drama has become an important vehicle for black expression. One reason that blacks have turned to the theater is that it is one of the few remaining forms of communication that remains uncensored. An outstanding example of this is the play *Sarafina* by Mbongeni Ngema (un-GAY-muh). This play uses *mbaqanga* (mm-BAH-kan-guh), the music of the black townships, to help tell the story of African students and their struggle for freedom.

Many South African artists were forced into exile. Among the best known is the singer Miriam Makeba. Banished from her native land in the 1950s, Makeba has long been a leading voice against apartheid.

Non-South African artists have also taken part in the battle. The 1988 film *Cry Freedom* powerfully portrays the life and death of the black activist Steven Biko. An American-produced television film *Mandela* tells the story of Nelson Mandela and the Freedom Charter.

The Future of South Africa.   Sooner or later black South Africans will gain the right to fully determine their own future. Is a post-apartheid South Africa likely to be just and prosperous? There is a reason to hope so. While economically deprived, the black community has great personal and intellectual wealth. This includes church leaders such as Archbishop Tutu and the Reverend Allen Boesak (BOH-sak), trade unionists such as Cyril Ramaphosa (rah-MAH-pho-suh), political thinkers such as Nelson Mandela, Oliver Tambo, and Albertina Sisulu (sih-SOO-loo), as well as many lesser-known figures. Finally, however, whether or not individuals such as these will be able to lead South Africa to a position of respect and influence in the world depends on how long it takes to end the effects of decades of apartheid.

REVIEWING THE CHAPTER

I. **Building Your Vocabulary**

In your notebook, write the correct term that matches the definition.

collectivization	referendum	guerrillas
tariffs	covert	sanctions

1. a special election held to determine the attitude of voters toward a particular law, policy, or question

2. taxes on goods traded between countries

3. bans or prohibitions against engaging in certain activities

4. group ownership of land

5. having to do with secret, undercover government activity

6. small bands of soldiers engaged in irregular military activity

II. **Understanding the Facts**

In your notebook, write the numbers from 1 to 5. Write the letter of the correct answer to each question next to its number.

1. Approximately what percentage of the African continent does Southern Africa cover?
   a. 8 percent **b.** 14 percent **c.** 20 percent

2. What independent nation was formed from Northern Rhodesia?
   a. Namibia **b.** Zambia **c.** Zimbabwe

3. What is the main problem that has kept Southern Africa from reaching its potential?
   a. drought **b.** water pollution **c.** politics

4. Which European country did *not* have a colony in Southern Africa?
   a. Great Britain **b.** France **c.** Portugal

5. What was the foundation of South Africa's wealth?
   a. manufacturing **b.** mining **c.** herding

III. Thinking It Through

In your notebook, write the numbers from 1 to 5. Write the letter of the correct answer to each question next to its number.

1. In an attempt to retain its power, the white South African government has
   a. gained a great deal of international respect.
   b. created chaos throughout Southern Africa.
   c. consistently turned in a poor economic performance.
   d. totally neglected its mineral resources to deprive blacks of jobs.

2. The majority of Southern Africans
   a. are immigrants from European countries.
   b. are descended from Arabian traders.
   c. have arrived in the area within the last 50 years.
   d. are descendants of Bantu-speaking peoples from Central Africa.

3. The use of migrant workers in the mines of South Africa has meant that
   a. South African minerals are very competitively priced.
   b. millions of black men are forced to live much of their lives away from their families.
   c. understanding among peoples has improved.
   d. agriculture has been neglected.

4. South Africa did everything possible to prolong the wars in Angola and Mozambique because
   a. these nations were economic competitors of South Africa.
   b. it wanted to force other African nations to use South Africa's ports.
   c. it was to its advantage to keep nearby black states weak and divided.
   d. it hoped to introduce apartheid to those countries.

5. Which of the following statements most closely represents the views of South Africa's African National Congress?
   a. South Africa belongs to all who live in it, black and white.
   b. Whites should play a very limited role in any government that comes to power after the end of apartheid.
   c. Whites should be banished from South Africa.
   d. The concept of private property should be abandoned, and all property should be owned and used by everyone.

DEVELOPING CRITICAL THINKING SKILLS

1. Show how the colonial policies of the Portuguese in Angola and Mozambique led to political instability in those two countries.

2. Discuss the role that Great Britain played in the formation of South Africa.

3. Explain how recent developments in South Africa do or do not offer hope for a better future.

4. Describe how the policies of Zimbabwe's Robert Mugabe have enabled the country to avoid economic collapse.

INTERPRETING A MAP

The map below shows the main railroad lines of Southern Africa. Study the map, and then answer the questions that follow it.

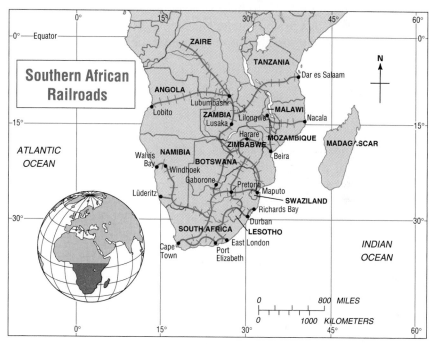

1. Which countries in Southern Africa have no railroad service shown on the map?

2. Cities and countries without rail service are at a disadvantage with respect to international trade. Why is this so?

3. Zimbabwe has a healthy agricultural economy. Which two ports are readily available to ship Zimbabwe's products overseas? What is the problem with these two ports? If they are closed, what alternatives are available to Zimbabwe's shippers? What are the problems associated with these alternatives?

4. If an additional rail line were built, what route might best serve the needs of both the Zimbabwe agricultural shipper and Zambia's copper producers for shipments to South America and the United States?

MAKING A TIME LINE

Use the material in the chapter to make a time line of the history of South Africa. Use the completed time line to make up a series of questions about the chapter to ask the rest of the class. There are two sample questions to help you get started: Which nations in Southern Africa received independence in the 1960s? Which happened first, the establishment of apartheid or the Freedom Charter?

ENRICHMENT AND EXPLORATION

1. Using standard library resources, conduct research into the Zulu people and the area of Southern Africa that they inhabit. Be prepared to present your findings in the form of an oral report. Be sure to present information on the origins of these people, their history, and the role they play today in Southern Africa.

2. Choose one of the five countries that was not closely studied in this chapter. Using standard library resources, gather information for a written report on the nation you choose. You may need to consult the *Reader's Guide to Periodical Literature* to locate up-to-date information. Be sure to include information on the country's early inhabitants, European settlement and colonization, its achievement of independence, its economy, the programs it provides for its citizens, and its current political climate.

3. Read a novel, story, or play by one of the South African authors mentioned in this chapter, or locate a similar work by consulting

your library's cataloging system. Report in class on the work that you have read. Be especially careful to explain what light it sheds on the racial situation in South Africa.

4. Working in small groups, collect current information on the situation in South Africa. Each group should look at contemporary South Africa from the point of view of a person who lives in that society, such as a black miner, an Afrikaner farmer, a non-Afrikaner white homemaker, a black railroad worker, an Indian teacher, and a white police officer. The information that you collect should come from contemporary sources, such as newspapers, news magazines, radio and television discussion shows, and television reports that focus on some aspect of South African apartheid. Plan a television documentary on apartheid that will feature interviews with these persons. Identify three or four questions that each person can be asked. Prepare a script for a twenty-minute documentary program, and stage the program in class.

10 *Africa and the World Today*

At the end of World War II, in 1945, the continent of Africa was not considered an active force in global affairs. During the war military campaigns had been fought in Africa, and Africa had given soldiers and materials to the struggle. Yet the continent was still held by non-African powers to be of little consequence. Only four African nations were independent in 1945—Egypt, Liberia, Ethiopia, and South Africa. Today, all that has changed. In 1991, 49 sub-Saharan nations had independent governments. All but Réunion were members of the United Nations. Africa now plays, and will continue to play, an important role in international affairs.

PROGRESS AND CHANGE

Within Africa problems exist that make headlines in the United States newspapers everyday. Poverty, famine, drought, political unrest, and violations of human rights are among the most severe. It is important to discuss these problems and how they affect the rest of the world. First, however, we should examine the areas of progress on the continent. Even with great differences between the countries, life has changed considerably for most African people since the early 1960s.

Literacy. The rise of literacy is especially significant. According to 1991 estimates, 47 percent of adults across the region are literate. This is the result of universal primary education and the increased number of educated people, including university graduates. Today many people can read newspapers. Mothers read labels on prescriptions, and farmers follow instructions for using fertilizer. Professionals in all fields can read up on the latest technologies.

Africa's writers, using local languages as well as such foreign languages as English and French, are reaching their own people. They are finding readers in other African countries as well as on other continents. Modern technology in the form of radio, television, and movies has increased communication among Africans. This communication is broadening the educational, cultural, and political aspects of African life. In Kenya, for example, villagers might gather to watch and participate in a play written in the Kikuyu language by internationally known Ngugi Wa Thiong'o. Across the continent in Cameroon, a university class might be discussing Ngugi's novel *A Grain of Wheat*. TV watchers in Abidjan, in Côte d'Ivoire, have a choice of local and international news broadcasts. They also can see popular American shows, an African historical drama such as *Shaka Zulu*, or locally produced educational and cultural programs. In London, Paris, New York, and Tokyo, African writers, film producers, and performing artists are becoming increasingly well known.

Health Care.   Health care is still far from adequate, but it has improved to the extent that life expectancy has now risen by ten years. As you have read, however, the birthrate continues to rise. And as you will read later, this means a problem of large and growing population, with serious consequences for the future.

African governments are continuing to expand their health-care programs. In this Ghanaian town, women bring their infants and young children to be weighed and examined at a well-baby clinic.

An important development in health care is the growing cooperation between Western-trained doctors—many of them African—and traditional African healers. They are working together to find the most effective preventive and curative approaches to such problems as malnutrition, malaria, and sleeping sickness.

A particular threat now sweeping the African continent is AIDS, or acquired immune deficiency syndrome. The World Health Organization (WHO) has estimated that more than half the total number of cases of AIDS worldwide have occurred in sub-Saharan Africa, particularly in the Central and East African nations. In Africa AIDS is transmitted mainly through heterosexual contact and affects men and women equally. Mothers, in turn, often pass on the virus to their babies. A complex interplay of medical, social, and economic factors has encouraged the rapid spread of the disease in Africa.

Although the virus that causes AIDS is the same in all parts of the world, the nature of the disease differs from region to region. In Europe and the United States, a type of pneumonia is the most common illness resulting from the breakdown in the body's inability to fight disease. In Africa most victims suffer from illnesses of the stomach and intestines. The poor quality of health care in many areas makes it difficult to treat AIDS effectively. Virtually everyone with AIDS dies within a few years, but in Africa the average patient dies in less than six months.

The Role of Women.   African governments are paying increasing attention to the needs of women. In particular, they are providing better prenatal and hospital care for mothers and their babies. Many women now receive special technical training that enables them to work in many areas of the economy. Women also hold elective office at every level of government and frequently represent their countries in such international organizations as the United Nations. One such representative, Anne Jiaggie of Ghana, drafted the UN Declaration on Elimination of Discrimination against Women.

Young People.   The youth of Africa are a major proportion of the population. Many of these young people find it difficult to get an education, especially beyond the primary grades. In addition, the scarcity of wage-paying jobs, even for the educated, has led many to disillusionment and disappointment. In spite of these obstacles, a number of young Africans have achieved international fame as athletes, and many more who are less famous have made their marks academically in European and American universities.

Family Life. Family life, too, has changed in many ways. For example, the movement of men to the cities or to other countries in search of work has had an impact on the family. Government-enforced living arrangements, such as those in South Africa, have been especially destructive. And the disruptions of war and famine have also disturbed family life. The separations that all of these situations create uproot the traditional African family system. Typically, each sex and age group has a particular and important role in the life of the family and the community. A special loss is the diminishing role of the elders, who are now considered more as objects to be cared for than as valued teachers. In the words of the Mali wise man Hampate Ba, "Each time an old man (person) dies, a whole library goes up in flame."

Family life today is also affected by marriage practices dictated by custom, religion, and government laws. Laws regarding polygyny, property rights, inheritance, and other family matters vary among the countries. Changing attitudes toward woman's rights, including those that have resulted from the influences of international women's organizations, are another factor affecting family life.

These and many other changes in the lives of Africans today will be discussed further in this chapter. First, however, we will consider some basic concerns that underlie present and future development in Africa.

POPULATION, ENVIRONMENT, AND FOOD SUPPLY

An African proverb says that "a child is born not only with a mouth to feed but also with two hands with which to work." In 1991 the 49 sub-Saharan countries had an estimated population of more than 516 million (slightly more than twice the United States, whose population is 250 million). This is 9 percent of the world's population. The birthrate averages 5.9 children per woman. Women have so many children partly because children are a valued part of the work force, especially in poor families. And because such a large part of the population today is young, the birthrate is likely to climb even higher, outstripping the death rate for at least 50 years. Some estimates predict a population growth of another 80 to 100 percent by the year 2020.

Although a majority of the population, at present about 75 percent, live in rural areas, urban growth is increasing rapidly. For example, in the 30 years between 1950 and 1979, the urban population in sub-Saharan Africa grew from 21 million to 93 million, an increase of 450 percent. For the 30 years from 1980 to 2010, the United Nations projects a 475-percent increase, to 441 million.

The pressures on city managers to plan for this growth are enormous. In Kenya, for example, about 3 million new housing units would be needed. That is equivalent to constructing 15 new cities the size of Nairobi by the year 2019.

Economic Diversity.   You have read how Africa is a continent of great diversity, in its geography and in its people. The economic situation is also greatly diverse, sometimes surprising in relation to the land's resources. For example, a small proportion of the population, about 11 percent, live in low-income, semiarid countries such as Burkina Faso, Chad, Gambia, Mali, Mauritania, Niger, and Somalia. Another group lives in countries with limited resources—Burundi, Lesotho, Rwanda, and Senegal. Another 30 percent, however, with higher per capita incomes, live in oil-exporting countries. Nigeria is the leading one, followed by Angola, Cameroon, Congo, and Gabon. Most of the other countries, with over half of Africa's population, are rich in natural resources but have seen slow economic growth. Many of these—for example, Ethiopia, Malawi, and Zaire—are among the poorest countries in the world. Yet some problems, such as an inadequate food supply, are not restricted to the poor or low-income countries. High-income countries such as Gabon, Kenya, and Nigeria import a great deal of their food.

The Threatened Environment.   Life-threatening environmental problems are a world concern today. These problems have been made worse by human activities, many of them in the name of progress. But only in Africa has there been such a great loss of life—some 150,000 deaths during the 1968-73 drought in the Sahel. Many more people have died in Ethiopia, where millions have suffered through year after year of far-below-average rainfall. Kenya, Mozambique, and Zimbabwe have also had long periods of drought, depleting cattle herds and reducing crop production. It is estimated that some 10 million people across Africa have been forced by drought to leave their homes in search of food, water, and shelter.

The disasters are not all natural, however. In earlier times Africans were much more in tune with nature, allowing the soil time to renew itself and moving their herds to avoid overgrazing. But the haste for development and commercialization, which began with the coming of European powers, has weakened the land. Overcultivation, overgrazing, **deforestation,** and many other human activities have resulted in soil erosion and climate changes. (*Deforestation* is the clearing of forests.)

*In Ethiopia in the 1980s, hundreds of people died daily
from malnutrition and hunger. Political unrest hampered
food distribution and added to the terrible famine
brought on by drought.*

In the Ethiopian highlands alone, more than 1 billion tons of topsoil
are lost every year.

Human beings are also to blame for the political conflicts that
disrupt food production and the delivery of relief supplies. For example,
the Ethiopian government stalled food deliveries to certain areas
because of a rebellion in the northern part of the country. In addition,
trucks carrying food were repeatedly attacked by the rebels them-selves.
In Mozambique the South Africa-supported Mozambique Na-tional
Resistance Movement has harmed food production. In Zim-babwe the
unequal distribution of good farm land, a carryover from the colo-nial
regime, has increased ethnic tensions. It has also caused some over-crowding
of already poor lands.

Resettlement of **refugees** from war-torn or famine-stricken coun-tries
such as Ethiopia and Chad has also taken its toll on the countries
receiving these immigrants, such as Sudan and Nigeria. In some cities—
for example, Nouakchott in Mauritania—refugees who have fled the
devastation of the Sahel make up more than half the population.

Other environmental problems, such as deforestation, water pollu-tion,
and the emission of dangerous chemicals, can be blamed partly
on nature. But they are also in large part the result of human careless-ness
and blindness to the environmental costs of development. Nature
might be blamed for the disease-carrying parasites that live in the rivers
and lakes in parts of Africa. These natural waterways have long been the

275

source of such diseases as dysentery, cholera, river blindness, malaria, and schistosomiasis, a parasitic ailment of the intestines, liver, and other organs.

In 1979 the World Health Organization and the United Nations Environmental Protection Agency (UNEP) launched the Blue Nile Health Project. This ten-year program was designed to eliminate schistosomiasis, one of the most common causes of infant death. Recently these organizations discovered that schistosomiasis and other water-borne diseases were found not only in the natural waters but also in the man-made lakes built to provide hydroelectric power. These include Ghana's Lake Volta, Zimbabawe and Zambia's Kariba Dam, Mauritania's Gorgol Reservoirs, and Mali's Serinque Dam.

Environmental groups are now pressing the World Bank and other possible lenders to back environmentally sound projects. One project recently questioned was a cattle-ranching program in Botswana. The program would have fenced off communal grazing land for a few ranches that would be owned by individuals. The planners of the project claimed it would help earn more foreign money (most of the meat produced would go to Europe) and create employment. Critics pointed out that it would destroy the grasslands and benefit only a few people.

DIVISIONS AND ALLIANCES

In addition to the geographic, ethnic, and language differences that are indigenous to the African continent, there are many more divisions that have resulted from changes brought about by non-Africans. As you have read, for example, the colonial powers cut across particular ethnic groups when they set up national boundaries. Some of the Ewe people found themselves in Ghana, others in Togo. One of the very few countries to have one dominant ethnic group is Somalia. That country has made some attempts to alter its borders to include Somali people now scattered in parts of Ethiopia, Djibouti, and Kenya. The effort has not been successful, however.

Although some ethnic conflicts involving border disputes continue, most countries now emphasize national unity. In some cases, especially in the cities, where different groups mix and often intermarry, ethnic divisions are fading.

Colonial occupation also left Africa with divisive issues. The continued use of European languages as official languages is one such

CASE STUDY:
A Bill of Rights

In 1981 the Organization of African Unity adopted the African Charter on Human and Peoples' Rights. In the charter "human rights" refers to the rights of individuals. "Peoples' rights" are understood to mean collective rights or the rights of an ethnic or minority group. Claude Ake, a professor of political science at the University of Port Harcourt in Nigeria, argues that because so many Africans are poor, they are more concerned with survival than with individual rights:

> In most of Africa, the extent of individualism is very limited. . . .
> Many people are still locked into natural economies and have a sense
> of belonging to an organic whole, be it a family, a clan, a lineage,
> or an ethnic group. . . . This means that abstract legal rights [for]
> individuals will not make much sense for most of our people. . . . Our
> people still think largely in terms of collective rights and express their
> commitment to it constantly in their behavior. . . . It underlies . . .
> our traditional land tenure systems, the high incidence of
> cooperative labor and relations of productions in rural areas. If the
> idea of human rights is to make any sense at all in the African
> context, it has to incorporate them in a concept of communal
> human rights. . . .
>
> African conditions shift the emphasis to a different kind of
> rights. Rights which can mean something for poor people fighting to
> survive and burdened by ignorance, poverty and disease. . . . If a bill
> of rights is to make any sense, it must include among others, a right to
> work and to a living wage, a right to shelter, to health, to education.
>
> Granted I have the freedom of speech. But where is this free-
> dom, this right? I cannot read, I cannot write. I am too busy trying to
> survive. I have no time to reflect. I am so poor I am constantly at the
> mercy of others. . . . [Thus] the people who are in a position to realize
> their [individual] rights are very few. . . . The [real] test for rights is
> those who need protection.

Claude Ake. "The African Context of Human Rights," *Africa Today* 34, nos. 1 and 2 (1987): pp. 5-12.

1. Why does he feel that many Africans cannot realize individual rights, such as the freedom of speech?

2. What does Ake mean when he says, "The [real] test for rights is those who need protection"? Is this true in other societies?

issue. Another is the lack of good transport systems within various countries. Most of these systems do not cross national borders, because the Europeans built them primarily to serve in the export of goods to Europe. In addition, economic and educational systems are still tied in some ways to those of the former colonial powers.

The Organization of African Unity. The purpose of the Organization of African Unity (OAU) was stated by Kwame Nkrumah, a founding member of the organization and Ghana's first president:

> A union of African states must strengthen our influence on the
> international scene, as all Africa will speak with one concerted voice.
> With union, our example of a multiple of peoples living and working
> for mutual development in amity and peace will point the way for
> the smashing of the inter-territorial barriers existing elsewhere, and
> give a new meaning to the concept of human brotherhood. A union
> of African states will raise the dignity of Africa and strengthen its
> impact on world affairs. It will make possible the full expression of
> the African personality.

The dream of a united Africa has not yet been fulfilled. But great progress has been made since Nkrumah spoke these words in 1963. Based in Addis Ababa, Ethiopia, the OAU brings together representatives from all over the continent to deal with African concerns. It has provided a forum through which African leaders can discuss the relations among African nations. Through the OAU they can attempt to voice concerns and solve disputes that arise.

The OAU does have its own problems, however. The division between a more moderate, pro-Western bloc and a pro-Soviet group is less strong now than it was in the 1960s, when the OAU was founded. Still, there are often opposing positions on issues. Throughout the 1980s, for example, African nations took different positions regarding the Soviet occupation of Afghanistan and United States activities in Central America. Conflicts relating to Arab nations—especially the activities of Libya's Colonel Muammar al-Qadaffi—have also created divisions. But the OAU is unanimous in its condemnation of South Africa's apartheid government.

In addition to the OAU, there are a number of regional organizations whose member countries cooperate on matters of common concern. Among them are the Economic Community of West African States (ECOWAS) and the Southern African Development Coordinating Conference (SADCC).

European Ties. In spite of their desire to become self-reliant, Africans maintain relations with their former colonial rulers. France especially has strong ties to most of its former colonies. It provides professionals to staff armies and departments of education, to help run banks, and to aid in rural development. The currency of all the countries formerly associated with France is based on the French *franc*. Though Belgium still maintains some relations with its former colony, Zaire, France has become closer to that country as well as to Rwanda and Burundi. For all these countries, France is the major trading partner.

Except for Sudan, all the former British colonies accepted membership in the Commonwealth of Nations, which recognizes Great Britain's ruler, Queen Elizabeth II, as head of the Commonwealth. South Africa's membership was dropped in 1960. The benefits of being part of the Commonwealth vary. One advantage is that it provides African nations with a forum for voicing opinion on international matters. For example, Africans frequently challenge Britain's weak stand against the apartheid government of South Africa. The Commonwealth also gives Africans access to economic and educational aid, as well as to a number of agencies with specialized resources.

Through their links with their former colonial rulers, some African states have recently been offered associate membership in the European Economic Community (the Common Market). Membership in this organization will give them access to investment funds and markets in Western Europe.

As you have read, Africans have been divided by their associations with one or the other of the superpowers, the United States and the Soviet Union. For example, there had been widespread reports of corruption and human rights violations in the administration of President Mobutu of Zaire. Nevertheless, in the late 1980s Mobutu still enjoyed the support of the United States because of his anticommunist declarations. Many countries, however, now belong to the nonaligned movement. They prefer to remain independent of foreign influences even though such a position could negatively affect the amount of aid they receive.

In spite of their desire to be independent, Africans cannot so easily overcome their divisions or remove foreign ties. Some of their alliances are necessary for their survival. Cross-continental transportation and communication systems, for example, are vital to better cooperation among the African nations. To build these, however, Africans must depend to a large extent on foreign aid. Thus they are reluctant to break the economic ties to nations beyond the continent.

TRANSPORTATION AND COMMUNICATION

Africans recently completed what governments designated as the decade of transport and communication (1978-88). Some progress was made and some future development plans outlined in these areas, especially for the expansion of rail lines and roads.

Developments in Transportation.   The most notable development since independence is the construction of the 1,100-mile Tanzam rail line joining Zambia and Tanzania (see Chapter 8). Built with help from the Chinese, this line reduced Zambia's dependence on the traditional import-export line through Zimbabwe during the pre-independence crisis there. It has served as a major route for the Southern Africa states ever since.

Africa has few railway systems—only 48,000 miles of track compared with Europe's 186,000 miles. Several countries have no railways at all. Future development will emphasize standardizing the railways. (Equipment left behind by the colonial powers did not match up from one country to another.) Management of most of the railway networks is coordinated by the Union of African Railways (UAR) under the OAU and the UN's Economic Commission on Africa.

Road development is expanding at a much faster pace. Many roads are now major connecting highways, paved with hard surfaces to withstand weather changes. Trans-Africa highways, in progress or being planned, include some 63,000 miles of roads stretching east-west and north-south across the continent. Each country is responsible for maintaining a section of these highways.

Transport on rivers and lakes is somewhat limited. As you have read, there are many waterfalls and other obstacles to navigation. Seasonal changes in the water levels of many rivers also occur. Africa's overseas trade is dominated by foreign-owned vessels. There are some African-owned lines, however, such as the Nigerian National Shipping Line and Zaire's Compagnie Maritime Zaïroise.

Most African countries operate their own airlines. Among those flying to other continents are Air Afrique, Nigeria Airways, and South Africa Airways. The combination of African and foreign airlines provides an excellent network between Africa and the rest of the world.

Developments in Communications.   Newsstands in major cities such as Dakar, Abidjan, Lagos, and Harare are likely to sell copies of international newspapers. Among them one can see the French *Le*

A train loaded with tractors makes its way over the Tanzania-Zambia Railway soon after it opened in the mid-1970s.

Monde, and the Herald-Tribune, an American paper published in Europe. One can also buy local papers and, occasionally, a paper or magazine from other African countries. The content, however, is often limited. This is because the press in many countries is controlled by the government, and the news is often censored.

Communication by telephone, radio, and television varies greatly from country to country. Wealthy individuals in Abidjan, Kinshasa, or Nairobi might boast the latest in electronic equipment—VCRs or even compact disk players. Many businesses keep in touch with offices elsewhere in the country and the world via computers, telex machines, and satellite computers.

In Africa, radio is still the major means of communication. Most radio stations are owned by the government, whose programming often tends to be dull. There are exceptions, however. One is a privately owned station called Africa No. 1, located in Libreville, Gabon. Begun in 1980, the station now reaches 15 million Africans. Its audience also includes listeners in Paris, New York City, and Canada.

Africa No. 1 presents a lively mix of music, quiz shows, and broadcasts of sports events, such as soccer games. Broadcasts also include health features, interviews, and morning shows for women. A program on dreams and one that features African tales of magic draw

281

large audiences. Music is also featured. Saturday evenings are reserved for nonstop dance music, which is heard and danced to in villages across Africa.

Experiments in mass education with the aid of television have been tried in Côte d'Ivoire, Senegal, and Ethiopia. However, the scarcity of equipment, the lack of a reliable electricity supply, and maintenance costs have discouraged this. Radio has been more successful in mass education. Countries such as Kenya, Ghana, Tanzania, and Zambia have well-established broadcasts under their ministries of education.

For those who do have access to them, radio and television offer wider contacts within Africa and to events and people beyond the continent. Through the media, young Africans have become fascinated with American pop stars such as Michael Jackson. Many have taken up the latest American fads, from various hair and clothing styles to the latest kind of dancing.

In South Africa all news—in print and on radio and television—is censored. This is to avoid airing critical comments about the government, especially by foreigners. Television was introduced to South Africa only a few years ago, and then it was only with strict government control of programming.

THE AFRICAN ECONOMY

The least developed region in the world, with two-thirds of the world's 40 to 50 poorest countries, Africa has the most to lose in the global recession that started in the 1980s. More than 150 million people in sub-Saharan Africa may be threatened by starvation. You read earlier that there are natural and man-made causes for these conditions. Among them are drought, famine, poor management by governments that concentrate on exports rather than food crops, political upheaval, and civil wars. These factors have contributed to a massive refugee problem. As people have fled hunger, oppression, and violence, Africa's refugee population has grown to 2.5 million. In proportion to its total population, this is the highest in the world.

Unequal Distribution of Wealth. It is important to remember Africa's diversity. Not everyone is starving. The quality of life is not better for everyone in the higher-income countries than it is in the poor countries. In some better-off African nations, like Gabon, Kenya, Zambia, and Botswana, the distribution of wealth is extremely unequal. Some 2

282

percent of the population receive about the same share of the total income as the poorest 50 percent. Life expectancy in Gabon and Côte d'Ivoire, another high-income country, is still below 50 years of age. In poorer Ghana and Tanzania, life expectancy is 50 and 55, respectively. Literacy rates in Ghana and Tanzania are also higher than those in Gabon and Côte d'Ivoire. And although Cameroon's per capita income is three times that of Somalia, the two countries have about the same ratio of doctors to the population.

The old African societies also had class systems and unequal wealth. However, the poverty of so many African people today is different from that of former times. Many people today have been "left behind." They do not have the technological skills necessary for better jobs. What skills they do have are no longer needed.

A number of changes have caused this social division. Among them are the commercialization of agriculture, the spread of Western education, and urbanization. The growth of government bureaucracies and the influence of official development programs have also contributed to this inequality. Development projects often emphasize new technology with little regard for traditional African skills and knowledge. Other changes have included the transfer of land to private ownership, which has been promoted by such countries as Kenya and Côte d'Ivoire. Private ownership in some places has replaced the traditional idea of community control of the land or control by community leaders.

International Trade. Since independence Africans have tried to change some of their economic policies. They are especially concerned with diversifying the kinds of products they export and finding customers other than their former colonial rulers. And to lessen their dependence on imports of manufactured goods, they have also begun to develop new industries. They want to produce their own goods from local raw materials. In all of these matters, they have had some success. Through the European Common Market they have found new trading partners in Europe. They are also increasing their trade with the United States, Canada, Japan, and other parts of the world. More trade also exists now between countries in Africa.

As Africa has developed its own industries, it has reduced the proportion of raw materials that it exports. This is so because it now needs these materials for its own industries. At the same time, industrial development has led to an increase in the proportion of raw material that is imported. For example, the amount of fuel that is imported has increased. In a recent period, fuel represented 37 percent of Kenya's

*Until they become more economically self-sufficient,
African nations depend on imports and exports. Oil
tankers and other large ships are common sights in
such port cities as Lagos.*

total imports. Food imports are also increasing. Overall, Africa is the largest per capita importer of food.

There are many reasons for Africa's economic problems. Among them are mismanagement, wasteful spending on "show" projects, greed and corruption among government officials, and political conflicts. Other causes, however, are beyond Africa's control. For example, to meet their development needs, Africans have had to borrow heavily from foreign banks and international agencies. Often these organizations attach strict conditions to their loans. These conditions continue to make African nations dependent. Consequently, Côte d'Ivoire, for example, used 45 percent of its income from exports in a recent year to pay off its foreign debt. Falling world prices, uncertain foreign markets, high export fees, and lack of capital are also to blame for Africa's economic woes.

Even among Western nations there is growing recognition of a need for change in the world economic system. As René Dumont, a French economist put it, "Europe cannot manage without Africa and the Third World because they supply [Europe] with cheap energy plus cheap metals, timber, and produce. It is, therefore, in Europe's interest that Africa survives."

WHAT THE PEOPLE SAY

Africans, like all peoples, have always expressed themselves not just in words. Today, as in the past, the material objects associated with African daily life reflect African ideas and feelings. They also reflect Africans' views about the people around them and the world in general. Their messages and ways of conveying their ideas and feelings have changed, however. These changes demonstrate Africa's ability to keep many traditional ideas while taking and using new ideas from the larger world.

Clothing. Clothing varies from place to place, often depending on the climate. In West Africa, with its large Muslim population, many people wear the traditional flowing robes of Islam. Elsewhere there is a mix of African and Western dress. Men go without neckties, dressed in colorful shirts and trousers. Sometimes they wear collarless suits in the style of those worn by Zaire's President Mobutu. For formal occasions and ceremonies, African-style dress is generally preferred. This is especially true among women, although more and more men are now adopting the African style. Brightly printed cloths and American-style T-shirts often carry messages of many kinds.

Some African T-shirts and other printed clothing carry words, while others have only a symbol or a picture. A particular message might be worn by a woman to scold her husband silently, something that she would not dare do out loud. Or a message might express a woman's feelings about someone else. *Adinkra* cloth, still worn by Akan women and men in Ghana and Côte d'Ivoire, carries symbolic representations of proverbs on such themes as cooperation, wisdom, and the all-powerful nature of God.

For school most students, from elementary grades through high school, generally wear uniforms. Recently, however, high-school students have begun to wear T-shirts with their school's insignia and, sometimes, messages related to education, sports, or national themes.

Modern Literature. As you have read, the works of established African writers are becoming an important part of international literature. In addition, some popular and children's literature has appeared, mostly for local consumption. There are women's and children's magazines, detective books, cartoon stories, and joke books.

Many earlier African writers criticized the disruptions in their culture that were caused by colonialism and other foreign influences. Today, both older and younger writers are more critical of their own governments for failing to live up to the promises of independence.

Another major concern of African writers is the change in family life. They note the breakup of families caused by urbanization and the disruptions of war, famine, and, in South Africa, apartheid policies. Among the increasing number of women writers, several focus particularly on this issue. Among them are Aminata Sow Fall of Senegal, Flora Nwapa and Buchi Emecheta of Nigeria, Grace Ogot of Kenya, and Bessie Head of South Africa. They write about the interaction between men and women, especially as it affects their children. They also voice concern about the special burden placed on many women who are single parents. Some children's books, for example, *No Place to Play* by Emecheta, who lives in London, picture the life of African children growing up in a foreign culture.

THE FUTURE OF AFRICA'S YOUTH

I wish the world to be rich and peaceful and to be healthy. Never ever should we let a world war break again. The countries should work together and be friendly. . . . To prevent starving to death every one should work hard for their nation. The governments should try to provide loans to farmers, so that their land can be improved, to avoid importing things like food, we can work hard on fields and earn more to feed the nation. . . . In future I wish to be a commercial farmer and feed the whole nation of Zambia.

Caroline Chipepe was a schoolgirl in Lusaka, Zambia, when she expressed these feelings.

Not far south of her home, the government of South Africa imprisoned an estimated 8,800 young people under the age of 16 for so-called security offenses. (The government admitted to only 256 of these arrests.) In spite of the efforts of the Detainee Parents Support Committee, most remained in prison until early in the 1990s. Even a special international conference on children under apartheid held in 1987 could not bring about their earlier release.

The situation among black youths in South Africa is perhaps the most dreadful. Yet many of the young people in other countries are also suffering from troubles that are not of their own making. They are in need of adequate food and other basics for survival. Another critical need for survival is education and job opportunities that can guarantee their future. Juvenile delinquency and drug and alcohol problems stem partly from the rootlessness that so many young Africans feel because they are denied such opportunities.

Governments have allocated large shares of their budgets to education. Efforts have also been made by Islamic and other private schools. Still, there are not enough schools and trained teachers to meet the needs, especially above the elementary level. There are many "school leavers." These dropouts are forced to leave school at an early age because they fail high-school entrance exams or for other reasons. Some, but not all, of these young people have opportunities for limited vocational training or special youth programs. But the scarcity of wage-paying jobs leaves many unemployed.

The general situation for African youth, in both the towns and villages, is difficult. Yet a considerable number of young people have had better opportunities. These and others promise much for the future. Africa has its share of young people who are privileged and upwardly mobile. While many are concerned most with fashionable clothes and being seen at stylish discotheques, there are also many outstanding students who do not take their privileges for granted. Like Caroline Chipepe, they feel that their education and other advantages require them to develop themselves as fully as possible. They also feel an obligation to serve other Africans. These future government, business, and professional leaders are the hope of Africa.

AFRICA AND THE WORLD

Many Americans, including legislators and businesspeople who can influence events abroad, know little about Africa. Yet recent media attention paid to events in South Africa and to the hunger crisis have aroused many Americans to lend support. It has also led many to become better informed about Africa. In addition, the Peace Corps and some student exchange programs have helped break down some of the American " jungle" images of Africans. These programs have also helped change the Africans' "Hollywood" images of Americans. Business exchanges between members of the Harlem Third World Trade Institute and African leaders have furthered mutual understanding. And American performers such as Harry Belafonte and Paul Simon who have worked with African musicians have also helped to break down traditional barriers between the continents. These examples show how much the world has to gain—in more than material terms—from Africans.

Whatever their problems, Africa's leaders want as far as possible to make their own choices. For many of them, the most urgent steps that must be taken to meet present needs and to allow for future development include:

The popular Nigerian musician King Sunny Adé in performance. Adé, a Yoruba chief, and his band play a style of dance music known as juju. *The lyrics often have a religious meaning. Like many other African musicians, Adé has found a worldwide audience.*

- Increased food production, with an agricultural program that meets the needs of small farmers and rural as well as urban areas

- Better prices for exports, with a more equal distribution of profits

- Better and more equal opportunities for health care, education, employment, and financial security

- Equal rights for all citizens, including representation in government

- Family planning and population control

- Environmental protection

Africans know that they live in an interdependent world. It is a world that forces everyone to give to and receive from others outside one's own country or continent. Recognizing this, Africans have asked for more equal participation in the planning and carrying out of development programs for their countries. In many cases, they have taken part in the work of aid agencies and multinational corporations. The United Nations, the World Health Organization, and many international religious, cultural, and scientific organizations bring

Africans together with others to share information and work on problems. The United States, through these organizations and through its own government agencies—such as the Agency for International Development—as well as through banks, corporations, and educational and cultural institutions, is closely linked to Africa's future.

Far more education and direct interaction is needed to make real Nkrumah's dream of a united Africa taking its place as a contributing member of the world family. Mazisi Kunene, the South African poet, put it this way:

Mother Earth
(or The Folly of National Boundaries)

Why should those at the end of the earth
Not drink from the same calabash
And build their homes in the valley of the earth
And together grow with our children?

REVIEWING THE CHAPTER

I. Building Your Vocabulary

In your notebook, write the correct term that matches the definition.

deforestation   urbanization   erosion

diversity   parasites   divisive

1. creating disunity or disorder

2. the process of clearing forests

3. organisms that live off other organisms

4. the condition of being different

5. the process of taking on the characteristics of a city

6. the process of wearing away soil

II. Understanding the Facts

In your notebook, write the numbers from 1 to 5. Write the letter of the correct answer to each question next to its number.

1. What is the only political entity in Africa that has not gained independence?
   a. Lesotho   b. Angola   c. Réunion

2. Which European nation has kept up especially strong ties with most of its former colonies?
   a. Portugal   b. France   c. Belgium

3. What do most countries in Africa now emphasize?
   a. ethnic groups   b. language families   c. national unity

4. Which of the following commodities does Africa *not* supply to Europe?
   a. automobiles   b. energy   c. produce

5. What percentage of the world's population lives in Africa?
   a. 6 percent   b. 9 percent   c. 24 percent

III. Thinking It Through

1. Which of the following statements reports on a development that has *not* yet occurred in Africa?
   a. The literacy rate throughout the continent has improved.
   b. Tremendous gains have been made in the war against AIDS.
   c. Modern technology has improved communication among Africans.
   d. African governments are paying increased attention to the needs of women.

2. Environmentally sound development programs are likely to come to Africa when
   a. land is more equally distributed among people.
   b. more progress has been made in the fight against disease.
   c. governments realize the wisdom of such programs.
   d. lenders of capital demand that such programs be environmentally sound.

3. Most of the existing transportation systems in Africa do not cross national borders because
   a. geographical barriers would make such crossings impractical.
   b. there is no need, since all countries have access to seaports.
   c. they were designed by their colonial builders to serve the need of exporting goods to Europe.
   d. the neighboring governments see no current need for such systems.

4. Which of the following statements best presents the original purpose of the Organization of African States?
   a. The OAS will allow the African nations to deal as a unit with their former colonial rulers.
   b. The OAS will allow all of Africa to speak with one concerted voice.
   c. The OAS will allow Africa to set fair prices for its exports.
   d. The OAS will allow Africa to show the world that its member nations take individual positions on issues.

5. In the area of transportation, which of the following statements represents a solution to Africa's most pressing need?
   a. Every nation should have its own national airline.
   b. Africa has too few railroads and ought to build more, since railroads offer the most economical means for moving goods.

c. African nations ought to invest in canals so as to eliminate obstacles to river travel.

d. Every nation ought to have a major road from its capital to the nearest seaport.

DEVELOPING CRITICAL THINKING SKILLS

1. Explain how AIDS is a threat to African society and what is being done to counter the threat.

2. Show how population growth is adversely affecting the development of Africa.

3. Discuss the benefits that many African nations receive by maintaining ties with former colonial rulers.

4. Describe the reasons for Africa's economic problems.

ENRICHMENT AND EXPLORATION

1. Choose a nation in sub-Saharan Africa. Over the period of a month, collect current information on the nation from newspapers and magazines. This information should be supplemented by consulting the *Reader's Guide to Periodical Literature* for articles published during the last year. Report orally in class on the current status of the nation you have chosen. Be sure to include in your report the progress that has been made in solving the problems faced by the nation.

2. Locate a short wave radio and tune in to Africa No. 1, a radio station that broadcasts from Libreville, Gabon. Record one or more of the station's broadcasts. Bring the tape to class and play it. Conduct a class discussion about the Africa No. 1 broadcasts. Identify program features that provide insights into contemporary African life.

3. Find out as much as you can about the current status of the Trans-Africa highway system by contacting the United Nations Development Program, the Organization for African Unity, or the embassies of specific African countries. Try to find out what the route of the road system is and the project's current status.

Glossary

Afrikaans: the language of the Afrikaners

Afrikaner: a descendant of the original Dutch settlers of South Africa

age grade: a group of people of the same age who pass through various stages and roles as a group

Agricultural Revolution: the period during which cultivation of crops and domestication of animals developed

apartheid: South African policy of strict separation of the races

autocratic: having total control

autonomous: self-governing

Bantustan: a national state, or "homeland," created by the South African government for a designated black ethnic group

basin: a depression in the surface of the land

batik: a process for dyeing cloth

Boer: an Afrikaner

bride-wealth: payment of money, goods, or livestock made by a suitor to the family of his bride

cash crop: a crop produced primarily for sale

cataract: a great rapids along a river

census: a count of the population

city-state: a self-ruling state made up of a city and its surrounding territory

clan: a group comprising a number of households or families

coalition: an alliance of two or more political parties

collectivization: socialist policy of group ownership of land

consensus: an opinion held by all or most of a group

coup d'état: the sudden overthrow of a government by a small group

deity: a god or goddess

delta: an area of soil deposited at the mouth of a river, often triangular in shape, as in Egypt

desertification: the transformation of semidesert land into true desert

domesticate: to tame wild animals for use by humans

drought: an extended period of little or no rainfall

dynasty: a ruling family, or the period of rule by members of one family

ebony: a tree that grows in Egypt, or its hard, black, heavy wood

escarpment: a steep cliff

ethnic group: a group of people who share common tradition, language, religion, and way of life

extended family: a family that includes several generations living together or near one another

famine: a great shortage of food in an area

griot: in West Africa, a person charged with memorizing and reciting the important historical and cultural events of a society in order to pass them from generation to generation

Gross Domestic Product: the total value of goods and services produced in a country each year

guerrilla: a member of a small band of soldiers engaged in irregular warfare.

hieratic: a cursive form of ancient Egyptian writing, simpler than the hieroglyphic

hieroglyph: a character used in a hieroglyphic system of writing

hieroglyphic: an ancient Egyptian system of writing that uses symbols and pictures to represent words

hominid: a member of the first human species to walk upright

imperialism: the extension of a nation's control over areas beyond its own borders

land alienation: requiring black Africans to live on overcrowded land while land in areas of white settlement remains unused

literacy: the ability to read and write

matrilineal: having to do with ancestry traced through the mother

mfecane: "crushing of peoples," a revolutionary upheaval in southern Africa in the late 1800s

monsoon: the wind that blows across the Indian Ocean and southern Asia

mummy: a body preserved by embalming and wrapping

nationalism: extreme devotion to one's nation

nationalize: to bring under government ownership and control

New Stone Age: the period between the Agricultural Revolution and the beginning of civilizations

nilometer: a measuring device of ancient Egypt used to record the level of the annual flood and to predict the size of the harvest

nomadic: having to do with herders who move from place to place so as to maintain a continuous supply of grazing land and water

obelisk: a four-sided pillar with a pyramidal top

papyrus: a writing material of ancient Egypt, made from the pulp of the papyrus plant

pass: identity papers that nonwhites in South Africa must carry at all times

paternalistic: treating people as if they are unable to manage their own affairs

per capita income: the average annual income of individuals in an area

pharaoh: an Egyptian king

phonetic: having to do with symbols that represent speech sounds

polygyny: the practice of having more than one wife

polyrhythmic: having to do with music that has several overlapping and interlocking rhythms played at once

polytheism: belief in or worship of more than one god

promontory: a mass of land that juts into the ocean

protectorate: a political unit that is dependent on a more powerful state for protection

rain forest: a dense, dimly lit forest with heavy rainfall year-round

reed: a hollow stem of a piece of grass, used as a pen

referendum: an election in which voters vote for or against a proposed law or policy

refugee: a person who flees his or her country in order to find safety and protection in another country.

regent: a person who governs in place of an underage, absent, or disabled ruler

relief: sculpture in which figures and forms stand out from a flat surface

rift: one of a series of deep valleys that run north and south through the African continent

savanna: a grassy plain with scattered trees and bushes

scribe: a member of a learned class trained to read and write

shifting cultivation: a system of farming in which land is used for several years, then allowed to lie unused for several years

slash-and-burn method: a method of farming in which brush is cut and set on fire, with the resulting ash fertilizing the soil.

sphinx: an image in the shape of a lion but with the head of a man, a ram, or a hawk

subsistence farmer: a farmer who grows only enough for his or her family's own use

surplus: the amount remaining when basic needs are satisfied

taboo: a rule forbidding certain actions for religious reasons

tariff: a tax on goods traded between countries

terra cotta: a brownish orange clay used for sculpture by early West African artists

terrace: a platform on the side of a hill, rising one above another, used in farming

tontine: a traditional African credit union in which a group of people pool their money and then lend it out to members of the group

tribute: payments to a ruler in exchange for protection

universal adult suffrage: the right of every adult person to vote

urbanization: the movement of people from rural areas to cities

veld: the region of short grasses in South Africa

wadi: a river that is dry most of the year but fills up during rainy periods

Bibliography

Chapters 1-2

Arnott, Kathleen. *African Myths and Legends*. New York: Oxford University Press, 1990.

Matthiessen, Peter. *African Silences*. New York: Random House, 1991.

Murray, Jocelyn, ed. *Cultural Atlas of Africa*. New York: Facts on File, 1982.

Stapleton, Chris, and May, Chris. *African Rock: The Pop Music of a Continent*. New York: Dutton, 1990.

Turner, Myles. *My Serengeti Years: The Memoirs of an African Game Warden*. New York: W.W. Norton, 1987.

Chapter 3

African Kings and Queens: A Gift of Heritage. Chicago: Empak Publishing, 1991.

Budge, E.A. Wallis. *The Mummy: A History of the Extraordinary Practices of Ancient Egypt*. New York: Bell Publishing, 1989.

Harris, Geraldine. *Ancient Egypt*. New York: Facts on File, 1989.

Hart, George. *Ancient Egypt*. New York: Knopf, 1990.

James, Thomas Garnet Henry. *Ancient Egypt: The Land and Its Legacy*. Austin, TX: University of Texas Press, 1988.

Morley, Jacqueline, and Bergin, Mark. *An Egyptian Pyramid*. New York: P. Bedrick Books, 1991.

Wilkinson, Gardner J. *A Popular Account of the Ancient Egyptians*. New York: Crescent Books, 1988.

Chapters 4-5

Mboya, Tom. *The Challenge of Nationhood*. New York: Praeger, 1970.

Monti, Nicolas, ed. *Africa Then: Photographs 1840-1918*. New York: Knopf, 1987.

Shellington, Kevin. *History of Africa*. New York: St Martin's, 1989.

Welles, Delta. *The Hominoid Gang: Behind the Scenes in the Search for Human Origins*. New York: Viking, 1989.

Chapter 6

Stevens, Stuart. *Malaria Dreams: An African Adventure*. New York: Atlantic Monthly Press, 1989.

Chapter 7

Tidwell, Mike. *The Ponds of Kalambayi: An African Sojourn*. New York: Lyons and Burford, 1990.

296

Chapter 8

Keneally, Thomas. *To Asmara*. New York: Warner Books, 1989.

Trzebinski, Errol. *The Kenya Pioneers*. New York: W.W. Norton, 1985.

Wubneh, Mulatu, and Abate, Yohannis. *Ethiopia: Transition and Development in the Horn of Africa*. Boulder, CO: Westview Press, 1988.

Chapter 9

Malan, Rian. *My Traitor's Heart*. New York: Atlantic Monthly Press, 1990.

Naidoes, Beverlay. *Chain of Fire*. New York: Lippincott, 1990.

Sparks, Allister Haddon. *The Mind of South Africa*. New York: Alfred A. Knopf, 1990.

Stefoff, Rebecca. *Nelson Mandela: A Voice Set Free*. New York: Fawcett Columbine, 1990.

Woods, Donald. *South African Dispatches: Letters to My Countrymen*. New York: Henry Holt and Company, 1988.

Chapter 10

Harden, Blaine. *Africa: Dispatches from a Fragile Continent*. New York: Norton, 1990.

Rosenblum, Mort, and Williamson, Doug. *Squandering Eden: Africa at the Edge*. San Diego: Harcourt Brace Javanovich, 1987.

Thomas, Maria. *African Visas: A Novella and Stories*. New York: Soho Press, 1991.

Index

298

Photograph Acknowledgments: Cover Photo: Farrell Grehan/Photo Researchers; 4, UN Photo; 7, Lynn McLaren/Photo Researchers; 8, H. Wolfe/UN Photo; 9, Georg Gerster/Photo Researchers; 11, Georg Gerster/Photo Researchers; 16, Bernard Pierre Wolff/Photo Researchers; 18, Lynn McLaren/Rapho/ Photo Researchers, 28, Bernard Pierre Wolff/Photo Researchers; 34, International Film Foundation; 36, George Holton/Photo Researchers; 38, Peter Buckley/Photo Researchers; 39, Georg Gerster/Photo Researchers; 43, International Film Foundation; 47, UPl/Bettmann Newsphoto; 53, UPl/Bettmann Newsphoto, 59, International Film Foundation, 65, Bettmann Archive; 67, George Gerster/Photo Researchers; 70, NYPL Picture Collection; 73, NYPL Picture Collection; 82, NYPL Picture Collection; 87, Bettmann Archive; 89, Bettmann Archive; 94, UPl/Bettmann Newsphoto; 98, Bettmann Archive; 101, Bettman Archive/BBC Hulton; 105, Bettmann Archive/BBC Hulton; 118, Georg Gerster/Rapho/Photo Researchers; 123, International Film Foundation; 126, UPl/Bettman Newsphoto; 128, Bernard Pierre Wolff/Photo Researchers; 132, UPl/Bettmann Newsphoto; 134, M. Desjardins/Photo Researchers; 143 Toni Angermayer/Photo Researchers; 153, Bettmann Archive/BBC Hulton; 154, UPl/Bettmann Newsphoto; 156, Photo, Jerry L. Thompson/Courtesy, Rolin Gallery Collection; 158, Shaw McCutcheon/UN Photo; 164, UPl/Bettmann Newsphoto; 167, UPl/Bettmann Newsphoto; 169, Georg Gerster/Rapho/Photo Researchers; 173, Bettmann Archive 183, Georg Gerster/Rapho/Photo Researchers; 186, Lynn McLaren/Rapho/Photo Researchers; 189, Bettmann Archive; 194, International Film Foundation; 198, T R. Pierson/Rapho/Photo Researchers; 201, Bernard Pierre Wolff/Photo Researchers; 205, International Film Foundation; 214, Georg Gerster/Rapho/Photo Researchers; 220, Georg Gerster/Photo Researchers; 223, UPl/Bettmann Newsphoto; 226, UPl/Bettmann Newsphoto; 228, Bettmann Archive/BBC Hulton; 234, Reuters/Bettmann Newsphoto; 237, Reuters/Bettmann Newsphoto; 247, Blair Seitz/Photo Researchers; 251, UPl/Bettmann Newsphoto; 257, UPl/Bettmann Newsphoto; 260, Georg Gerster/Photo Researchers; 264, Any Freeberg/Retna Ltd.